# MANAGING
## to Change the World

---

## The Nonprofit Leader's Guide to Getting Results

**by Alison Green and Jerry Hauser**
**The Management Center**

ISBN 978-0-615-27341-9

## A Note About the First Edition

We believe this book will get better as you put the concepts here into practice and let us know what works and what doesn't. Please send any comments – things you like and things we could improve – to jerry@managementcenter.org.

# Contents

# List of Tools

*Introduction*

# The Job of a Manager

I bet you had trouble finding the time to read this. If so, it's probably because, like many of the nonprofit leaders with whom I work, you're feeling serious stress. You're under pressure from funders, from your staff, from constituents, and ultimately from yourself, to be getting more done. Too much of the burden of making things happen is falling on you.

Effective management – how you get things done through other people – could help you accomplish more with less stress, but you may not know where to start. And if that's the case, you're not alone. Nonprofit leaders often end up in their roles not because they're skilled at management, but because they're talented, dedicated people committed to a particular issue, or because they have excelled at a specific function like policy analysis or communications. Up until now, you may have been fantastic in getting results on your own, but you might not have had to get results through others.

> *Effective management lets you accomplish more with less stress.*

Fortunately, good management isn't rocket science. In fact, it's pretty straightforward. My co-author, Alison Green, and I have tried to create an easy-to-use manual that will help nonprofit managers get better results by equipping them with hands-on, practical advice and tools. We'll cover a range of skills, representing what we think are the most important areas for managers to master – from delegating tasks, to setting and holding people accountable to clear goals, to hiring and firing, to staying organized and using your time effectively, to managing your boss. Exercised properly, these practices will make your life much easier.

Most importantly, though, not only does good management make your life easier, but it also makes it easier for you to get results. And that brings me to the fundamental premise of this book, which I want to be clear about from the start: **your job as a manager is to get results**.

While this probably sounds obvious, I didn't always fully grasp it. My first real management experience came at Teach For America, a large national nonprofit where, as the chief operating officer, I was responsible for managing the day-to-day work of the organization. As a former teacher myself, I had been drawn to management partly because I liked seeing people learn and develop to their full potential. I wanted staff members who were happy and fulfilled in their jobs, and I viewed it as my job to mentor them so that they grew and developed.

That was fine as far as it went, but at Teach For America we had very ambitious aspirations: we were trying to triple in size, raise the quality of our teachers, strengthen our alumni network, raise more money, and build a stronger organization to make it all happen. Early in my tenure, when I was more focused on mentoring and viewing my staff members' satisfaction as an end goal, I wasn't producing the kind of progress we needed. Most of my staff members worked extremely hard, but not everyone did. And many excelled at their jobs, but in several critical cases the organization's needs had outgrown my staff members' skills.

One day I was complaining to a friend about how much pressure I was under and how difficult it was to get things done without making people hate me. She looked at me and said, "Well, if you're doing your job, you might just be the least popular person there." With those not-so-reassuring words, my friend helped me realize that I was thinking about my job the wrong way. The organization was never going to achieve its aims without my making some people unhappy. I needed to hold people to more ambitious goals, I needed to be clearer with people when they weren't meeting expectations, and ultimately, I would need to tell some of my staff members that they weren't the right people for the job.

Through this stage in my work, I came to more fully appreciate what my true job was as a manager. Yes, it was good to develop people, to empower them, to help them be fulfilled at work, and to mentor them. Those things helped make my job enjoyable, and in some cases they helped make my people better at what they did, but ultimately, they were means to an end. *Fundamentally, my job was to make sure we got the results we aspired to.* That's why we existed as an organization, and it's what I was getting paid to do. Our donors funded us to help expand opportunities for students in low-income communities, not to make our staff happy. If I wasn't doing what it took to make us as effective as possible in pursuing our mission, then I wasn't doing my job.

As it happens, I believe you can get things done *and* be well-liked, at least most of the time. In fact, by being clear about what you expect, helping people meet your expectations, ensuring people are in roles in which they excel, and getting everyone aligned around a common purpose, you'll build your staff's morale in the long run. Treating people well also happens to be the best way to sustain your results over the long haul, because you'll never get good people to work for you otherwise. Time and time again, though, I've found that managers confuse being "supportive" bosses who "empower" their people with being effective managers who actually get things done. And in the short term, getting things done sometimes requires you to do things that will make people unhappy with you.

> *Too many managers confuse being "supportive" bosses who "empower" their people with being effective managers who actually get things done.*

Two examples from clients of ours might help illustrate what happens when managers do – or don't – fully feel the weight of responsibility for getting results in their realms. In the first case, a manager directly oversees the field operations for her organization. The organization realized that it needed to put more energy and resources into one part of the field program in order to improve its results. The manager, however, made only incremental changes in staffing levels to meet that need, changes that would almost certainly not suffice to generate the results needed. At a meeting with the head of the organization, she explained her plan, saying, "Imagine the uproar if I had proposed really shifting people around." Her explanation made it clear that she was weighing the potential staff reaction to changes (or perhaps better put, her own discomfort with that reaction) more heavily than the important results that the organization needed her to generate. Fortunately, the senior manager's own manager caught the issue before it was too late.

In contrast with this approach, our client in the second case did what it took to get results. This client is the executive director of an organization whose work gets carried out through multiple state offices, with those offices overseen directly by a regional director. The executive director and the regional director had agreed on ambitious new, critically important goals for what each state office would produce over the coming four months, before the organization's next fundraising cycle began. After even a couple of weeks, it was painfully clear that the regional director was proceeding under "business as usual," and that the state offices were nowhere near on track to producing the results they needed to.

In this kind of situation, many managers would continue to work through the regional director, checking in periodically, hoping the regional director would deliver when all was said and done, and perhaps blaming him if he didn't come through. In this case, though, the executive director understood that if things failed, he himself was ultimately responsible. He also understood that in this case the results *had* to happen: the organization would not fulfill its mission without them, and it would not be able to raise funds to keep supporting itself. Given that, the executive director took a much more hands-on approach, insisting on daily calls with each of the state offices with the regional director and the executive director himself to discuss what steps the states were taking to produce the results. After a few days, the energy at the state level changed, and within a couple of weeks, dramatically different results began to appear. The regional director, who was initially not thrilled with the executive director's "heavy-handed" approach, learned a valuable lesson in how to generate results. Interestingly, he is not only more effective in his job but is actually more satisfied than he was before all this happened. And now that things are on track, the executive director is able to step back and take a more "normal" approach to managing by working through his regional director.

When we highlight examples like these and stress the importance of being results-oriented, people sometimes ask us whether that means we think nonprofits should be run like hard-nosed businesses. Our answer is that because the work nonprofits do is so important, we need to be *more* hard-nosed about management than for-profit enterprises. Given what nonprofits do, we have a moral imperative to commit to strong, effective management practices. What's at stake is much more important than a business's bottom line.

And that's the main reason Alison and I wrote this book. We want to see more strong, effective nonprofits that are out there changing the world.

> *The work of nonprofits is so important that we need to be more hard-nosed about management than businesses.*

Inside this book, you'll find the tools you need to make it easier for you to get results. We intend for this book to be helpful to new managers as well as to those who have some experience, and to managers of individual teams or departments as well as to executive directors of entire organizations. You won't find information on fundraising or working with the media or other topics on specific functions already covered by myriad other books. Instead, you'll find step-by-step guidance on how to effectively manage any single area or an organization as a whole.

As I noted earlier, management is *how you get things done through other people*. There are three components to that definition: there's getting things done, there's the other people, and there's you. We've divided the book along the lines of those three pieces, covering in each part the practices in which the best managers we've seen excel:

- Managing the Work. We begin with "getting things done," because this is what most people think of when they think of management, and it's the most immediate challenge that most new managers face. We'll start with the most specific level of things you might want to get done, which is looking at how you delegate a discrete task or project. We'll then look at how you can assign bigger pieces of work and broader responsibilities by using clear goals with concrete measures of success. Then, knowing that beyond the things you discuss explicitly with your staff there are simply thousands of tiny actions that people take every day within your organization, we'll look at how you can use culture to guide your staff members on those items. Finally, we'll try to bring it all together by looking at a couple of easy-to-implement management systems that help you stay on top of it all.

- Managing the People. Using practices to make sure you have the right "other people" to get things done for you may be the single most important lever you have, and yet it's the area most neglected by managers. We'll discuss how to build a staff of superstars – hiring them, developing them, making sure you hold on to the best, and letting go of those who fall short.

- Managing Yourself. In the last section, we'll discuss how to apply to yourself the same rigor that you apply to your management of others, including using your time effectively, staying organized, working with your boss, and exercising authority. As a manager, what you do in this area sets the limits on – or, hopefully, removes the limits from – the results you can get.

The practices in this book will help you build a high-performing organization that gets results over the long haul. And for nonprofits working to change the world – and the people who run them – that's what it should be all about.

- Jerry Hauser
CEO, The Management Center
Washington, D.C.

# Section I
# Managing the Work

**SHARING THE BURDEN**

Whether you're managing a single team or an entire organization, there's going to be more work than you can handle on your own. And if you accept the fundamental premise of this book – that managing well is about getting results in your realm – then you're going to be feeling a lot of pressure.

In this section, we'll talk about how to manage the work – ideally, how to transfer some of the weight on your shoulders to your staff members. If you do this right, your staff members will feel energized because they will have real responsibility, your team will get much more done than you were able to previously, and you'll be freed up to focus on work of even higher impact.

Sounds great – so how do you do it? Whether the work you're trying to get someone to do is as straightforward as handling logistics for a meeting or as complex as raising your organization's visibility in the mass media, the same basic principles apply. You have to be clear about what you expect, you have to stay engaged along the way to increase the likelihood of success, and you have to hold people accountable for whether they deliver.

In this section, we'll look at how you can apply these principles of expectations, engagement, and accountability to manage different types of work.

- The most common thing most managers do is hand off specific tasks or projects. In Chapter 1, we look at how you can do this through strong delegation. Once you've mastered basic delegation, all the other ways in which you'll manage work follow easily, because the same principles apply.

- Ultimately, you'll maximize your impact when you can hand over not just specific tasks, but broader responsibilities. In Chapter 2, we look at how you do this by setting and reinforcing clear, measurable goals for your staff, which will enable you to fully share the pressure (and joys!) not just of day-to-day tasks but also of driving your organization forward.

- Whether in pursuit of specific projects or broad responsibilities, your staff members are going to perform thousands of tiny activities that you never discuss explicitly, but which will be key to the quality of the results you attain. In Chapter 3, we look at how you can create a powerful culture that will guide how your staff members approach and execute every aspect of their work.

- Finally, in Chapter 4, we'll look at a couple of systems that will help you bring all of this together – how in the real world with multiple staff members each handling a range of projects and responsibilities, you can stay on top of it all to ensure good results.

As you'll see, the exact details will vary depending on the context, but the basic principles of making sure people know what you expect of them, engaging with them to maximize their chances of success, and holding them accountable at the end of the day are the same.

# Chapter 1
# Managing Specific Tasks: Basic Delegation

Does either of these scenarios sound familiar to you?

> You ask your staff member to write a fundraising appeal for your new campaign. When you review the draft, the emphasis is on the wrong points and key pieces are missing, so you start making edits – and soon find that you've rewritten the entire thing. Your staffer is frustrated because it's not her letter anymore; it's yours. "Why didn't you just do it yourself to begin with?" she wants to know.

> The next time you assign your staff member a piece of writing, you try to give her more leeway so she doesn't feel micromanaged. But when you look at what she's written on the day it's scheduled to be mailed out, the tone is off, the pitch for funding isn't strong enough, and it doesn't feel compelling to you. You're frustrated and unhappy with it and when you tell her, you can tell she's frustrated, too.

If you're like most managers we work with, one, if not both, of these will ring true. In fact, many managers we know go back and forth between being too hands-on and too hands-off. Frequently a manager will start off at one extreme, discover that it doesn't get the desired results, and react by moving to the opposite extreme, only to find that doesn't work either. For instance, after giving staffers a great deal of leeway to run with a project and not having it go according to plan, a manager may vow to be involved in every step of the next project. And managers who get feedback that they've been too intensively involved will often start suppressing their natural desire to sit in on crucial project meetings and get interim project reports, only to inevitably find out at the end of the project that they should have listened to their gut. At that point, it can be tempting to throw up your hands in exasperation and feel that you're "damned if you do, damned if you don't."

It's no wonder managers get exasperated, because neither extreme works. In this chapter, we'll discuss how to get the balance right, and we'll then walk through each component of good delegation.

### Exactly How Hands-on Should You Be?

Wouldn't it be nice if there were an easy answer to that question? ("Finally – now I know that I should be 58% hands-on!") While there's no one-size-fits-all formula, from our work with managers we've come to a paradoxical-sounding belief: **most managers need to be more hands-on than they are, and also more hands-off**.

Huh?

Contrary to the popular belief that managers just need to empower their people and let them go, we believe managers need to be significantly more hands-on in key respects. They need to be more hands-on in clearly communicating their expectations for the outcomes of the work, in making sure they and their staff are on the same page about how the work will proceed, in monitoring the work while it's ongoing, and in creating accountability and learning on the back end.

At the same time, managers need to be more hands-off in actually doing the work. For every manager we see who's too hands-off in making expectations clear on the front end and in monitoring ongoing work, we see another (or often the same) who's too hands-on in pushing the day-to-day of the work forward and often doing much of it herself. The point of managing other people is to get more done than you would on your own, but too often we see managers fail to gain the benefit of having other people make the work happen.

Given all this, if you're like many of the managers we see, we can sum up our advice to you this way: **guide more, do less**.

*Guide more so you get better results, and you'll be able to do less.*

Won't this take more time? In the long run, definitely not. *Guiding more* means that you may spend more time than you otherwise would in explaining a project at the start. You also might spend five minutes more than before reviewing data on progress along the way. By doing this, though, you'll radically increase the chances that whatever you're delegating will be a success. Everyone will be happier, and you'll ultimately get to *do less* because you won't end up redoing the work (and dealing with an unhappy staff member), and over time you'll be able to delegate bigger and bigger pieces of work and know that they'll come out successfully. And when that happens, you can focus your energies on the work that only you can do.

## THE COMPONENTS OF GOOD DELEGATION

As we mentioned in the introduction to this section, there are three key steps to managing work generally, and in the delegation process more specifically:

1. Agree on Expectations. Ensure you and your staff are on the same page about what you want achieved.

2. <u>Stay Engaged</u>. Make sure the work is on track to succeed before it's too late.

3. <u>Create Accountability (and Learning)</u>. Reinforce responsibility for good or bad results and draw lessons for the future. (If you remember things only with acronyms, you could change "accountability" to "enforcement" and think of the 3 E's.)

How exactly these principles apply depend on the context, so we'll discuss a fourth principle, which most people do intuitively: adapting your approach to fit the person and project.

The figure below summarizes the basic process:

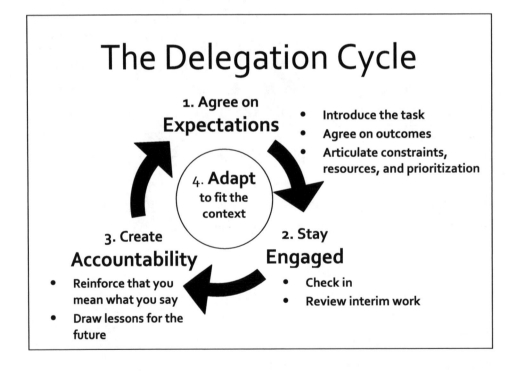

**Step 1: Agree on Expectations**

The first step in launching the work is for you and your staffer to come to a clear, shared understanding about what results you expect. Sound straightforward? It can be harder than you might think to get to the point where you and your staff would give the same answers to questions like, "What are you trying to accomplish?" and "What does success look like?" Just giving a quick rundown of the project won't get you there. Rather, there are four distinct stages to this step: assigning the job; agreeing on what success looks like; articulating details like the project's constraints, available resources, and priority level; and confirming that your staff understands the assignment and has a plan for moving forward. Let's look at each of the stages.

### *Assigning the job*

Assigning the job to your staffer is fundamentally about articulating what you are delegating and what role you want your staff member to play. While this sounds easy, we frequently see managers define the task more narrowly than they might. To take a very simple example, you might ask your assistant to check on whether there are enough pads and pens in the conference room for an upcoming meeting. A broader approach – one which will make the assistant's job more challenging and your life easier – would be to tell the assistant that she is in charge of all logistics for the meeting. Similarly, it's one thing to ask a head of development to send a thank you note to a potential donor after you have met with the donor, but another thing to delegate being in charge of all written donor communications. (Even better, as we'll see in Chapter 2, is to delegate the broad responsibility of "Ensure we raise our budget this year.")

However broadly you ultimately define the task, be unambiguous with your staff members that they are responsible for it at the end of the day. Too often we hear managers say, "Can you help me with logistics for the meeting?" when what they really mean to say is, "You're in charge of making sure logistics for the meeting go smoothly." Your staff member still might call on you or others for help or input as appropriate, but as the "owner" (a word we love) of the responsibility, their job is to ensure a successful outcome.

**Keep the Monkey On Your Staffer's Back**

Once you've delegated a responsibility, make sure you keep the ownership for the project squarely with the staff member. Authors William Onken, Jr., and Donald Wass suggest thinking of each project or task as a monkey someone is carrying around on her back. When you assign a project to a staffer, you're handing over the monkey. But often, that staffer will find ways to return the monkey to your back. For instance, if you see that a phone bank script isn't working well, don't "take the monkey back" by rewriting the script. Rather, after you talk with your staffer about the elements that need changing, she should do the rewrite – so that the monkey stays on your staffer's back and doesn't hop back to yours.

Very commonly, "taking back the monkey" happens in response to a seemingly legitimate question. Whenever possible, rather than suggesting solutions yourself, try to get the staff member to propose solutions herself. "What do you think?" is a great question to use in ensuring you don't inadvertently take on monkeys you have delegated.

*For a more complete explanation of how to ensure that staff members do not "pass the buck" back to their managers, see "Management Time: Who's Got the Monkey?" by William Oncken, Jr., and Donald Wass in* Harvard Business Review, *November-December 1999.*

### Agreeing on clear outcomes

Most managers we know hate being labeled micromanagers. Micromanagers tell staff exactly how to do a project, or worse yet, do (or re-do) the work for them. What lets you delegate effectively while not micromanaging is *setting clear expectations for success.* By being extremely clear about what success looks like, you free your staff up to figure out the best way to get there.

*Establish the aim.* In cases where outcomes are basically pre-determined, such as getting a bill passed that your organization has determined is a priority, you can simply state that the desired aim is bill passage by the end of the year with certain key provisions in it. In cases where the ideal outcome is less clear, you might ask your staff to take the lead in proposing outcomes, particularly if they have some experience in the area. For instance, you might say, "You're in charge of logistics – what do you think doing that successfully looks like?"

> *"Make sure your staff members can answer the question, 'What do I have to do to delight my boss?'"*
>
> *- Peter B. Lewis, Chairman, Progressive Corporation*

In either case, the outcomes that you and your staff agree to should be as specific as possible. Quantitative targets are often ideal, since they leave little room for misunderstanding what is desired. Quantifying outcomes is not always feasible, though, so you can also agree to qualitative aims. In these cases, you should be as specific as you can about what the qualitative target is – i.e., how you will "know it when you see it." For the staffer you put in charge of logistics, the qualitative aim of having things "run smoothly" might more specifically be "everything is set up and ready to go on time; if we run out of supplies we have extras at the ready; we anticipate basic needs and provide for them; and we have someone ready to deal with extraordinary requests."

Sometimes even qualitative outcomes are hard to pin down. In these cases, making sure that your staff member understands the full context of what you're trying to accomplish can go a long way. For instance, in delegating a piece of writing, you might explain that you need the document to appeal to a particular funder, and you could give context about the things that the funder cares about and what will turn the funder off.

*Samples and templates.* When possible, offering samples can be an incredibly useful way to give your staff a clearer idea of what you're looking for. For example, if you and your head of communications agree that the new Web site she is developing should look "clean and crisp," you might send her links to sites that you think feel that way. Similarly, you could give your new development director a successful grant proposal from last year to show her what tone and style she should be striving for in this year's report.

If the assignment is a new type of work, providing a template can help structure the work in the way you're envisioning. For example, rather than simply asking a staff member to give you research about other organizations working on a particular issue, you might create a chart with the specific headings you are looking for (e.g., organization name, mission, budget, etc.) and have her fill it in.

### Articulating constraints, resources, and prioritization

Most work assignments have some constraints and resources attached, and you should articulate these, as well as making it clear how high of a priority overall the work is.

*Constraints.* What are the constraints on the process (e.g., who needs to sign off on an item before it goes out the door?) and the substance (e.g., items to include in the budget)? In the Web design example, you might ask your communications director to submit draft design options to the head of development before she makes a final recommendation (process constraint). You might also indicate that the organization's logo must appear on every page (substantive constraint).

*Resources.* What money, people, supplies, and other tools can your staff member use? Within that list, one of the most valuable resources you can offer your staff is your own time. Make it clear that staff members can approach you to clarify expectations, answer questions, review interim progress, and help brainstorm solutions. In doing this, keep in mind the "monkey" principle (*see page 16*) and make sure that staffers maintain ownership for the project – so a staffer can say, "I'm wrestling with X – the best solution I can come up with is ABC, but I worry that it's not the most cost effective approach. Do you have any suggestions about other options I might consider?" Staffers should not say, "I'm stuck on X. What should I do?" That said, if you have input about the project, you should give it to your staff member on the front end. There are few things more frustrating for staff members than spinning their wheels to figure out something you already knew. If you know from experience that having a Web site vendor in a different city has been a nightmare in the past, don't hesitate to tell your head of communications that.

---

### Process Constraints: When Projects Involve Multiple People

Because nonprofits often place a high value on inclusion, projects often end up involving lots of different people. Getting multiple perspectives can be a good thing, but too often we see it devolve into confusion when people are not clear on their roles and projects languish for lack of a clear driver or decision-maker.

In projects where multiple people are playing roles, then, part of your job is to articulate who should play what role throughout the work. Many of our clients have found it very helpful to have a standard vocabulary within the organization for how people might be involved. There are different models you can use, but one option is the "MOCHA" model. (You can remember "MOCHA" because if you get this right, your job becomes easier and you can sit at a café all day sipping mochas.)

**M**anager: Assigns responsibility and holds owner accountable. Makes suggestions, asks hard questions, reviews progress, serves as a resource, and intervenes if things are off-track.

**O**wner: Has overall responsibility for the success or failure of the project. Ensures that all the work gets done (directly or via helpers) and that others are involved appropriately.

**C**onsulted: Should be asked for input and/or needs to be brought in.

**H**elper: Available to help do part of the work.

**A**pprover: Signs off on decisions before they're final. May be the Owner or Manager, though might also be the executive director or board chair.

---

*We adapted this model from the "DARCI" model taught in some programs, which stands for: Decider, Accountable, Responsible, Consulted, Informed.*

### Give Work to the Right Person

We sometimes see managers fail at delegation because they assign a project to the wrong person in the first place, trying to fit a round peg (e.g., creating a detailed project budget) into a square hole (the artistic director who is a creative genius but a disaster with numbers). When delegating work, be sure to consider who actually has the talent and skills to get the job done rather than who *should* be able to do the task at hand given her background or position. (Of course, if you repeatedly find yourself reluctant to delegate a responsibility that the staff member in that position should be able to handle, you need to assess whether that person is a good fit for the role and determine an appropriate course of action. We talk more about this and other performance issues in Chapter 8.)

*Prioritization.* Make sure your staff member knows where the project falls relative to her other priorities. You've likely had the experience of assigning a project, expecting it to be finished or at least well underway a week later, checking back in, and discovering that the staffer hasn't started it yet. Again, it comes down to being clear about your expectations: state the timeline you expect and how the work fits with other priorities. (It's okay to leave the timing up to the staffer as well, if you truly mean it – but be specific about any qualifiers attached to that. You might say something like, "There's no rush for this, so it's fine to do it as time allows, but it should definitely be wrapped up by August.")

### *Agreeing on How to Move Forward*

Once you've shared your expectations for the project, the final step in the "expectations" stage is to close the loop by making sure your staff member actually understands the assignment and, where relevant, creates a plan of attack.

*The repeat-back.* Time and time again, we see managers who think they have been crystal clear about their expectations shocked to discover that their staff members have heard something very different. We're often reminded of the children's game of telephone, where a whispered message gets passed from person to person and comes out humorously different at the end than at the beginning.

The best way to prevent "telephone syndrome" and to be sure your staff member understands the project the way you do is simple: ask. That is, find a way to get your staff to repeat back to you what they've taken their assignment to be. In simple cases, the repeat-back might be verbal. Before ending a discussion about an assignment, you might simply say, "So, just to make sure we're on the same page – can you tell me what you're taking away from this?" When an assignment is more complicated or will take more than a day or two to complete, you might ask the staff member to send you a quick e-mail summarizing the assignment, including expected outcomes and next steps. This might feel awkward at first, but you can even blame your own fallible memory by saying something like, "You know how I sometimes change my mind about a project without realizing it? To make sure that doesn't happen, can you take five minutes to capture what we've agreed to here and e-mail it back to me, so we both have down what we've agreed to?" Almost invariably, in looking back over the e-mail, you'll find one or two details where you and the staff member weren't on the same page, so you'll now have an opportunity to clarify.

*See page 34 for a sample e-mail repeat-back.*

*The plan.* The quick verbal summary and the five-minute e-mail are simply less formal versions of what can become a more extensive plan on more complicated projects. The level of detail will vary from situation to situation, but the basic ingredients of any plan include the key activities needed to reach the desired outcomes, a timeline for when those activities will occur, and who is responsible for each step – in other words, plans should spell out **"who will do what by when."**

For complex projects, you should ask your staff member to create a written plan so that the two of you are on the same page about how she intends to move forward. This plan will be the staff member's tool for juggling the work's many moving pieces, and it should include information about each step, interim deadlines, and notes on MOCHA-type stakeholders *(see sidebar on page 19)*. For instance, if your staff member is organizing a conference, the plan would cover steps associated with choosing the venue, designing and printing invitations, developing the agenda, and confirming speakers. The plan should be in a format that is easy to update, since your staff member will likely be making small adjustments to those interim deadlines as the work progresses. Because this sort of planning requires your staff member to think through each step and plan backwards, she may spot early steps (like securing a venue) which could otherwise have slipped until too late.

---

### Project Planning: The Five S's

In creating a project plan, your staff members might think through the Five S's:

1. <u>Success</u>. What are the desired outcomes of the project?

2. <u>Stakeholders</u>. Who else needs to be involved, and how? Use MOCHA as a tool to think through who needs to be involved in what.

3. <u>Stages</u>. Are there key dates by when certain phases of work must be complete? For instance, there might be a planning stage, a rehearsal stage, and an execution stage.

4. <u>Streams</u>. What are the main categories of work? What should be the MOCHA for each stream?

5. <u>Steps</u>. What are the specific, detailed steps that need to happen within each stream of the project?

*See page 35 for a sample project plan.*

---

While your staff members should take the lead in proposing the plan, as the manager you should ensure that it's realistic and as comprehensive as it needs to be. This might mean asking hard questions about the plan ("Is it really possible for you to go from mock-ups of the Web pages to having the pages coded within two weeks, as you've proposed?") and making recommendations based on your expertise and experience ("I worked with vendors on a Web site remotely once and it was a disaster – you might think about finding someone you could easily meet with in person"). Don't be shy about playing the role of "skeptic," pushing against the plan and the results to date to help the staff member refine the plan. The ideal outcome of the back and forth is a plan that is better than either you or your staff member might have developed on your own.

## Step 2: Stay Engaged

Once there has been significant discussion about the expectations and the plan of attack, many managers assume that the actual work will be completed almost as a matter-of-course. They are then often surprised by the "implementation gap," where what happens in practice looks very different from what they expected. In fact, the number one way managers fail at delegating is by not staying involved to check on progress.

You can avoid the "implementation gap" by continuing to engage with your staff during the course of the work, getting a feel for how the work is proceeding, and making sure that tasks are either completed according to plan or that the plan is adapted as needed. Managers sometimes feel awkward about doing this, but you can be direct with your staff. Tell them that you're hoping to check in on things along the way, both to see how things are going so you can avoid any implementation gap and so that you can serve as a better resource to your staff.

> *The number one way managers fail at delegating is by not staying involved to check on progress.*

There are three main ways to get your hands dirty and ensure your staff is making progress: checking in with staff directly, reviewing interim work, and seeing the work for yourself firsthand.

### Checking in with staff directly

This can be done by e-mail, phone calls, or in-person conversations, including regular weekly meetings, ad hoc meetings on specific topics, and quick stop-bys to see how things are going.

Regardless of the forum, in addition to serving as a resource on whatever issues your staff member might raise, your job is to ask probing questions that get beneath the surface to make sure that work is on track. For instance, in preparing for an upcoming conference, rather than simply asking, "So, is everything going okay?" and receiving a "yes" answer, you might ask your staff to review progress against the plan, to discuss steps around a particularly tough issue ("How are you approaching the issue of diversity on the panels?"), and to report on RSVPs and speaker confirmations.

In formulating these questions, think critically about what could go wrong and probe around those areas in particular. Don't let yourself assume things are proceeding smoothly; assume your job is to look for trouble. (But do this in a tone that won't make your staffer feel you lack confidence in her.) Remember, your job as a manager is to make sure you, your team, and the organization get results. For instance, in the example of the conference, you might ask, "Do we know how the hotel will deal with malfunctioning equipment?" and "Is there anything we can do to be prepared to accommodate attendees with disabilities?" You could even ask, "What could go wrong? What's your worst case scenario?" and brainstorm about ways to address those possibilities.

### Reviewing interim work

It happens over and over: you assign a piece of writing, your staff member spends two weeks on it, and when it comes back to you it's not at all what you were picturing. Many managers think to ask for a draft in advance, but even at that stage your staff member has put significant time into the project. A less common but very helpful technique here can be to ask to see a small sample of the whole before the person has put substantial energy into getting all the way through it. For instance, you might ask for a short segment of a document, an outline of an argument, or one page from the new Web design before the whole site is created. In many cases, discussing a "slice" of a project before the staff member gets too far saves tremendous energy and frustration down the road.

In addition to reviewing either partial or more complete products, managers can review reports on progress. Sometimes progress reports might be simple narrative updates from staff members, ideally covering topics that the manager and staff member have agreed upfront are most important. Managers can also ask to see regular reports with data indicating progress toward the desired outcome – for instance, a weekly report on progress toward a fundraising goal, a monthly chart showing Web site traffic compared to prior months, or a weekly list of targeted lawmakers and their position on a pending piece of legislation.

### *Seeing the work firsthand*

The least common but perhaps most powerful way to see how things are really going is to directly observe the work in action. Staff members might be completely upfront in reporting on progress, but managers often find that getting a feel for the actual work leads them to a much greater understanding of what is going on. For instance, joining your staff on a lobby visit, sitting in on a media training, attending a meeting with a prospective funder to hear your staff's pitch, or observing a phone bank to see how volunteers actually deliver an agreed-upon appeal can all offer valuable insights into how what is happening in reality compares to what has been outlined in the plan. Even taking a sample from something as simple as a stack of letters that a staff member is addressing to donors can lead to surprising insights about how a task is being completed. However you do it, seeing a sample of the work firsthand allows you to catch any disconnects before too much time goes by.

With work that's happening in the field, seeing it firsthand is particularly important, since – unlike with, say, a report where you'll see the final product – it's possible to never actually see work that's happening remotely. Since you can't effectively manage a program without seeing what's happening, find ways to see field work in action. If your organization runs training programs, sit in on some trainings. If you're running a ballot initiative campaign in another state, make site visits to how things are being run on the ground. One executive director we know

*One executive director was shocked by how different what was happening in the field was from what he had been assuming.*

started sitting in (with permission) on randomly selected calls between his head of regional operations and the organization's regional staff, and was shocked to discover how different what was happening in the field was from what he had been assuming.

Firsthand observation also helps you serve as a resource to your staff as they consider changing the plan to reflect how things are playing out in the real world. Ideally, you would conduct observations like these with your staff member at your side, so that you have the same fact base about how things are unfolding. Following these observations, you should debrief with your staff to share your impressions and make sure that there is agreement about any changes going forward. In the example above, the executive director sat down with his head of regional operations so they could debrief the calls, acknowledge where things were off-track, and generate solutions.

### Step 3: Create Accountability (and Learning)

We recently met with a manager who was incredibly frustrated. He had delegated the task of writing an important memo to one of his staff members. He set expectations appropriately and made sure the staff member understood them, and then reviewed a draft along the way to make sure it was on track. The end product produced by the staff member, though, was still missing a crucial ingredient. The manager's reaction was typical: "This just shows that you can't delegate anything and expect it to get done right!"

While we shared his frustration, we reminded him that there was one more piece to the delegation process he needed to pursue: creating accountability. He needed to go back to the author of the letter and, in a direct, assertive (but not hostile – see Chapter 9) way, share his reaction to it. By doing this, the manager would not only get the product he wanted, but perhaps more importantly he would also set himself up for better results the next time by sending a clear message that slipshod work was not acceptable. Creating accountability at the end of a process is the first step in setting expectations for the next iteration of the delegation cycle – fundamentally, the message is, "I mean what I say." Of course, this goes for rewarding positive outcomes as well. When staff members have done a good job and produced the desired results, managers should recognize their effort and celebrate their success.

> **Don't Punish the Whole Class**
>
> Remember when you were in school and one student did something wrong but the teacher yelled at the whole class? We occasionally see managers make a similar mistake, trying to hold a group accountable for the actions of individuals. When you're trying to make clear that you mean what you say, you'll be much more effective if you deliver that message to one person at a time. For instance, if three of your staffers miss a deadline you've set, you'll create a culture of accountability more quickly by going to each of the three individually (even if it's sending each an identical e-mail, customized just with their name) than by talking to the whole group to stress the importance of deadlines.

*Fundamentally, the message is "I mean what I say."*

In addition to reinforcing responsibilities, the accountability stage can produce lessons for the future. Even when things have gone well on a project, both you and your staffer have likely learned from the experience and picked out things that could be done differently next time to get even better results. A write-up of these lessons – even as just a quick bulleted list – can be an invaluable resource to have on hand the next time you conduct a similar project. One small step that can make a large difference in producing lessons and accountability is to schedule – or better yet, to have your staff member schedule – a brief reflection meeting for the end of a project, and to get it on the calendar right from the start.

---

### The Value of Debriefs

Harvard Business School researchers found that among a group of surgeons learning a new operating technique, those who discussed each case in detail and debriefed with team members after procedures managed to halve their operating time... while those who didn't discuss and debrief hardly improved their time at all. (See Atul Gawande, "The Learning Curve," The New Yorker, January 28, 2002.)

---

## Step 4: Adapt to Fit the Context

When assigning work to your staffers, you should apply the three steps in the delegation cycle above, but how you apply them will vary depending on the person to whom you're delegating (the "who") and the nature of the project (the "what").

When it comes to the "who," consider your staff member's skill and will.

### *Skill*

You will likely learn from experience who is best at turning around a high-quality written assignment and who is a superstar at building connections with an external constituent (rarely the same person). Yet when assessing skill level, don't automatically assume that stellar employees need little guidance, since even the best employees have areas where they need closer management. You might have an otherwise outstanding worker who has trouble meeting deadlines, so you might ensure she creates a timeline with built-in room for unexpected delays on the front end. Or you might have someone who simply hates putting plans in writing, but who always delivers high-quality work on time. With that person, you might waive your normal expectation of a written plan and instead agree verbally on a path forward.

A subset of skill is the person's experience in your organization. You may have just hired a master fundraiser, but because the person is new to your organization, you will still want to work with her more closely on early projects than you would on the same projects three months from now.

### Will

Considering will means assessing what people like and dislike. Your program manager's well-known hatred for doing budgets should lead you to take a more hands-on approach, because it's reasonable to think she might be inclined to put the work off or put less energy into it than into work she loves. (Of course, if she does an otherwise excellent job as a program manager, it might be reasonable to find someone else to handle those budgets, since you'll likely get better results by assigning that work to someone with more enthusiasm for numbers.)

Beyond the "who," you need to consider the "what" – the nature of the task and how difficult and important it is.

### Difficulty

Obviously, the more difficult the assignment, the more time you'll want to spend discussing it on the front end and checking in as the work progresses. And conversely, relatively easy, straightforward tasks will require less input and oversight from you. For instance, if you are asking your experienced advocacy coordinator to create letter-to-the-editor templates for activists to use, you might simply talk about what topics you want to cover and show her templates that have been used in the past. But if the same person has been assigned to devise and implement a plan for a new initiative to establish local chapters, you'll want to talk in-depth at the outset about the goals, process, and potential pitfalls, check in regularly to give advice as the plan develops, and stay in very close contact as the implementation begins.

### *Importance*

How important is the assignment? What are the potential ramifications of success or failure? For instance, if your organization's most important ally in the Senate is speaking at your conference, you would want to be more actively engaged in ensuring that everything goes smoothly than you would be in supervising the set-up for your management team's monthly meeting.

After weighing all these factors, you'll want to decide on a general approach. Should you take a highly hands-on approach? Should you be moderately hands-on? Or should you be fairly hands-off? If your consideration of these factors leads you to determine that a particularly hands-on approach is called for, it can be helpful to let your employee know this upfront. You might tell her, "I'm going to be checking in pretty closely since this is the first time you've done this and we really can't afford to have any delays in getting these out to our funders."

Allow yourself and your staff to work through a couple rounds of the delegation cycle to get the hang of it. Once the principles of agreeing on expectations, staying engaged, and creating accountability are in place, your team will produce stronger work products with a lot more efficiency, helping you get the results you need.

> **Managing Sideways**
>
> What about overseeing a project or delegating work when you don't have authority over the people involved? Actually, most of the same principles still apply. Determine how hands-on you need to be based on the nature of the project and what you know about the people involved; agree on clear outcomes, constraints, resources, and prioritization; and check in during the course of the work.

*See page 33 for a delegation worksheet.*

## Key Points

- Remember the basic rule of **guide more, do less**.

- Guiding well means setting clear expectations, staying engaged enough to ensure corrections get made along the way, and creating accountability on the back end.

- In setting expectations, you can avoid micromanagement by focusing on clear outcomes, and letting your staff member propose the best way to get there.

- A simple "repeat-back" of expectations from your staff member can do wonders to avoid miscommunication.

- The most common way managers fail at delegating is by not staying engaged to monitor progress. If you don't get a feel for how the work is proceeding once you've assigned it, you will almost always experience a serious implementation gap.

- When a project ends, you and your staff should reflect on results, draw lessons learned, and create accountability. You need your staff to understand that you mean what you say.

- Consider the skill and will of your staffer as well as the difficulty and importance of the assignment and adapt your approach accordingly.

## 📖 Additional Reading

- Stephen R. Covey, "Delegation: Increasing P and PC" in *The 7 Habits of Highly Effective People: Powerful Lessons in Personal Change* (Free Press 2004 edition), pages 171-179.

- Atul Gawande, "The Learning Curve," The New Yorker, January 28, 2002.

- William Oncken, Jr., and Donald Wass, "Management Time: Who's Got the Monkey?" Harvard Business Review, November-December 1999.

- Situational Leadership Theory, see http://en.wikipedia.org/wiki/Situational_ leadership _theory and http://12manage.com/methods_blanchard_situational_leadership.html.

## ✎ Tools

- Delegation worksheet

- Sample e-mail repeat-back

- Sample project plan

## Delegation Worksheet

*Setting your people up for success*

I am assigning _____ the responsibility of _____.

Given the difficulty and importance of the task and my staff member's will and skill for this task, my approach should generally be:

        Very hands-on      Moderately involved      Relatively hands-off

### Step 1: Agree on expectations

1. What background and context does your staffer need to understand where the work is coming from and what you are trying to accomplish?

   _____
   _____

2. What would success look like? What are the ideal outcomes?

   _____
   _____

3. What are the constraints on process? What is the timeline? What samples or resources are available? How big a priority is this task relative to other work?

   _____
   _____

   | The MOCHA for this task is: | Manager | Owner | Consulted | Helper | Approver |
   |---|---|---|---|---|---|
   | | | | | | |

4. What other input do you have?

   _____
   _____

5. How will you make sure you and your staffer are aligned on key points and next steps?

   ☐ verbal or written repeat-back    ☐ project plan    ☐ other _____

### Step 2: Stay engaged

1. With what frequency will you check in? What hard questions should you ask?

   _____
   _____

2. What specific products or activities will you want to review or see in action?

   ☐ a draft or outline    ☐ key data    ☐ other _____
   ☐ an interim piece of work    ☐ rehearsals/walk-throughs    _____

### Step 3: Create accountability (and learning)

When and how will you debrief how things went?

_____

## Sample E-mail Repeat-back

**From**: Alice Lee
**To**: Jenny Ray
**Sent**: Tue Jul 29 16:05:56 2008
**Subject**: Newsletter production (repeat-back)

> The e-mail repeat-back should be short and informal, and should not become a long, bureaucratic process.

Hi Jenny,
Here's what I took from our discussion about newsletter production:

Tasks (delegated 7/29/08)

1. Printing
- Look into printing options (several hundred copies, depending on cost)
- AL, JR to touch base on or before August 1 about results of initial search

2. Layout
- Look for people/companies who can do the layout (one possible lead: freelancer used by West Africa team to produce their Liberia report)
- Remember to make the newsletter usable—include samples?
- Touch base on this early and often

3. Editing
- As early as September 1, begin super-micro edit/proofreading of all articles

> When your staff knows they'll need to do a repeat-back, they'll be far more likely to take notes and therefore to remember what you said.

4. Online Strategy
- Which parts should we put online – all? Articles only? Are there other options?
- Goal: Want a way to track not just how many, but who is reading the newsletter
- Come up with a few good options on this

**Context**:
Our reports contain useful information and right now we have no systematic way to share them beyond our contacts. Other orgs use newsletters successfully, both online & printed.
**Budget**:
Rough at this point – could cost $10,000 but shouldn't cost $40,000. ER will find out what was originally set aside in annual budget.
**The final product should be**:
Impressive, useful (including easy to use), and, ideally, viral
**Timeline: TBD (ideally by Oct. 1)**

Side notes:
- Think ahead of time about who needs to be involved – and in what capacity – before starting the project.
- Start with the deadline in mind and work backward to determine interim due dates.
- It is often helpful on larger projects to list key overall stages with deadlines upfront.

## Sample Project Plan

### Training for 2008 Fellows

| Stream | Steps | End product/deliverable | Due Date | Stakeholder notes (MOCHA)[1] | Status/notes |
|---|---|---|---|---|---|
| Overall | Produce and deliver top-notch training | Great trng! Avg. participant satisfaction of at least 9.2 (of 10) | Jan. 15 | M = Dan, O = Sue C = John, Rachel, H = Teresa, A = Dan | In Process |
| | Make decision on whether to conduct training | | Oct. 21 | | Done |
| | Dft presentation to John | | Dec. 1 | | |
| | Final presentation to John | | Dec. 15 | | |
| | Conduct training | | Jan. 9 | | |
| | Evaluate training and do necessary follow-up | | Jan. 15 | | |
| Research/dev. | | | | | Done |
| | Review materials from last year's training | | Oct. 15 | | Done |
| | Do additional research as needed | | Oct. 22 | | Done |

[1] Manager, Owner, Consulted, Helper, Approver

| | | | | | |
|---|---|---|---|---|---|
| | Make decision on whether to conduct training | Confirmation e-mail to JR | Oct. 23 | Nina should also be C | Done |
| | Send background materials on training | Monkey article and chapter on managing up | Oct. 23 | Teresa is O | Done |
| **Content** | | | Oct. 24 | | In Process |
| | Meeting to discuss content and next steps, including delegating specific pieces | Delegation worksheet on training | Oct. 28 | | |
| | Develop content for training: outline | Outline | Oct. 30 | | Pending (add mats from TL's group) |
| | Develop content for training: PowerPoint | Draft ppt. deck | Nov. 12 | | |
| | Develop worksheets and handouts | Revised outline and ppt. deck | Nov. 14 | | (See '07 training wkst) |
| | Send materials to DS | | Nov. 17 | | Pending (key question re: audience) |
| | Get comments from DS | | Nov. 21 | | |
| | Revise materials based on DS input | | Nov. 26 | | Pending |

| | Finalize presentation and send to JR | Final deck and handouts | Dec. 15 | | Pending |
|---|---|---|---|---|---|
| **Logistics/ execution** | | | Jan. 15 | Teresa = O for all logistics, Sue = M | Pending |
| | Set up call with JR to finalize logistics | | Dec. 20 | | Pending |
| | Practice giving training to staff | Full run-through | Jan. 7 | | Pending |
| | Print out final materials | | Jan. 8 | | Pending |
| | Save presentation on disk and bring to session | | Jan. 8 | | Pending |
| | Set up debrief session | | Jan. 5 | | Pending |
| | Conduct debrief of training w/ JR, DS, & RJ | | Jan. 15 | | Pending |

## Chapter 2
# Managing Broad Responsibilities: Setting and Using Goals

In the last chapter we talked about how to set expectations, stay engaged, and create accountability to successfully delegate specific tasks or projects to your staff. For many managers, delegating even discrete projects will represent an important start to getting better results.

In the long run, though, managers will only generate the kinds of results they need to – and free themselves up to take on the pieces that only they can do – when they are able to assign not just specific tasks but broad responsibilities to the people around them. Jerry first learned this lesson from Wendy Kopp, the founder of Teach For America. Like many founders, when Wendy first started the organization she was basically responsible for everything: she drove the fundraising, she made sure the recruitment and training efforts were successful, she oversaw the design of marketing materials, and on and on. She had people to help with each piece, but the real energy was coming from her and the ultimate weight of responsibility was falling on her. Not surprisingly, this was exhausting for Wendy and, as she tells it, demoralizing for her staff.

Wendy came to realize that she needed to have people truly in charge of each area of the organization and responsible for its progress. She needed a head of fundraising who would lie awake at night until she was sure the revenue would come in, she needed a head of "program" to ensure recruitment and training were top-notch, and she needed a head of communications to oversee marketing efforts. How, though, could she hand over such broad responsibilities while making sure Teach For America got the results it needed?

Wendy learned that the key to delegating broad responsibilities was to ensure that the people assigned to each area had very clear goals for what they needed to accomplish. Goals with clear, measurable outcomes became a key part of how Teach For America operated, and to this day they are an essential part of the organization's success.

In this chapter, we'll talk about how you can use goals to hand off broad responsibilities so others can help drive significant pieces of your organization forward. First we'll look at what a goal is and what makes for a good one. Then we'll look at the process of creating and using goals, applying at a broader level the lessons from the last

> *The key to delegating broad responsibilities is to give people clear goals for what they need to accomplish.*

chapter about setting expectations, engaging along the way, and creating accountability. Finally, we'll take a look at how to use goals and their precursor, mission statements, to manage not just specific responsibilities but the direction of an entire organization.

Before we dive in, we want to warn you: some of what follows may look a little daunting at first. But know that every time you and your team go through the process of setting goals, things will get a little easier and a little more natural. So don't let the perfect be the enemy of the good. The important thing is to put goals in place and to begin capturing their benefits, and then you can keep improving them over time.

## PART I: WHAT'S A GOAL?

Goals establish what a person will achieve, how that achievement will be measured, and what the target for success over a particular time period is. Thus, goals consist of three component parts *(see page 80 for a summary chart)*:

1. <u>Objectives</u> to describe what the person aims to achieve;
2. <u>Metrics</u> to gauge the extent to which the objective is attained; and
3. <u>Targets</u> to define what "success" looks like on any given metric.

For instance, a development director might have an objective of expanding the organization's base of high net worth individual donors. As a metric, she might use the number of donors giving at least $5,000, and the target might be to increase the number of such donors from 10 to 18.

While others use different terminology to describe similar concepts, the key point is for managers and staff to agree on expectations: what the staff member should accomplish, how they will measure the degree to which they accomplish it, and the bar for what success looks like.

### Setting SMART Goals

Not all goals are created equal. Strong goals share a number of qualities, captured by the acronym "SMART" – Strategic, Measurable, Ambitious, Realistic, and Time-bound.

### *Strategic*

Goals are strategic when they reflect the most important dimensions of what the person responsible for them seeks to accomplish. While this sounds obvious, we frequently see staff members set lofty sounding goals that don't actually reflect their most important work. For instance, we recently met with a client who manages the head of finance for her organization, and who was reviewing the finance head's goals. We asked the client to turn the draft goals over so she couldn't look at them, and then asked her to tell us what she most wanted the finance head to accomplish in the coming year. Without hesitation, she told us that the most important thing was for the finance head to provide quick and accurate revenue and expense information to help shape the organization's decision-making as it shifted resources from one area to another. We then turned the paper over and saw that the finance head's goals related to things like increasing the speed with which the finance department paid its bills. This was a classic case of reasonable-sounding goals not being strategic.

In addition to reflecting the most important work of a team or individual, goals that are strategic are aligned at every level of the organization. Individual staff members have goals that add up to the department's goals, and department heads have goals that add up to the most important organizational priorities. Goals whose underlying objective is not connected in one way or another to the broad direction of the organization are not strategic and should be discarded.

---

### A Common Pitfall: Confusing Data with Goals

Your team members might track a wide variety of data. Remember, though, that collecting data on something does not in and of itself make it a goal you should be managing to. For instance, it might be smart for your head of communications to look at your monthly Web site traffic to inform your strategies. That doesn't mean, though, that she should be expending effort to increase that traffic – unless doing so is an explicit and deliberate aim that makes sense.

---

### *Measurable*

Consider the difference between an aspiring athlete who says, "I want to get in shape" versus one who says, "By the end of the year, I will be able to run six miles in under an hour." The former is a wish, the latter a commitment. Effective goals produce that sort of commitment by creating a clear finish line, a way to judge whether or not the goal has been attained.

*What if your goals are hard to measure?* The easiest way for a goal to be measurable is for it to be quantitative, as in the runner example, but that doesn't always need to be the case. Coming to a qualitative agreement about what success looks like can be an extraordinarily powerful tool for managers when success is hard to quantify, as it often is in the nonprofit context.

The trick in creating qualitative goals is to tap into the instinct that you would "know success when you see it" and to articulate the specifics beneath that instinct. For instance, an advocacy director's goal might be to

> *To create qualitative goals, think about how you would "know it when you see it."*

generate significant attention to the organization's issue during the presidential campaign. The director might word the goal this way: "Our issue will become a salient issue in the presidential campaign, meaning that it will be included prominently in candidate materials, questions will be asked about it in debates and town hall meetings, candidates will mention it in ads and at events, and polls will show it among the top 10 issues on voters' minds." Or your receptionist might make one of her goals to "always make visitors feel welcome and give them the sense that we're a professional, upbeat organization." This isn't quantitative, but it still establishes a bar for expectations.

---

### The Power of Goals

Specific and measurable goals are far more likely to be adhered to than more general ones. As Time magazine's Sanjay Gupta reported, "Investigators at Berlin's Free University found that people who set general goals, like 'I will exercise in my free time,' did a far worse job of sticking to that plan than people who made a firm commitment, like 'I will walk to my friend's house and back every Monday, Wednesday, and Friday.'" ("Stuck on the Couch," Time Magazine, February 22, 2008.)

*Activities vs. outcomes.* Measurability also raises questions about what exactly should be measured – activities or outcomes?[1] For instance, the advocacy director of a health care organization might set goals around activities *and* outcomes, such as the number of meetings held with legislators (activity) and the number of legislators met with who agree to support a bill (outcome). Activities tend to be easier to measure, and there is a direct correlation between the staff member's efforts and the metric. With outcomes, it can be harder to attribute the result to the staff member's effort. In this example, target legislators might decide to support the bill, but for reasons having little to do with the group's efforts.

Nonetheless, effective managers do push to set goals around outcomes whenever feasible. By doing this, they are articulating an answer to not just, "What do I want you to do?" but more fundamentally, "What do I want you to achieve?" When everyone within an organization is clear on the answer to this second question, they are free to think of new ways to approach problems. Continuing with the example above, if the staff member is clear that the real goal is to get eight legislators to support the bill, she might think of better ways to make that happen than holding direct meetings (perhaps persuading large campaign contributors to place calls instead, for instance). In this way, outcome-oriented goals can be an antidote to micromanagement, as they let the manager and the staff member focus on what the result should be, with the staff member's job then being to figure out the best way to get there.

### Ambitious

While measurability means that goals must contain a clear finish line, ambitiousness means that the finish line must represent significant

---

[1] For the sake of space and our readers' sanity, we've simplified a broader spectrum of terms that you may hear about. Most commonly, the full range goes from inputs ("spend $5,000 on publications") to activities ("write monthly e-mail updates") to outputs ("e-mail updates sent to 12,000 people each month") to outcomes ("at least $25,000 in donations generated by our e-mails") to impacts ("successful advocacy efforts in 3 states funded"). Of these, the most commonly used – and we believe, the most useful – refer to activities and outcomes.

progress. Goals should not simply be "predictive," laying out what the staff member would be likely to achieve that year if she simply did what she always does.

"Stretch goals" – goals that require staff members to reach far in terms of effort and tactics – can drive enormous progress within your organization. For instance, with the health care organization above, if the advocacy director currently had secured the support of just three legislators, then a goal of adding 15 more within a year might be a stretch goal. The director would need to focus significant energy here, leaving little room for distraction.

The habit of setting ambitious stretch goals is one of the key practices that distinguishes high-performing individuals (and organizations). While others might go about the ordinary course of business each year, perhaps making incremental progress, organizations where staff members must think about how much progress is possible and set ambitious goals reflecting an aggressive sense of possibility often make dramatically more progress.

*What happens if we don't meet stretch goals?* Staff members who set stretch goals often worry about the consequences of not reaching those goals. The answer is more art than science, as there is a delicate balance between rewarding risk and ambition on the one hand and ensuring that staff members take goals seriously on the other. When a staff member sets a goal representing dramatic progress, there needs to be an implicit understanding that the task is difficult. Even in failing to meet the goal, the staff member could make significant progress, which merits reward rather than rebuke. At the same time, failure to meet a goal should cause reflection on what could be done differently going forward, and a pattern of failing to meet goals over time should be cause for concern.

From an external perspective, leaders might also fear that funders will cut support if goals aren't met. The key here is to communicate with your funders directly, perhaps flagging from the start that a goal is particularly ambitious so that you correctly set expectations. Ultimately, though, fear of what your funders might think should not deter you from setting ambitious goals. In our experience, funders are more likely to reward you if you make significant progress, and ambitious goals help you do that.

### Realistic

At the same time that you want your people to have ambitious goals, implicit in the idea of taking those goals seriously is that they cannot be so ambitious that they simply represent wishful thinking – goals must be more than purely aspirational. The best goals lie just at the intersection of ambitious and realistic. When goals are not realistic, staff members do not commit themselves to meeting them. The staff might mouth the words of the goal, but deep down they will not have decided to do whatever it takes to reach it, which is the type of commitment leaders need from their teams.

> *The best goals lie just at the intersection of ambitious and realistic.*

Making goals realistic has several important implications.

*Goals must have plans behind them.* Setting a goal – especially a stretch goal – generally makes sense only if staff members have at least some sense of how they might reach it. Without that understanding, the goal is more of a wish than a commitment. So as goals are being developed, part of the conversation must be what tactics the staff member envisions using to achieve them. For instance, when setting annual fundraising goals at Teach For America, the directors of the local offices submitted plans showing a realistic list of potential sources of funds. No director would be able to set a goal of $1 million without demonstrating that there was a realistic path to get there. Of course, your staff member's tactics may change during the year as she reacts to new developments and adapts her plans. But the important thing is to have thought through a road map and had meaningful discussion about it before solidifying a goal. (We talk more about plans at the end of this section.)

> *A goal without a plan to reach it is a wish, not a commitment.*

*Goals may need to represent interim progress.* Particularly in advocacy work, there are times when the only realistic outcomes are interim ones. An advocacy director might have the long-term goal of getting a housing bill passed through the state legislature, but for this year, her realistic (but still ambitious) goal might be to get the desired bill out of committee in the state house, or perhaps endorsed by the leading candidates for governor. These are still outcome goals (because they capture the result of the organization's activities and not just the activities themselves), but they represent interim progress toward a longer-term end.

*Sometimes goals may need to change.* In general, managers should be reluctant to change goals during the course of the year, because once a target is established, the team should commit to doing anything and everything to reach that target. However, extraordinary circumstances may make reaching a goal simply impossible, in which case a leader would change the goal. For instance, an organization's advocacy director might have had an ambitious legislative agenda for 2001, but after the September 11 attacks, she might have had to recognize that significant legislative progress that year was not going to happen, regardless of her efforts. She might have instead focused on laying the groundwork for the future, perhaps building a cadre of committed "grasstops" leaders who would speak on behalf of a desired bill the following year.

*Account for unknown variables.* Don't get hung up on the presence of unknown variables in your goals. For instance, your legislative director and her team might be engaged in state-level fights in 12 states. She might reasonably argue that she will need to react to developments in the states to decide where to focus her efforts, so she cannot set meaningful goals specifying exactly how much progress will happen in each state. You and she might agree, though, that a successful year would include making significant legislative progress in four states. Her goal then might be, "Of the following 12 states, make significant legislative progress in four."

*Measurability should not become a project unto itself.* Being realistic about goals means examining not just the content of the goals themselves, but also the energy needed to measure them. Your advocacy director might decide that in an ideal world, she would set goals for the total number of activities that your grassroots members engage in – attending meetings, calling legislators, selling tickets to fundraisers, etc. She might, though, decide that the energy it would take to keep tabs on every member activity would be prohibitive and that a reasonable, more easily-tracked proxy for total activity would be the number of members who attend meetings. In some cases, devoting significant energy to assessing progress toward a goal might make sense, but managers should use their judgment about how much effort is merited. In the end, your people should devote energy appropriate to the importance of each goal, but not more.

### Time-bound

Being time-bound simply means that goals should contain not just a clear finish line, but also a deadline for reaching it. For instance, the goal, "Increase the number of donors giving at least $5,000 per year from 10 to 18" should be accompanied by "before the end of our fiscal year" or "by June 15." In most organizations, goals are set annually, so the time is at least implicitly a 12-month window. In situations where there's not necessarily a natural cycle (as there might be, say, with a legislative session or a school year), we've sometimes seen clients make faster progress by setting goals covering shorter periods, like six months.

Whatever the time period, once you have agreed on final goals, you should also ask your team members to establish milestones for interim progress, so that you and they will know throughout the year whether they are on track toward meeting their goals. There are two types of milestones:

1. Milestones that directly measure interim progress toward a goal. For instance, if your development director's goal is to raise $100,000, she might agree that to be on track she needs to raise $20,000 by March, $50,000 by June, and $75,000 by October.

2. Activity-based milestones. Sometimes the only useful milestones are about completing activities, rather than actual outcomes. For instance, your organization might receive the vast majority of its contributions in December, so your development director might not know how many people will end up contributing until after the holidays. She might, then, set activity-based milestones, like having at least three "friend-raisers" by July 1 and having follow-up meetings with 15 donors by October 1.

**Bringing It All Together**

Before moving on to the process of creating goals, let's look at some sample goals and address a few common questions.

***What does a SMART goal look like in practice?***
Here's an example for an advocacy director:

> Goal: Qualify a state health care initiative for the Arizona ballot by October 31.

> *Milestone 1:* Initiative language drafted and vetted by lawyer by February 1
> *Milestone 2:* 50,000 signatures collected for ballot certification by April 30
> *Milestone 3:* 80,000 signatures collected for ballot certification by July 31

*Milestone 4*: 125,000 signatures submitted to the state by
September 30
*Milestone 5*: Initiative certified by the state by October 31

And here's an example of a SMART goal for a chief operating officer in a context where "measurability" requires the use of a qualitative definition describing "how we'll know it when we see it":

> Goal: By March 31, all "low-performing" staff will have raised their performance significantly or left (with "low performers" defined as staff who only sometimes meet goals and rarely exceed them, who do not demonstrate our core values, and/or who would be relatively easy to replace with someone as good if they left).

*Milestone 1*: By January 15, list of all low performers created (identified either in annual performance review or by managers after quarterly check-ins)
*Milestone 2*: By February 15, all supervisors of low performers have placed them on improvement plans or have coached them out

### *What about "maintenance" goals?*

Some of the work your staff is responsible for is more about running a tight ship day-to-day than stretching to meet a new, ambitious goal. For instance, ambitious new fundraising initiatives aside, a development department also needs to send out renewal mailings on time, respond to donor inquiries in a timely and informative way, maintain an accurate development database, and process donations quickly. These sorts of things are important tasks, but if your staffers created goals around them and every other item in their purview, they would likely end up with 25 or even more goals apiece, which can dilute the impact of having goals in the first place.

To avoid goal overload, we recommend grouping these day-to-day duties together as "maintenance" goals, referring to responsibilities that are important but don't move the organization significantly forward (perhaps putting them all under one goal of "running a tight ship"). This helps you keep the staff's energy primarily focused on major "growth" goals. For instance, in the case of the development department, the day-to-day, maintenance work needs to happen, but if the primary goal is to raise $3 million by the end of the year, that's where you want to see much of the development director's emotional energy focused. (She could, though, ensure that the staff member directly responsible for maintaining or reducing the turnaround time for external inquiries includes that as one of her goals.)

Speaking of which...

### How many goals are too many?

In general, the number of goals for a person or department should be in the rough range of three to five. Going slightly over this (say, to eight) isn't a disaster, but having way too many – we've seen organizations in which one person will have 32 significant goals for the year – means that you can't truly focus on many of them.

> "If you can't tell me what your goals are without looking at a piece of paper, then you don't have real goals."
>
> - Jon Cowan, President, Third Way

In fact, having just a single, clear, overriding goal can be incredibly powerful. For instance, your development director might have several goals around adding new major donors, raising a certain amount from an event, and so forth, but ultimately you want her to be obsessing over a single bottom-line goal for dollars raised during the year.

In cases where a person does have multiple goals, consider indicating their relative weight. For instance, you might decide that while broadly educating legislators on your issue is a goal, it represents only 10% of success for the year, and passing your bill out of committee is worth 60% and thus much more important.

---

**Goals Makeover**

Take a look at how these goals were made over into SMART goals.

BEFORE: Work with activists to build grassroots support for health care legislation.
AFTER: We will have quality grassroots activists (meaning they respond to the vast majority of our requests, they can articulate our messages, and they come off as "normal" people) working in 20 of our 25 targeted congressional districts by June.

BEFORE: Manage publications schedule.
AFTER: 90% of our mailings and publications will be issued on time, and 100% will meet our quality guidelines.

BEFORE: Maximize the amount of earned media coverage that includes our messages.
AFTER: At least one-third of news stories on all major, national, events related to our issue will have included our perspective. Additionally, we will publish an average of at least three letters-to-the-editor per month, reaching an average of at least 300,000 readers (based on average circulation) per month or 3.6 million readers for the full year.

---

### *What about plans?*

Goals answer the questions, "What are we trying to accomplish?" and "How will we know whether we accomplished it?" Plans answer the question, "How will we get there?"

As we noted in Chapter 1, the basic ingredients for a good plan include:

- the key activities needed to reach desired goals;
- a timeline for when those activities will take place; and
- an assignment of responsibility for each step.

Put more succinctly, plans establish **who will do what by when**. Within those broad outlines, plans can take a variety of forms within organizations. In many cases, department heads will establish a high-level plan for the year, laying out the main tactics they plan to pursue and when they will implement them. A year is a long time to plan for, though, so many of our clients create annual plans to articulate general initiatives around their goals, and then rely on quarterly plans for the specifics (as we describe in Chapter 4). For instance, a development director's annual plan might include the general tactic, "Expand circle of high net worth donors by convincing current donors to host 'friend-raisers' for us." Her quarterly plan then, would be more specific: "By February 15, Joanna meets with Alan, Robin, and Marty to see whether they'll host events for us." *See page 68 for a sample set of departmental goals.*

*Good plans establish who will do what by when.*

## PART II: HOW TO CREATE AND USE GOALS

Now that we've talked about the ingredients of strong goals, we'll look at how you can develop them and use them. As with delegation, the key is to agree clearly on the expectations on the front end, to stay engaged to increase the chances of success, and to create accountability on the back end.

In describing how the cycle applies in this context, we'll assume that the goal-setting is occurring not with one person in isolation, but rather as part of a broader, organization-wide process with everyone establishing goals. With this more complicated picture in mind, though, you can easily simplify it as appropriate to establish goals for just one of your staff members.

## Setting the Goals: Agreeing on Expectations

### *Lay out the timeline*

Depending on the size of the organization, there may be a lot of moving pieces to consider in a goal-setting process, so creating a timeline will help you keep the process on track. *(See the sample goal and plan development process on page 77 for an example of how this might work.)* Your timeline should leave plenty of time for back-and-forth between you as a manager and your staff members (and among staff members as well). If you are managing people who are in turn heads of their own teams, you should give them time (a week or two, say) to draft their goals in a way that involves their team members. You might meet with your team leaders before they begin so that you are all on the same page about the general direction, or you might wait until they produce a draft. Either way, once there is a draft, there should be plenty of time for back-and-forth.

While in theory people might create goals in the span of a day or a week, we've found that it can take a month or two in the press of the day-to-day to gather relevant data, reflect on lessons from prior results, and have rigorous back-and-forth between managers and staff members at all levels.

### *Engage intensively*

As your staff members propose their goals and tactics, you should engage rigorously to test their thinking, to ensure goals truly are SMART, and to challenge the assumptions underlying them. For instance, if your development director proposes a goal of 50% growth in annual revenue, you'll want to understand what she will do that is different from prior years to produce that growth before you sign off on the goal – since without a plan to reach the target, the goal is merely wishful thinking and thus fails the "realistic" piece of SMART. Similarly, let's say your development director proposes a goal to increase the number of "members" who donate $50 over the Internet. You, however, think the energy should be going to high net worth donors, so the two of you need to work that out. A significant part of the power of goals, in fact, comes not from the final words on the page, but rather from the process of alignment that results from real discussion around what you expect your staff members to accomplish.

> *The power of goals comes as much from the process of creating them as from the final words on the page.*

### *Solidify the final product*

While the process might be as important as the final product, you should make sure that there is indeed a final product. Set a date by which you want the final, final version of each of your staff member's goals, and put the goals in an easily accessible place (like a "goals" folder on a shared server). Since each staff member will ideally have just three to five key goals for a given time period, their list of goals and the accompanying high-level plan will generally be no more than a couple of pages. *See page 72 for a sample of individual goals.*

Once goals are created, they should be circulated to the relevant parts of the organization. Department heads might share their goals with one another, which not only ensures that leaders of the different parts of the organization know what the others are doing, but also helps create a sense of mutual accountability where departmental leaders feel responsible to their peers for meeting their goals. (In all of these cases, this sharing could also occur before the plans are final, giving staff a chance to comment on the plans of others whose work might be connected to their own.)

## Using Goals Throughout the Year: Staying Engaged

Once goals have been created, they can be either an incredibly powerful tool for managers or an empty bureaucratic exercise that sits on a shelf gathering dust. To be meaningful, goals must shape the regular course of business.

*Managers and staff members should refer to goals regularly*

First, every individual should refer to the goals for which they're responsible on a regular basis. Ideally, at the end of each week, staffers would each review their goals, consider what needs to be done to remain on track, and then shape their plans for the following week to accomplish those tasks. Perhaps more realistically, as the manager you can declare that at one meeting a month with each of your staff members, the two of you will look at the staff member's goals and assess the extent to which things are on track. (Some clients of ours have started incorporating these as "first Monday check-ins" at the beginning of each month.)

*Managers should engage meaningfully to assess progress*

As we discussed in the last chapter in the section on staying engaged, the best managers ask probing questions to get beneath the surface so that they can truly understand how things are progressing. For instance, instead of asking a simple, "Are things on track?" managers might ask, "Can you review for me how you're moving forward in getting us established in Arkansas? What indicators do we have of whether or not we're on track? How many active members do we have so far? What are you worried about?" By using goals as the basis for regular conversations, managers can ensure their teams stay focused on what everyone has agreed up-front is most important and can work with their teams to evaluate what's working and adapt tactics as needed.

In addition to asking questions and

---

**Managers play the critical role**

Throughout the process of creating and using goals, their success or failure will hinge on how well you use them as the manager. If you give goals only a cursory look when they are proposed, if you do not refer to them in the regular course of business, and if you do not hold your staff members accountable for meeting them, they may well be nothing more than a bureaucratic hassle. If, however, you reinforce their importance throughout the process, you will find that your staff pursues them vigorously, taking on more and more ownership and freeing you up to focus on new and higher impact work.

---

looking at data on progress toward goals, managers should also see how broad priorities are playing out on-site. For instance, if your IT department has a goal of providing same-day solutions to staffers' technical problems, you might sit in on some conversations between the IT staff and end users to observe the work in action. Or, if your development staff has a goal of prompt, friendly answers to member inquiries, you might look through some of the member e-mails they've received and the replies they've sent. Since you're responsible for the results at the end of the day, and since there's often a gap between plans and reality, you should look for concrete examples of how your staff members' work is actually playing out in practice.

## Reflecting on Attainment of Goals: Creating Accountability

It sounds obvious, but too few organizations put it into practice: the extent to which your staff members achieve their goals should be an important component of their performance evaluations. We like to see managers evaluate their staff members on both what they did – i.e., whether they achieved their goals and produced strong results – as well as how they did it. Frequently, managers' evaluations focus only on the "how" component, commenting on whether a staff member collaborated well, showed up to work on time, or demonstrated particular skills. The "how" part does matter, but it should not overshadow the "what." And if you want your staff to really work to achieve their goals, you

*Evaluate your staff on what they achieved, not just how.*

must hold them accountable for the extent to which they succeed at that. One specific implication of this is that if you set goals on a calendar year cycle, your evaluations should happen around that cycle as well. We frequently see organizations with goals based on the calendar year but evaluations based on "service anniversaries," or dates of hire, which makes it next to impossible to include an assessment of whether staff members have actually met their goals for a given time period.

Accountability for achievement of goals (or lack thereof) should include a learning component as well. By stepping back with your staff to assess their performance against goals, you can discuss why they succeeded or fell short, and you can work with them to draw lessons that will inform the pursuit of their goals in the next cycle.

## PART III: USING GOALS (AND MISSIONS) TO STEER THE ORGANIZATION

Up to now we have considered goals primarily as a tool for individual managers to use in managing their staff members. If you're leading an entire organization, setting goals for what the organization as a whole will accomplish can be a similarly powerful device.

In the sections above, we talked about how goals let you shift the burden of driving forward some of the responsibilities that would otherwise fall to you. For instance, an executive director whose head of fundraising does not have a fundraising goal has basically said, "Can you help me with fundraising?" An executive director whose fundraising head has a goal of ensuring the organization raises $7.2 million this year has said, "You're responsible for making sure we raise our budget."

Setting goals for the organization as a whole can take real energy, but you gain additional benefits:

- Fresh thinking. Leaders often find that by putting the focus on big-picture goals, they and their staff discover effective new tactics and discard old methods that may no longer be working.

- Internal alignment. At their core, goals are a communications tool. They are the leader's mechanism for sending unambiguous signals about where energy within the organization should (and should not) go, so that everyone in the organization can be pushing in the same direction. The process of setting goals creates that alignment, and the end product reinforces it. In addition, organizational goals help individual staff members connect their work to the bigger picture of what the organization is trying to accomplish.

- Better external communication. Goals are also powerful communications tools for external constituents. By capturing the organization's most important priorities, they make it easier for the leader to explain the direction of the organization to everyone from funders to allies to the media.

- Shared urgency and focus. Ambitious goals keep complacency at bay and create a healthy sense of urgency. That urgency, in turn, tends to prevent other issues from becoming distractions, as staff are too focused on meeting goals to let other matters seize their attention.

- Continuous improvement and accountability. Setting clear targets against which success will be judged lays the groundwork to reflect on what went well and what could have been improved. It also establishes the basis for accountability, so that managers and staff alike know when someone has lived up to expectations and when they have fallen short.

- Traction. Most importantly, clear, ambitious goals ensure that all of the activity within an organization actually leads to real progress. It's too easy for an organization to spin its wheels, working frenetically but not ultimately moving forward. Setting a clear goal – such as "Get from 35% of the public supporting our issue to 60%" – helps ensure that the activity adds up to actual results.

Just as we did at the individual level, let's look briefly at what good organizational goals look like and how you might put them into practice.

**Contents of Organizational Goals**

There's no real substantive difference between organizational goals and goals for an individual. In fact, many of your organizational goals might in fact be goals owned by specific individuals (for instance, your overall fundraising goal might rise to the level of an organizational goal, but ultimately your development director might be responsible for it). As such, the criteria for good organizational goals are the same as for individuals: you want them to be SMART (Strategic, Measurable, Ambitious, Realistic, and Time-bound).

In order for your organizational goals to be strategic, they need to represent the broad direction of the organization. Organizations differ in how they establish this. Many engage in formal strategic planning processes in which they lay out a three-to-five-year vision for where they want to be and how they plan to get there. Others might skip the full strategic plan but still establish longer-term goals – say, for three years – articulating how much progress they want to make. Finally, other organizations might feel they operate under so much uncertainty that setting longer-term aims is meaningless and may not look beyond more than one year. *Refer back to pages 41-49 for more on making goals SMART.*

Just as with goals for individuals, you should have a relatively small number of goals for the organization as a whole that capture the most important work for a given time period. As with individuals, one way to think of good organizational goals is to answer the question, "If we accomplish nothing else, what would we need to achieve for this year to be successful?" Given that, you don't want to establish 30 different organizational goals. Finding the most important three to five goals can be incredibly powerful. These goals often fall into two main areas: programmatic priorities, which are goals directly connected to the organization's mission, and capacity-building priorities such as fundraising, staffing, or technology.

*See organizational goals samples on pages 74 and 75.*

## Mission Statements

Whether or not your organizational goals are grounded in a longer-term plan, setting goals and managing to them presumes you know what broader end they're for – i.e., that you know what your organization is really trying to accomplish. That's where your organization's mission statement comes in.

If you've ever seen meaningless mission statements posted on walls ("Our mission is to delight our customers" hanging behind the counter of the local deli with the rude wait-staff), you might approach the idea of mission statements with a bit of cynicism. We've found, though, that getting clear on your organization's fundamental purpose – its reason for being – can be incredibly powerful. For instance, one of our clients has struggled because half of his staff thinks the organization's fundamental purpose is to deliver a product, while the other half thinks the purpose is to train the people who deliver the product. That basic lack of alignment plays out on a daily basis in tension over how to prioritize different activities.

What makes for a good mission statement? People approach this differently, but in our view, a mission statement should be a concise, action-oriented statement of your organization's fundamental purpose. The best mission statements we've seen begin with a verb (like "reduce" or "protect" or "make") and then a description of the problem you want to address or the conditions you want to foster. For instance:

- Make quality, affordable health services available to all Americans.
- Protect the rights of women to make safe and informed reproductive choices.
- Confront and end national and global cruelties to animals.

As a leader, you should use your mission statement constantly. When you describe what you do in your literature or to someone new, your mission statement should be a standard refrain, so that everyone has a shared, fundamental understanding of what you're about. And in deciding whether or not to take on major new streams of work for the organization, the first question you ask should be, "Does this advance our mission?" Fundamentally, your mission should be the compass you steer by.

[Once they've defined their fundamental purpose, organizations sometimes then add on a statement of strategies, which explains how they will go about achieving their purpose. For instance, the mission statement of Venture Philanthropy Partners in Washington, DC, is "to concentrate investments of money, expertise, and personal contacts to improve the lives of children and youth of low-income families in the National Capital Region (*purpose*). We do so by helping effective community leaders build strong nonprofit institutions and by cultivating an engaged donor community to generate funding and influence in support of these institutions and of social change (*strategy*)." Parentheticals added.]

**How to Create and Use Organizational Goals**

Creating and using organizational goals requires the same process as the one we described for individual goals. In fact, the best way to think of organizational goals is to consider them the executive director's own goals, which they essentially are. In the same way a department head would create her goals by taking the lead but involving her team, so too should the executive director create her goals by driving the process but involving her staff.

*Creating the Goals*

Whether organizational goals get set before or after departmental goals depends on the context. In some cases, goals for the organization will simply be the "sum of the parts" of the work of each department. When that is the case, and when the overall direction of the organization is clear, then the organizational goals are simply a synthesis of each department's chief goal and can be established after the departmental process.

In other cases, an organization might have cross-cutting goals that are the product of multiple departments' efforts – think of a newspaper where circulation totals might stem from the quality of the editorial department's work and the efforts of the subscription and newsstand sales teams. There might also be situations in which a department's goals depend on the overall direction of the organization. For instance, a marketing team may need to know whether its organization will place a higher priority on raising the group's public profile than on ramping up programmatic work before setting team goals.

In cases like these last two, the organizational goals should be set first and departmental goals should flow from them. In practice, the process will be iterative – so the executive director and her team might decide that they would like to put energy into raising the organization's visibility. The marketing department might then consider what it would take to do that and develop goals and a plan to reach them, and then those goals might in turn inform the organizational goals.

Whether the process is more top-down (where the organizational goals get determined before the departments') or bottom-up, there should be significant back-and-forth around the content of organizational goals. The executive director might take the lead in developing an initial proposal, or sometimes just a set of questions to consider. Typically, she would then involve key members of her senior team in intensive discussions about the goals and whether they capture the most important work of the organization. The executive director's own manager – in this case, the board – should also be engaged in the process. In practice, this might mean that the board reviews an early draft of goals and gives initial input, and then reviews and eventually approves a more final version.

In considering individual goals, we noted that the goal-setting cycle should align with the cycle for performance evaluations. Beyond that, organizations should also align the goal-setting process with their budgeting process, since goals should impact decisions about resource allocation. Here too, the exact process might vary, but the important thing is for organizations to make explicit choices about how best to align the cycles.

### Using the Goals

Just as with individual goals, having organizational goals can either provide tremendous focus and shared urgency, or it can be a meaningless exercise. The key is to reflect on progress against the goals

> *Creating goals can be a meaningless exercise – unless you use them to guide your actions.*

regularly, restrategizing about how to reach them as needed.

Since the executive director is the ultimate "owner" of the organizational goals, she should look at them frequently, assessing progress toward them and determining any additional steps that are needed. To ensure her team stays focused on and invested in the goals, she should review them not only on her own, but also with others. The frequency of review will vary depending on the circumstances and how regularly updates are available, but most organizations find that to be meaningful, these "step-backs" need to happen at least once a quarter. For organizations that conduct monthly reviews, one option is to quickly review all the goals and pieces of the plan, and then delve more deeply into one or two particular areas. Executive directors might also call ad hoc meetings to hear about progress and to strategize around areas of particular import or concern.

### *Creating Accountability*

As with individual goals, at the end of the day there should be accountability around whether or not the organization as a whole meets its goals. One of the best ways to ensure this is through reporting to the board and to funders, both of whom can hold the organization and its leaders accountable. In the case of the board, an assessment of the organization's progress against its goals should form a significant part of the executive director's annual evaluation. Funders, of course, will make up their own minds about whether the organization made significant progress toward goals, and will act accordingly. (This manual is not about fundraising, but we will note that we see time and time again the power of being honest and transparent with funders. If your organization falls short of its goals, explain in direct fashion what happened, what you learned, and what you will do differently going forward. Most funders appreciate the candor and the determination to press on after a difficult year.)

The executive director can create real accountability internally as well. Executive directors can publicly share their assessments of progress with their staffs, and they should openly discuss their thoughts on how the organization might improve in the future. Depending on the results, executive directors can also ensure that their organizations celebrate accomplishments, a critical step too often neglected in the rush to begin pursuing goals for the next cycle.

**Summing Up: Expectations, Engagement, and Accountability Writ Large**

We warned you that our discussion about goals might be a little lengthy. Fundamentally, though, this chapter presents nothing more than the same lessons we talked about in the delegation chapter, just on a broader scale. Goals help you set clear expectations for what you want to see accomplished so that you can hand over broad responsibilities. Checking in on progress against the goals is your way of staying engaged, so that you maximize the chance of success at the end of the day. And creating accountability around the extent to which your team meets its goals reinforces the importance of the goals and begins setting expectations for the next cycle. Simple, no?

**Key Points**

- Goals help managers assign broad responsibilities rather than just specific tasks to staff members.

- SMART goals are Strategic, Measurable, Ambitious, Realistic, and Time-bound.

- Goals should measure outcomes rather than activities whenever possible.

- Goals should contain milestones for interim progress so that you'll know throughout the year whether you are on track toward meeting them.

- Managers should ensure goals have realistic plans behind them.

- To be effective, goals must be used in the normal course of business throughout the year: staff should check them regularly, managers should hold regular meetings to check on progress, and executive directors should be deeply committed to doing everything possible to hit them.

- Goals should be aligned with other organizational processes, such as annual budgeting and personnel evaluations.

- At the organizational level, executive directors can use goals to set broad priorities and to steer the direction of the organization.

## 📖 Additional Reading

- James C. Collins and Jerry I. Porras, "Big Hairy Audacious Goals" in *Built to Last: Successful Habits of Visionary Companies* (Harper Collins 1997 edition), pages 91-114.

# ✎ <u>Tools</u>

- Sample departmental goals and action plan

- Sample individual goals

- Sample organizational goals (1-year)

- Sample organizational goals (longer-term)

- Sample goal and action plan development process

- 3 components of a goal

## Sample Departmental Goals and Action Plan

### State Health Care Now

Legislative Department Goals for Jan. 1, 2008 – Dec. 31, 2008

*Last Updated January 8, 2008*

| **Objectives**<br>Big-picture, what are you trying to accomplish this year? | **Measures of Success**<br>At the end of the year, how will you know whether you are successful in this area? | **Milestones**<br>How will you know if you are on track along the way? | **Activities**<br>Who will do what by when over the next 90 days? |
|---|---|---|---|
| 1. Create significant traction for universal coverage legislation | 1. By Dec. 31, universal state health coverage bill introduced in one chamber with public support of either key committee chair or leadership.<br><br>2. By Dec. 31, secure commitment of at least 75% of declared governor candidates to include universal state coverage in campaign platform. | • Majority party sponsor and 2 cosponsors in relevant committee secured by Jun. 30.<br><br>• Majority leader's office in one chamber publicly pledges support for draft bill by Aug. 15. | • Legislative Director and Advocacy Manager meet biweekly to check on political strategy. Initial meeting held by Jan. 15. (Rodrigo)<br><br>• Set-up at least 8 meetings and briefings with staff and/or members of relevant committees and leadership caucus by Mar. 31. Executive Director joins meetings and briefings when possible. (Rodrigo) |

In setting goals, focus on the concepts and avoid getting hung-up on terminology (others may call Objectives "Priorities" and Measures of Success "Goals," for instance).

Specify an owner for every step, where possible.

Goals and plans can either be captured in a chart like this one or in outline format. See the individual goals sample on page 72.

| Objectives | Measures of Success | Milestones | Activities |
|---|---|---|---|
| | | | • Draft bill language by Mar. 31 (final by May. 1). (Carmen)<br>• Write and produce health care resource guide for candidates in collaboration with Communications Assistant, by Jan. 31. (George)<br>• Create brief on all declared candidates' positions on universal state coverage by Mar. 1, updating as candidates' status changes. (George)<br>• Contact all candidates by Mar. 15 to offer "meet and greet" briefings with ED. (Carmen) |
| 2. Intensify and broaden grassroots support | 1. By Dec. 31, quick grassroots response capacity created (for 3 major calls to action, an average of at least 6,000 grassroots supporters contact state representatives and senators). | • By June 30, at least one major action held with over 6,000 supporters.<br>• Tracking sys. up by Feb. 15.<br>• Launch super activist recruitment campaign by Apr. 30.<br>• By June 30, at least 7% of supporters are super activists. | • Identify consultant or temp to clean up grassroots supporter database and create mechanism to track "tell a friend" forwards by Jan. 30. (George)<br>• Meet with Care2 advocacy relations staffer and at least two online advocacy consultants for mobilization strategy advice by Mar. 15. (Rodrigo) |

| Objectives | Measures of Success | Milestones | Activities |
|---|---|---|---|
| | 2. By Dec. 15, 10% of existing (i.e., in database as of Jan. 1) grassroots supporters categorized as "super activists," as defined by having forwarded each action alert to at least 10 friends or having organized an in-person mobilization event (e.g., a house party). | | • Identify and pitch at least 4 press-worthy opportunities for calls to action and draft action alert language for each (on the assumption that at least 1 will actually be launched to grassroots supporter list) by Mar. 31. (George)<br>• Build organizational profile that can be "plugged-in" to and serve as platform for outreach and action alerts on Facebook, MySpace, and other online social networks by Mar. 1. (George)<br>• Identify and pitch at least 2 opportunities for distributed events (e.g., a house party) by Feb. 28. (George) |
| 3. Build a strong staff | 1. All open positions filled by June 30.<br>2. 90% of staff identified as high performers at start of year have committed to stay another year. | • Performance improvement plans in place for all relevant individuals no later than March 31.<br>• Policy Director hired by June 30. | • Develop individualized plans for retaining each high performer, including strategies like private recognition, increased responsibility, direct discussions about future plans, and conversations with ED by Feb 1. (Carmen) |

| Objectives | Measures of Success | Milestones | Activities |
|---|---|---|---|
| | 3. All department staff identified as low- or mid-performers have raised performance significantly, are in the midst of performance improvement plans, or have left. | | • Evaluate department staff on 2007 performance by Jan. 10, categorizing and notifying staff of Executive Director-approved categorization by Jan. 15. (Carmen)<br>• Develop performance improvement plans for all low and mid-performers and meet with all individuals with low and mid-performance 2007 reviews by Feb. 28. (Carmen)<br>• Launch Policy Director search by Feb 15. (Carmen) |

71

## Sample Individual Goals

**State Health Care Now**
**George Alvarez, Program Associate**
Jan. 1, 2008 – Dec. 31, 2008
*(Last Updated Jan. 8, 2008)*

> Goals and plans can either be captured in outline format like this or in a chart like the departmental sample on page 68.

**Objective 1:  Build a base of "super activists" and grow membership**

**Measure of Success 1:** By Dec. 15, 10% of existing (i.e., in database as of Jan. 1) grassroots supporters are "super activists," as defined by having forwarded each action alert to at least 10 friends or having organized an in-person mobilization event (e.g., a house party). (60%)

> Noting what percentage of workload should be devoted to each measure helps ensure alignment about prioritization.

**Milestone 1:**  Launch super activist recruitment campaign by Apr. 30

**Milestone 2:**  At least 10 leaders sign on to be activist recruiters by May 31

**Milestone 3:**  By June 30, at least 7% of supporters are "super activists"

*Key Activities (next 90 days):*

➢ Identify consultant or temp to clean up grassroots supporter database and create mechanism to track "tell a friend" forwards by Jan. 30.

➢ Develop full plan for super activist recruitment campaign by Feb 15.

➢ Generate list of targeted leaders for activist recruiters by Mar. 1.

➢ Build organizational profile that can be "plugged-in" to and serve as platform for outreach and action alerts on Facebook, MySpace, and other online social networks by Mar. 1.

➢ Hold all one-on-one meetings with prospective recruiters by Mar. 31.

➢ Identify and pitch at least 4 press-worthy opportunities for calls to action and draft action alert language for each (on the assumption that at least 1 will actually be launched to grassroots supporter list) by Mar. 31.

**Measure of Success 2:** By Dec. 31, increase our membership by 40%, from 10,500 to 14,700. (30%)

> **Milestone 1:** At least 20 grassroots-led mobilization events held with average attendance of 25 each
>
> **Milestone 2:** By June 30, increased membership by 10%

*Key Activities (next 90 days):*

➤ Identify and pitch at least 2 opportunities for distributed events (e.g., a house party) to at least 10 members by Feb. 5.

➤ Develop membership building plan by Feb. 28.

➤ Present plan to membership committee and get feedback by Mar. 15.

➤ Revise plan and develop accompanying tools (e.g., mobilization event toolkit) by Mar. 31.

**Objective 2: Serve as useful resource in universal coverage effort**

**Measure of Success 1:** 100% of published products (e.g., health care resource guide, candidate brief) are produced in a timely way, are factually correct, and add significant value (as reported by Legislative Director and rest of advocacy team). (10%)

> **Milestone 1:** Health care resource guide completed by Jan. 31 and distributed to targeted allies by Feb. 15
>
> **Milestone 2:** Candidates brief published and distributed to media by Mar. 31

*Key Activities (next 90 days):*

➤ Manage communications assistant to format guide and send to Rodrigo by Jan. 15.

➤ Finalize distribution plan and delegate to communications assistant by Jan. 15.

➤ Hold initial meetings with Rodrigo and Carmen to discuss candidates brief by Jan. 31.

➤ Produce outline of candidates brief and send to Rodrigo by Feb. 5.

➤ Meet with Communications team to discuss plan for candidates brief by Feb. 15.

➤ Get sign-off on communications plan from Rodrigo by Feb. 28.

➤ Develop system for tracking changes to candidate positions by Mar. 15.

## Sample Organizational Goals (1-year)

### State Health Care Now
Jan. – Dec. 2008

> It can be powerful to have your organization's goals on one page.

**programmatic**

**OBJECTIVE 1: Create significant traction for universal coverage legislation**

**Measure of Success 1:** By Dec. 31, universal state health coverage bill introduced in one chamber with public support of either key committee chair or leadership.

**Measure of Success 2:** By Dec. 31, secure commitment of at least 75% of declared governor candidates to include universal state coverage in campaign platform.

> You may want to have milestones and tactics supporting each measure of success (on a separate document to preserve the clarity of a one- or two-page goals document).

**OBJECTIVE 2: Intensify and broaden grassroots support**

**Measure of Success 1:** By Dec. 31, quick grassroots response created (for 3 major calls to action, an average of at least 6,000 grassroots supporters contact state representatives and senators).

**Measure of Success 2:** By Dec. 15, 10% of existing (i.e., in database as of Jan. 1) grassroots supporters are "super activists," as defined by having forwarded each action alert to at least 10 friends or having organized an in-person mobilization event (e.g., a house party).

**OBJECTIVE 3: Raise profile of state health care crisis in the media**

**Measure of Success 1:** By Dec. 31, at least one major national media hit (estimated viewership/readership of 1 million+) and at least 5 minor (state or regional) media hits generated.

**Measure of Success 2:** By Jul. 31, editorial support received from at least one of the three major regional daily papers.

**capacity**

**OBJECTIVE 4: Strengthen our financial sustainability**

**Measure of Success 1:** By Dec. 31, a total of at least $1,850,000 raised, including $1,600,000 in general support.

**Measure of Success 2:** By Dec. 31, 70% of 2006 donors renewed at same giving level or higher.

**OBJECTIVE 5: Build strong staff and culture of performance**

**Measure of Success 1:** All open positions filled by Jun. 30.

**Measure of Success 2:** By Dec. 31, 90% of staff identified as high performers at start of year have committed to stay another year, and all staff identified as low- or mid-performers have raised performance significantly, are in the midst of performance improvement plans, or have left.

## Sample Organizational Goals (longer-term)

### Teach For America
### Organizational Priorities & Measures of Success
### 2000-2004
### *(Initial draft, June 2000)*

**Overarching goal: To build a truly effective movement to realize our vision that one day all children will have the opportunity to attain an excellent education.**

> Having a "headline" goal that encapsulates your focus for the period can be helpful.

1. **Ensure corps members experience real success in closing the achievement gap between their students and students in more privileged areas**

   *Key measures*
   - ➢ 50% of our teachers demonstrate gains in student achievement of at least 1.5 grade levels
   - ➢ 90% complete their two-year commitment

2. **Foster the leadership of alumni in pursuing the systemic changes needed to realize our vision**

   > You should have only a few (ideally four to six) primary objectives in order to focus your staff's efforts.

   *Key measures*
   - ➢ 80% of alumni feel part of a national movement working towards ensuring that all children in this nation will have an equal chance in life
   - ➢ 2,000 alumni participate in at least one event or activity created by the Alumni Association
   - ➢ 80% of alumni report that they feel very positive about Teach For America

3. **Ensure our movement is as large and ethnically and racially diverse as possible**

   *Key measures*
   - ➤ 3,800 corps members teaching by September 2004
   - ➤ More than double the applicant pool (to 10,000)
   - ➤ 40% of incoming corps members are people of color

4. **Develop a sustainable funding base to support our efforts**

   - - - | You should have long-term capacity-building objectives in addition to programmatic ones.

   *Key measures*
   - ➤ $29 million/year revenue by FY 2004
   - ➤ 100% operating reserve built
   - ➤ Annual expenses not to exceed $29 million per year by 2004

5. **Build a thriving, diverse organization capable of consistently producing outstanding results over time**

   *Key measures*
   - ➤ 85% feel very positively about working at Teach For America
   - ➤ 80% of high-performing staff retained until next year
   - ➤ Racial/ethnic make-up of the staff mirrors that of the corps

## *Sample Goal and Action Plan Development Process*

*This sample goal and plan development process serves as a guide to help you design your organization's own process. The exact steps, dates, and duration for each phase will depend on your organization's size, its previous experience with setting goals, and the existence of a longer-term strategic plan, if any, that sets out priorities. The example here assumes an organization operating on a calendar year cycle (i.e., Jan. 1 – Dec. 31).*

> The sample below outlines a lengthy, intensive process that may not be realistic for you. Remember, though, not to let the perfect be the enemy of the good. It's still better to set goals through a shorter process than to have no goals at all.

### I. Set timeline

➢ Executive Director (ED) drafts rough timeline for setting next year's goals and action plans, and shares with senior management team. (Aug. 1)

➢ ED meets with Finance and HR Directors to align goal and action plan cycle with budget cycle and personnel evaluations. (Aug. 8)

### II. Identify organizational priorities based on broad strategic direction
*This phase may be substantially shortened or skipped if your organization has an existing strategic direction or plan (formal or informal) from which it can easily derive the upcoming year's priorities.*

➢ ED reflects on broad strategic direction: is it generally to continue down current or identified path, or should there be broader discussion? If continuing down current path, skip to step III.

➢ If broader discussion, ED starts discussion with an e-mail to senior managers, including department heads, that articulates initial sense of "big-picture" initiatives and areas of focus for the coming year. (Sep. 5)

➢ In one meeting or more, ED and department heads discuss and ultimately agree on a list of initiatives, and identify high-level implications for each department. (Sep. 10 – 20)

### III. Develop departmental goals and plans

➢ With general organizational priorities in mind, department heads brainstorm on their own or with their teams to reflect on past year's progress and identify potential areas of focus for the year ahead. (Sept. 25)

➢ Department heads (and relevant team members) meet separately with ED to discuss department's progress from prior year, lessons learned, and potential areas of focus and goals for the year ahead. (Sept. 28 – Oct. 10). *(Note that for departments where key results are not yet in, the timeline would shift to later in the year.)*

➢ Department heads take ED input and draft actual goals and plans for the year ahead, getting further input from team members as desired. Department heads send draft to ED.

➢ ED drafts goals and plans for any areas for which ED is directly responsible. (Oct. 20)

➢ Department heads and ED meet to review draft goals and plans. (Oct. 25 – Nov. 5)

➢ Department heads make any revisions and send new version to ED. (Nov. 7)

## IV. Finalize key organizational goals

➢ ED pulls from departmental and own plan to create summary goals and plans document, reflecting key areas of organizational focus for the year ahead. ED ensures key goals collectively add up to desired organizational progress toward strategic direction. (Nov. 10)

➢ ED sends draft of summary organizational goals and action plans to chair of board of directors and has call to discuss initial feedback. (Nov. 13)

> Get input from key board members and other important stakeholders early enough in the process for their input to be integrated into the final product, if appropriate.

➢ ED discusses any additional changes (based on board chair feedback or further developments) with department heads, and sends plan to full board. (Nov. 20)

➢ ED discusses proposed final draft of organization's goals and action plans with full board of directors. Board approves final draft (as is or with changes). (Dec. 1)

➢ ED creates final version of organizational goals and action plans. (Dec. 3)

## V. Create individual action plans

➢ Department heads direct
staff to draft individual goals
and short-term action plans based on departmental goals and action
plans. (Nov. 15 - 30)

> Individual goals will become part of each staff member's performance evaluation.

➢ Department heads meet with individual staff to refine individual goals
and action plans and ensure teams collectively cover areas of
departmental responsibility. (Dec. 3 - 13)

➢ Department heads approve all individual goal documents and compile
them into one document (per department) for easy reference. (Dec.
16)

➢ (Department heads meet with staff for performance evaluations
covering prior year.)  (Dec. 10 – 23)

## VI. Roll out organizational goals and action plans

➢ ED convenes full staff for meeting to discuss goals for the year ahead.
1-pager version of organization's key goals distributed in hard copy for
easy posting and reference. (Dec. 5)

➢ Development Director highlights organization's topline goals in
holiday fundraising drive. (Dec. 8 – 31)

> Potential funders will love the fact that you have meaningful goals.

## 3 Components of a Goal

| | Description | Example 1 | Example 2 |
|---|---|---|---|
| **OBJECTIVE** | What you are trying to achieve | Convince more state legislators to support universal health care reform | Raise media profile of organization's expertise in early childhood education issues |
| **METRIC** | How you will measure progress toward your objective | The number of state legislators who have made their first public written or verbal statements in support of universal health care reform, using our language | The number of news hits in which the organization's frame is represented and the organization is mentioned by name<br>• "major" hit = in outlet with average audience of >400K<br>• "minor" hit = in outlet with average audience of <400K |
| **TARGET** | What success looks like on a given metric | 10 | 10 major hits, 20 minor hits |
| **GOAL** | Specific, measurable statement of what you are trying to accomplish | By Nov. 5, 10 state legislators will have made their first public written or verbal statements in support of universal health care reform using our language. | By Dec. 31, organization will have attained at least 10 major and 20 minor hits in which the organization's message and name are referenced. |

## Chapter 3
# Managing the "In-Between": Building a Culture of Excellence

Up to now, we've talked about how you set and reinforce expectations so your staff can take on specific tasks and broad responsibilities. Along the way, though, whether as part of those assignments or just in the course of day-to-day business, your staff will perform thousands of activities that you may never see, or even know about – from greeting prospective job candidates with a friendly smile rather than a curt, "Follow me," to making sure that e-mails to important stakeholders are typo-free. Just as in other areas, here too you need to make sure your staff is clear about your expectations. In this case, your expectations are as much about *how* people operate as about *what* they do. The way you set those expectations is by creating and reinforcing a strong culture.

Culture is the invisible force that transmits messages about "how we do things around here." If you're wrestling with feeling like you have to tell your staff exactly how to handle every situation or aren't confident that they'll perform well in your absence, culture is likely the culprit – and the solution. Whether you're managing a single team or an entire organization, culture is an incredibly powerful tool for shaping how your staff members get work done.

> *Culture is the invisible force that tells people "how we do things around here."*

Whether you shape it deliberately or not, your organization will have a culture, so the real question is whether that culture is sending the kinds of signals you want it to. In this chapter, we'll talk first about the kind of culture you might aim to create. We'll then talk about how you shape and reinforce it, as well as how you hold people accountable for acting in accord with it.

## ELEMENTS OF HIGH-PERFORMING CULTURES

First, let's talk about what you should be aiming for in your culture. While no two cultures will be identical, we've been struck by how often we see the same elements on high-performing teams run by the best managers.

- <u>Relentless pursuit of results</u>. High-performing managers run processes smoothly, but at the end of the day what they care most about is results. They emphasize concrete achievements and, when they're not getting the results they want, they persist until they do.

- <u>Transparency and commitment to continuous improvement</u>. Because they're determined to be successful, high-performing managers are fairly ruthless when it comes to identifying ways they could perform better, and they put a premium on being open (at least internally) about their flaws so they can search for ways to improve. They're generally obsessive about learning from experience, incorporating lessons into practice, and adapting their approach to make it as effective as possible.

- <u>High bar for performance</u>. In teams determined to make an impact, the bar for performance is high. There's often a sense that "not just anyone can work here," and employees know that the manager demands great, not merely good, performance.

- <u>Accountability</u>. Staffers know that if they do a mediocre job on a project, they'll need to redo it, that they need to follow through on

82

commitments (i.e., nothing just disappears), and that they'll be held accountable for their performance.

- Mission integrity. Leaders are focused on the actual impact of the organization's work, not on appearances. Their goals represent what they truly believe would be meaningful progress, rather than just predicting results that would have come about regardless of the organization's actions. For instance, one high-performing organization we know had a goal of recruiting new progressive candidates for local office. It wouldn't permit itself to count toward that goal candidates who likely would have emerged on their own – even though listing them might impress funders.

- Authenticity of all of the above. We can't say enough about the importance of all of these elements being authentic, because cultures are only as powerful as they are genuine. While some organizations pay lip service to these concepts, on high-performing teams what we describe here is truly how things work.

## CREATING AND REINFORCING A HIGH-PERFORMANCE, RESULTS-ORIENTED CULTURE

How, then, can you establish these elements so that they shape the work that gets done on your team? As with delegating tasks or using goals to assign broad responsibilities, the best approaches involve making your expectations clear on the front end, engaging along the way, and holding people accountable to meeting those expectations. Here are four of the most effective ways we've seen managers do this:

1. Modeling. First and foremost, lead by example. Whether you're creating a culture from scratch or trying to turn one around, modeling by leaders is easily the most powerful way to transmit the cultural values and behaviors you want your staff to demonstrate, such as

"always follow up on things," "treat constituents with respect," and so forth. In fact, your culture will look a lot like you. For instance, if you're an executive director who gossips and complains about your volunteers, you can bet your staff is going to do the same. On the other hand, if you talk about your volunteers with respect and appreciation, your staff will reflect that approach themselves.

2. Explicit articulation. Formally articulating the values you expect all staffers to live up to is a simple, worthwhile process that can send strong messages about how people should approach their work. However, in order to be worth doing, this *must* be authentic: we've all seen well-intentioned but laughable posters listing the alleged values of a poorly run business – often claiming that "customers come first" even as we're facing clear evidence that their customers decidedly *don't* come first.

> "A lot of the best organizations that I see are organizations where the role of the manager is primarily to reproduce the culture, because if people have that basic understanding of what the effort is about and how it's appropriate to pursue it, they can be freed up to make all kinds of decisions and take all kinds of initiative. There's a less intensive management workload with a higher return on investment."
>
> - Ricken Patel, Executive Director, Avaaz

But if your core values are genuine, explicitly articulating them can help assimilate newcomers into your culture and reinforce the behaviors you want to see in existing employees.

Once you've established values you want staff members to aspire to, you can reinforce them ongoing through explicit discussions. For instance:

- During new employee orientation, discuss each of the values and what they mean in practice. You could even discuss hypothetical scenarios and how the values would play out. *See point three below.*

- In performance evaluations, measure employee performance against each of your core values. *See point four below.*

- Consider posting a list of core values in the office, and provide the list to all employees.

- Periodically review and edit your list of values with your entire staff or your most senior people – it's a great way to reinforce the meaning behind the words.

*See page 87 for a sample list of core values.*

3. <u>Reinforcement during hiring</u>. You begin sending messages about your culture from the moment a job applicant first contacts you: How responsive are you? What sorts of questions do you ask? Do you start the interview on time? The hiring process is a microcosm of your culture, and smart candidates – exactly the people you want to hire – will be picking up loads of messages about how you do things.

   In addition, we recommend including a discussion of your organization's culture as part of the interviewing process. And you might also ask some of your staff members who best exemplify your culture to speak with top candidates, both in order to give candidates a better sense of your culture and in order to get input from your cultural stars about their sense of a candidate's fit.

4. <u>Performance evaluations and consequences</u>. Performance evaluations are one of the easiest and more direct ways to reinforce culture, since they're an opportunity to formally comment on what values you're looking for and how the staff member is measuring up. In addition to measuring the extent to which the staffer met her goals, the evaluation should also include explicit ratings against your organization's core values. *See page 178 for a sample evaluation form.*

   Having real consequences for performance (in terms of fit with your culture, as well as the results a staff member generates) sends strong messages about what is and isn't expected from staff members. High performers should see their behavior reinforced through positive consequences like promotion, additional responsibilities, lavish praise, and/or extra pay, and low performers should see consequences like serious warnings and terminations (or self-selection out).

---

### Key Points

- Culture is made up of and reinforces the hundreds of daily signals about "how we do things here."

- High-performing managers create cultures that place high value on relentlessly pursuing results, being transparent and committed to continual improvement, meeting a high bar for performance, and exhibiting fundamental integrity. And it's all authentic; this is really how things work.

- Powerful ways to reinforce culture include leading by example, explicitly articulating the core values you expect all staffers to hold, displaying and discussing those values during hiring, and having meaningful consequences for performing in accord with the culture.

---

## 📖 Additional Reading

- Jim Collins, "A Culture of Discipline" in *Good to Great: Why Some Companies Make the Leap... and Others Don't* (Harper Collins 2001), pages 120-143.

- James C. Collins and Jerry I. Porras, "Cult-Like Cultures" in *Built to Last: Successful Habits of Visionary Companies* (Harper Collins 1997 edition), pages 114-139.

## ✏ Tools

- Sample statement of core values

## Sample Statement of Core Values

### TFA Core Values[1]

Teach For America's core values reflect how we as an organization want our staff to operate, individually and collectively. Our core values are central to our culture and represent the style of operating that we believe to be critical for moving us most quickly and purposefully toward our goals.

- **Relentless pursuit of results:** We assume personal responsibility for achieving ambitious, measurable results in pursuit of our vision. We persevere in the face of challenges, seek resources to ensure the best outcomes, and work toward our goals with a sense of purpose and urgency.

- **Sense of possibility:** We approach our work with optimism, think boldly, and greet new ideas openly.

- **Disciplined thought:** We think critically and strategically in search of the best answers and approaches, reflect on past experiences and data to draw lessons for the future, and make choices that are deeply rooted in our mission.

- **Respect and humility:** We value all who are engaged in this challenging work. We keep in mind the limitations of our own experiences and actively seek out diverse perspectives.

- **Integrity**: We ensure alignment between our actions and our beliefs, engage in honest self-scrutiny, and do what is right for the broader good.

[1] From the Teach for America Web site, at http://www.teachforamerica.org/about/corevalues.htm

# Managing the Day-to-Day Work of Your Team: Structures to Bring It All Together

In this section on managing work, we've talked about delegating specific projects, using goals to hand over broad responsibilities, and using your culture to manage all the things that fall in between the cracks. In theory, it's all pretty straightforward. In practice, it can be a lot harder. You might have half a dozen staff members, and for each of them you might have agreed on multiple goals, and have added several specific projects for each of them. You want to follow the principles of setting clear expectations, staying engaged, and creating accountability, but what does that look like in the day-to-day when there's so much to stay on top of?

We've found that there are two very helpful systems that make it significantly easier to manage the day-to-day work of your staff members and to ensure that it's connected to the big-picture goals you want them to accomplish:

1. <u>Mid-range plans</u>. These help bridge annual goals with the shorter-term by getting you and your staffers aligned about what the next several weeks to months should look like and where energy should be going.

2.  <u>Weekly check-in meetings</u>. Even if brief, having a regular time to touch base with your staff about their work keeps you focused on their results and creates a forum for agreeing on expectations, getting engaged, and creating accountability.

In this chapter, we'll explore how to put both of these systems into practice.

## MID-RANGE PLANS

One challenge facing every manager is how to make sure that the ways your staff spends their time each day are well-aligned with what their big picture priorities should be. This can be harder than it sounds, since in the press of day-to-day work, dozens of opportunities come up to work on items that could be useful. Part of your job as manager is to help your staff stay focused on the most important priorities and not get distracted by worthy but less important projects.

Of course, to stay on track, you and your staff need to be clear on what the big-picture priorities are in the first place, and in Chapter 2 we talked about how to use goal-setting as a way to do that. Your goals represent the priorities that the day-to-day work should align with – but a year is a long time, so most people find it easier to break those annual goals and plans down into more manageable chunks. We've found that plans covering somewhere between one and three months are the most effective way of doing this.

Simply put, *a mid-range plan lays out what a staff member's priorities are for the next block of time*, providing a bridge between her broad goals for the year and her daily work. Without this sort of deliberate planning, it's easy for anyone to get caught up in focusing reactively on the work immediately before her – and the next thing you know, it's November and your staffers haven't focused on the important projects you had wanted them to devote time to. (This is true for managers *and* their staff, so as you'll see in Chapter 10 we recommend that you create quarterly plans for yourself as well.)

Just as with annual goals, a major part of the value of mid-range plans comes from the process of creating them: going back and forth with staff members about their mid-range plans helps get you on the same page about your expectations.

> *"I've had to learn the discipline of, in a constantly changing environment, saying that my team needs specific work plans and to build in flexibility for change but still say that over the course of six months, this is what we're going to be doing."*
>
> *- Brian Komar, Director of Strategic Outreach and Alliances, Center for American Progress*

Mid-range plans can be very simple. A single page of bulleted points can suffice, as long as they're specific, the items are reasonably actionable, and your staff member attaches dates wherever appropriate. One way to organize these is by having your staff member list each of her annual objectives and then note what she'll be doing this month (or quarter) to meet each. *(See page 100 for a sample quarterly plan.)* This approach is useful because it forces her to think through her goals and ensure that she doesn't get caught up in activities for activities' sake. Then, apart from the mid-range plan, for any piece of major work she might also create a more detailed project plan (as discussed in Chapter 1) that lays out the more nitty-gritty steps to get there. *See page 35 for a sample project plan.*

> *A simple bulleted list of actionable items and rough dates can suffice as a mid-range plan.*

As with most aspects of managing, you should adapt your approach to fit the person and the context. For an experienced employee with a strong track record, you might just look for a plan that gives you a high-level sense of where the person's energy will be going, whereas with an employee who needs more structure, you'd want to see a plan with more specifics and dates.

## CHECK-IN MEETINGS

We think everyone should create mid-range plans because they're such a helpful way of getting on the same page about priorities and expectations. But even if you choose not to have your staff create these, one managerial tool you definitely shouldn't pass up is the regular check-in meeting.

Check-ins are periodic meetings between a manager and a staff member to discuss ongoing work. Check-ins serve a variety of purposes:

- Advancing individual projects. By spending a few minutes on each of the major items on the staff member's plate, the manager has a chance to ask probing questions, spot areas of concern for further work, and serve as a resource to the staff member. Often the manager's "one level up" perspective allows her to fairly quickly see solutions to problems that the staff member may have missed.

- Balancing priorities across projects. By looking across all the work on a staff member's plate, managers can help their staff focus on the most important pieces and can suggest areas that the staff member might deprioritize. Without check-ins, it's very easy to miss when a staffer's workload is too heavy or too light, when a staffer is focusing too much time on one project at the expense of another, or when a staffer is letting less visible tasks fall through the cracks.

- Coordinating the team. Managers can spot ways in which different staff members' work intersects and can ensure the different parts of the team act in concert. (Regular staff meetings can help with this, too.)

- Providing feedback. In theory, managers should provide feedback in the moment, but it's sometimes easier to do this during a regular check-in meeting than in the rush of the day-to-day.

- Connecting personally. Staff members need to know that you care about them as people, and having a regular time to meet outside the course of daily work also gives you a better chance to ask about their morale, as well as their lives outside of work.

**Putting Check-in Meetings into Practice**

Let's look at how you can put check-in meetings into practice.

- How frequently should you have check-in meetings? In our experience, a weekly check-in meeting works well for most employees. However, as always, you should adapt your approach to fit the context – some employees need more frequent interaction, while others might benefit from less frequent (say, every other week) but longer discussions, so you should determine how much is appropriate for each employee.

- Who should attend? Typically, a check-in meeting involves just you and the employee. Unlike department meetings or staff meetings, where the goal is more about fostering coordination and communication across a team of staff members, check-ins work best when they are one-on-one.

- How long should the meetings be? The length of the meeting will vary, but in general, allow between 30 and 90 minutes per meeting, depending on the complexity of the staffer's work and her needs.

- Use an agenda. This sounds so obvious that we hesitate to say it, but we see practices to the contrary all the time: meetings are much more productive if you don't walk into them cold. Preparing for a check-in can run the gamut from asking the staffer to e-mail you an agenda beforehand to taking a minute at the beginning of the meeting to agree on the what topics to cover.

- Consider using weekly (or biweekly) reports. Some managers swear by having their staffers submit weekly or biweekly reports, summarizing their current and upcoming projects. These reports can then form the agenda for your check-in meetings: you'll flag items from the report you want to raise for discussion, and the staffer will come prepared with her own questions for you. And having a comprehensive list of everything on the staffer's plate can prompt both of you to ask questions or raise issues about tasks that might not otherwise be on your radar screen.

On the other hand, other managers (including one of your authors!) worry that these reports can be a bureaucratic drain on valuable staff time. If you do decide to use weekly reports, keep in mind that the goal is to put you and your staffer on the same page about priorities and to create accountability, not to simply force the staff member to document where her time went that week.

*See page 102 for a sample check-in meeting agenda.*

## Making Check-in Meetings Effective

We believe that check-in meetings are such a powerful tool that you'll begin to see better results just by implementing them as a regular practice. But here are a few ways to really get the most out of them:

- <u>Think beforehand about what you want to get out of the meeting</u>. Again, it sounds obvious but few do it. Taking two minutes in advance to force yourself to think through "What am I most worried about? What do I want to make sure we focus on?" can have a big impact.

- <u>Don't just go through the motions</u>. Check-ins are one of your key management tools, so make sure to fully engage during the meeting. Put away that Blackberry! We've both been guilty of sneaking a glance at e-mail during a check-in, but we've also learned that resisting the temptation and staying focused saves us time in the long run.

- <u>Keep the big picture in mind</u>. Be guided by a broader sense of whether you and your team are on track to reach your most important goals. Keep asking yourself whether the projects at hand are the most important things to be spending time on.

- <u>Keep track of items you want to raise</u>. While ideally the onus should be on the staffer to make sure you cover everything that needs to be discussed, it's ultimately your responsibility. Develop a system for keeping track of check-in topics that come up during the course of business. This could mean jotting them down on your weekly action list (see Chapter 10), or you might keep track in whatever electronic calendar you use. Not only will this help you remember important topics, but when your staff members see that items don't slip through the cracks, they'll feel more accountable and will keep better track themselves.

- <u>Give feedback</u>. Reflect on what's gone well recently ("Great report to the board") and what didn't meet expectations ("Let's talk about what went wrong with the phone banking"). This one-on-one time is a good opportunity to discuss what can be learned from recently concluded projects, as well as to provide both positive and, when needed, corrective feedback.

- <u>Make sure next steps are clear</u>. Few discussions should end without an agreement about what should happen next, even if it's just, "Let's both think this over and then you should bring it up again next week." It can be especially useful for your staffer to e-mail you a summary of everything that was agreed to, or at least for her to give you a verbal recap of next steps at the end of the meeting (just as you would ask for a "repeat-back" when delegating a single project).

- <u>Include a human element</u>. Take a few minutes to make a personal connection and find out how the person is doing generally. How is the person's life going outside of work? Now is a good time to ask about significant others, kids, and non-work projects.

- <u>Adjust your approach to fit the staffer</u>. For instance, some staffers will need you to be more directive and hands-on, whereas with others, you can switch into more of a "how can I be helpful to you?" mode. Or you may learn that one staffer needs help not losing sight of the big picture, while another needs prompting about specific items that may be slipping through the cracks.

---

### Getting Beneath the Surface

One of managers' biggest challenges in a check-in is figuring out how to get beneath the surface to understand what's really happening. If you simply run down a list of projects without digging deeper, you're likely to miss important information about what obstacles might be looming and how you might be a resource to your staff in avoiding them. Here are some questions that can help you get beneath the surface:

- What one or two things would make this week a success for you?
- How do you know you're on track?
- How are you checking to make sure that's working?
- How are you handling X [a specific element]?
- What seems to be working well?  Why do you think that's working?
- What could go wrong?  What are you most worried about?
- Have you thought about what you'll do if Y happens?
- What's most important out of all those things?
- What makes you say that?
- What kind of data do we have to inform how that's working?
- Roughly how much of your time are you spending on that?
- What's your timeline for that?
- Can you give me a specific example of that?
- Can we take one specific instance and talk through how you're approaching it?
- Can we role-play what that might look like?
- What does your agenda for that look like?
- What other options did you consider?

*See page 103 for a sample check-in script.*

---

## Monthly Step-Backs

Ideally, your check-in meetings include discussions of big picture progression toward goals, morale, development needs, and lessons learned – but in reality, these bigger picture topics will often get pushed aside in the press of day-to-day business. So it's a good idea to have one check-in per month to deliberately focus on these issues (Jerry and his staff members hold "first Monday step-backs" every month). During these meetings:

- Pull out the staffer's goals and check how her progress is matching up against them.

- Focus in on how she's doing, both personally and with the job. Is she happy? Frustrated? How is she feeling overall?

- What might you both be able to do to help her develop further? (See Chapter 6 for a discussion of staff development.)

- What lessons have been learned from recent work and how should they be applied in the future?

**Reminder: See the Work in Action**

> ### Managing Other Managers
>
> When the person you're managing is a manager herself, part of her job is to get work done through other people. So instead of, or in addition to, asking about how's she's spending her own time, ask about what her team is focused on. Who is working on what? How is she managing Casey on that project? How is it going? How does she know?
>
> And here too, getting your hands dirty will help. Be enough in touch with the people on her team that you have a good sense of what's going on. And consider doing a joint visit with the manager to observe the work of her team.

As powerful and important as check-in meetings are, don't forget that they're not the only way to check on progress. You should get out from behind your desk and see things in action, too. Often what you see actually happening will look different from what you pictured when you were just talking about it. As we discussed in the first chapter, finding ways to observe the work in action can give you a much deeper understanding of how plans are really playing out.

### Managing Work Outside Your Area of Expertise

If you're charged with managing an area of work outside your main expertise, such as IT, here are five tips to do it effectively.

1. Get aligned about big, important goals, with clear ambitious deadlines. For instance, agree with your IT team that "We need an interactive Web site up and running in time for our big legislative push, which means launched, tested, and ready to use by February." This keeps you focused on the end product, and then you can ask questions about the process – "How will we know whether this is on track? Are there milestones you could set to hit along the way?"

2. Manage by asking good questions rather than suggesting answers. Even without knowing the substance, you can pose basic, useful questions like, "How do you know that XYZ is true?" or "What will you do if ABC happens?" or "What do other organizations do about DEF?"

3. Use your ignorance to your advantage. Try a lot of, "Help me understand why..." and probe the answers.

4. Connect the person to her "customers." Your staffer may be doing work that few others understand but where many know whether or not they're getting what they need. Often you find yourself in the middle between "customers" (staff members in other departments) who tell you they want something, and an "expert" whom you manage. Your job is to bring the two sides together. Make sure your managee is talking to customers and agreeing with them on what they'll have by when. Ensure there's an ongoing channel for communication and feedback, including periodic surveys or other means that let you and your staffer see how the customers feel.

5. Judge by what you do know. Often you won't have any clear idea whether 90% of what the person does is good because you don't really understand the subject matter. You will, though, understand 10% of it (even if it's just something like, "Did this person explain what she was doing in a way customers could understand?" or – with IT – whether or not your e-mail and network are running smoothly). Extrapolate from what you *can* understand, and assume the 90% you don't get is similar. If the small pieces you get seem great, it's reasonable to assume that the rest probably is – and if the piece you get seems off, it's likely that the rest may be, too.

## Key Points

- Quarterly plans can get you and your staffers aligned about what the next few months should look like and where energy should be going. These plans provide a bridge between an employee's broad goals for the year and her daily work.

- Holding regular weekly check-in meeting with each staff member is essential to monitoring ongoing projects, ensuring that problems are spotted and addressed, balancing workloads, providing feedback, and generally "checking in" with the employee about how things are going overall.

## Tools

- Sample mid-range plan

- Sample check-in meeting agenda

- Sample script – check-in meeting

## Sample Mid-range Plan

*Julie, VP Marketing, 3-Month Plan*
*July – September 2008*

**Goal 1: 85% of senior staff from teams we support (Regions, Recruitment, Alumni, Development) feel the Marketing team consistently delivers high-quality products on time (as measured by end-of-year survey)**

> Organizing mid-range plans by goal helps keep the ultimate end in mind so you can be sure your activities listed below align with it.

- Create guidelines/best practices for regional galas (event and diaries) (*nice-to-have – if so, by 9/30; at minimum, start informal running list of ideas*)
- Create materials for summits in Houston/DC/Baltimore – due 7/15
- Revise Continuum (contingent upon hiring new Dir of Alum Comm)
- Hire new Director of Alumni Communications – create job description and place ad on Idealist and craigslist by 9/1
- Ensure Lynette develops letterhead (without address/vision statement) for press kits/development packets/recruitment packets, etc. by 8/15

> Clear due dates will make it easier to determine at a glance which items need to be prioritized in your daily work.

**Goal 2: All written materials reflect our desired messages and 80% of staff (as determined through random sampling) can deliver concise, accurate messages on basic questions about our organization**

- Conduct message training for RDs/CDs (I go on at least 2 site visits and work one-on-one w/RDs)
- Revise guidelines and templates for regional matriculation packets, ensure Lynette completes new version by 8/31
- Web site
  - Public site: identify contacts for recruitment, HR, development by 7/15
  - Maintain quality control of public and CMA Web site per system established – ongoing
- Ensure new ED training on media/PR is ready for ED conference 9/2

**Goal 3: Increase in significant national and regional press hits – i.e., stories about us, not just mentions in passing – by 50% (from 8 to 12 national and 52 to 78 regional)**

- Explore hiring firm to help on the PR front for short-term. Convene meeting with Connie and Thomas by 7/15
- Web site
  - Have press center up and running by 9/30
- PR strategy finalized (*may change per PR consultant/agency*)
  - Prepare calendar of announcements
  - Capitalize on annual round-up stories (i.e. *NY Times* Giving section—November deadline; *Worth Magazine* 100 Best Charities; *Chronicle of Philanthropy* Year-end Round-up)
  - Establish PR advisory board (top targets: Ms. Jackson at ABC Bank; Mr. Goldstein at MSNBC; etc.)
  - Finalize more detailed plan for all of this by 8/15

**Goal 4: New glitch-free Web site that reflects our identity and desired positioning and enthusiastically signed-off on by top 3 execs in the organization launched by December 31.**

- Ensure Juan gets phase 2 of Web site up by 9/1
  - Online giving capabilities
  - Replace regional "supporters" list with regional one-pagers
- Redesign regional pages (content and layout) to be more effective/engaging by 8/1

***Longer-term (on hold for now):***

- Explore possibility of desk side briefings with Abby/Wendy (around issues, studies)

> Specifying what you will NOT do helps you get aligned with your manager and your staff about what your priorities really are.

- Redo 2008 national brochure (winter/spring as part of annual report)
- Corporate sponsorship guidelines (with development)
- Early planning for national alumni summit
- Welcome packet for new alumni

## Sample Check-in Meeting Agenda

**This week will be successful if... (i.e., my priorities for the week)**

1) All materials for training finalized and out the door by Thursday night
2) Housing bill drafting started, and on track to be done by end of next week
3) Newsletter draft complete, ready for layout

> Weekly priorities should be few in number (two to four) in order to focus on the most important areas, and they should be presented as outcomes so it's clear at the end of the week if they've been achieved.

1. Key program updates
   a. Training
      i. Outline/agenda completed
      ii. Materials for 1st training
      iii. Sample evaluation form – quick thoughts?
   b. Housing
      i. New coalition members – others?
      ii. Bill drafting – need lawyer recommendation
      iii. Action – location/organizers/targets/number of attendees
   c. Outreach
      i. Newsletter draft and timeline
      ii. Membership database update
      iii. Training agenda

2. Ongoing business
   a. Staffing/personnel
      i. Interviewing three Program Associate finalists for this week
   b. Topics for management meeting

3. Other items/misc.
   a. Summer internships: candidates/posting/hiring process

4. Longer-term projects
   a. Annual conference – *planning meeting July 6*
   b. Train the trainers – *curriculum due July 15*

## Sample Script – Check-in Meeting

*Here's an example of what a typical weekly check-in meeting between a manager (M) and staffer (S) – in this case a communications director – might sound like.*

M: Hey, come on in. How's it going?

S: Busy, busy, busy. You?

M: Things are good. You'll be happy to know that Tony [son] got the lead in the musical. No pressure, but I'll expect to see you and the family on opening night. *[Pause for nervous laughter.]* How's Denise?

> Be real and take an interest in your staff members' lives.

S: She's feeling a lot better – thanks for asking.

M: Glad to hear it. So I know you're busy – should we dive in?

S: Let's do it.

M: Your e-mail agenda looks great. The areas I've highlighted that I want to discuss are framing of our messaging in next week's press release, progress on the new Web site, how last week's meet-and-greet went, and next steps around hiring your assistant. I'd also like to add the e-mail we got from John and how you're thinking of following up. Anything else on your list?

> Your staff should propose topics for discussion (could be as formal as a weekly report or as informal as a short e-mail with bullets of key items), ideally in advance so you can give thought to the topics and add your own.

S: Nope – that covers it.

M: Let's start with the messaging for the press release. How are you thinking you'll frame it?

…

That sounds good, but have you thought about including some sound-bites on the key points from the research?

…

How will you handle it if a reporter asks YYY?

> Ask probing questions and try to get beneath the surface to see whether the staffer is on the right track.

S: I'm torn. We could frame it as a states' rights issue, or we could try to make it more personal and use anecdotes. I'm really wrestling with that.

M: Which way are you leaning?

> You don't want to shy away from giving your opinion, but asking questions "keeps the monkey" on the staff member to do her best thinking first.

S: I guess for this context, the individual anecdotes are more likely to get coverage, so that's my inclination.

M: That sounds right to me, too. Have you gotten Joe's input on this whole thing? - - - - - - - - -

> Remind the staffers of others who should play a role.

S: Not yet. I was thinking of setting up a meeting for the three of us in the next day or two – would that work for you?

...

M: So how are you coming with the Web site? As I said in my e-mail, I thought you did a really good job with the templates I saw.

S: Yeah, thanks. I think we're in good shape.

M: So can we delve into this a bit? It certainly seems like things are good, but as you know, these kinds of projects have run into glitches in the past for all different reasons. What do you think could happen that would slow things down and make you miss the deadline we discussed?

> Probe about potential problems before they have the chance to develop.

S: The only issue I see is the vendor – they haven't returned my calls the past two days. I'm worried that they're overwhelmed.

M: That's a good point. How are you thinking about taking that on?

S: If I don't hear back in the next day, I'm going to call their VP. I'm not sure it'll be necessary, but if it feels like it is can I have you call the CEO to reinforce the importance of this?

M: Absolutely. And in terms of reaching out to the VP, my instinct is not even to wait another day – I'd let them know right now that you're focused on this and can't have any delays.

> Where you do have ideas, don't hesitate to share them.

S: That makes sense, I'll do that.

M: So stepping back from all these, what would you say your biggest priorities are right now?

S: Well, the press thing isn't that critical, but it's urgent – so I'm on that. Then there's the Web site and getting ready for the conference.

M: Where does hiring to fill your assistant position fit in?

S: Good question. It's definitely important, but I just haven't been able to find the time. ------ Make sure nothing big is missing from the staffer's radar screen.

M: Could you pull Jackie in more on the conference to free up some of your time?

S: Hmmm... that's a good idea. Yeah, I'll talk to her about that. Assuming that works, it'd be press, Web site, and hiring.

M: Sounds great. And can we just quickly run through next steps on those?

S: Yup. On press, by Tuesday I'll send you...

M: That all sounds good. Anything else?

S: Nope. Tell Tony congratulations for me.

# Section II
# Managing the People

## IT'S ALL ABOUT THE RIGHT PEOPLE

As we've just discussed, managing the work well is critically important –
but having the right people to do the work in the first place might be even
more important. Managers, though, often overestimate their own abilities
to get people to produce results when their team members aren't as strong
as they should be.

To illustrate the flaw in this approach, let's talk sports. If you were
coaching a basketball team and your job was to win, would you want to
take players who were chosen for you and then work your hardest to shape
them into a strong squad, or would you rather choose your players (say,

Michael Jordan and Scottie
Pippen), even if it meant
you couldn't do a thing to
alter their performance
once they joined your
team? No matter how
good a coach you are,
you're never going to get
a squad of Jerry Hausers
and Alison Greens to beat
Michael and Scottie.

Clarify goals all you want – your
5'9" co-author isn't going to dunk
on Michael.

The impact of having a team of high performers in the workplace is similarly dramatic. We're not talking about small gains in productivity and effectiveness, like 5% or 10%. We're talking about massive, startling gains – think of the difference between the number of points Jerry would score versus the number Michael would (trust us on this – it would be big). In our experience, we've seen that in a variety of situations high performers outperform lower performers by *five times or more*. Consider:

- When Jerry was at Teach For America, he replaced one regional director with another, and in one year fundraising in the region went up from $43,000 to $285,000 (and within two additional years, to $1 million).

- We've both had assistants who struggled to handle the volume of work and who swore that there was too much work for any one person to juggle. In each case, when they left, their replacements were able to handle all of the duties and then some, to the point that we ended up loading them up with entire new areas of responsibility to make the best use of them.

- In the development department at one organization, a processing clerk couldn't keep up and created a six-month backlog of checks to process. A new person came in and *within one month* had processed the six-month backlog and was fully caught up.

We could go on and on with examples like this. One high performer can have the same impact as five or more lower performers – so imagine the impact of having an entire organization of people operating at this level!

If the right people make an enormous impact on your results, and getting results is your fundamental job, then you should put significant energy into getting and keeping the right people on board and moving out the ones who don't meet that bar. And in this section, we'll discuss how to do that:

- In Chapter 5, we'll talk about how to find and hire superstars.

- In Chapter 6, we'll discuss how (and when) to develop the skills and performance of your staff.

- In Chapter 7, we'll look at ways to make sure your best employees stay.

- And in Chapter 8, we'll tackle how to address performance issues, including terminating employees who aren't meeting the high bar you need.

Just as with managing the work effectively, managing the makeup of your team pays enormous dividends. When you have the right people with the right skills on board, you'll get dramatically better results.

*Chapter 5*
# Hiring Superstars

Little about management is more important than hiring well, since you'll never get great results without having the right people on your staff. But we've found that even when managers say they know how crucial it is to have the right people on staff, they often don't use the hiring practices that should stem from that belief.

Just to take one example, probably the key determinant of success for any hiring process is the quality of the candidates a manager has to choose from. That is, most hiring mistakes occur not because managers select the wrong person, but rather because they don't have the right person to select to begin with. The secret lies in proactively building a strong pool of candidates. Many managers pay lip-service to this idea, but then end up spending very little energy doing anything beyond posting jobs on popular Internet sites.

In this chapter, we'll talk about how to do hiring the right way, so that you maximize your chances of ending up with a staff of superstars. We'll cover five key steps:

1. Figuring out who you're looking for by articulating the critical qualities needed for the role;

2. Building a high-quality pool of candidates;

3.  Gathering information about your candidates through interviews, exercises, and reference checks so you can make your hiring decision based on the *actual* rather than the *hypothetical;*

4.  Making your decision; and

5.  Selling the position and making the offer.

### FIGURING OUT WHO YOU'RE LOOKING FOR

The very first step in hiring well is to get a detailed picture of who you are looking for. Who would your ideal candidate be? In order to answer this question and produce an effective job description for potential hires, you'll need to clarify the role and think critically about what skills and qualities you should look for.

**Get clear on the job responsibilities**

First, organize your thoughts about what the person will do (and won't do). The more specific you are about likely activities, the more helpful your list will be. For instance, rather than saying, "manage our brand," your list for your head of marketing might include "create list of brand attributes," "design collateral materials," and "conduct trainings so staff can identify messages that do and don't fit our brand." If the position has an existing job description, look at it critically and make sure it captures what you need now, which may be different from what you needed when the job was first designed.

**Consider what skills, knowledge, and general qualities the position requires**

Once you're clear on what the person will need to do, think about what type of person would thrive at those things. What skills, background knowledge, and general qualities should the person have? For instance, if you are hiring a research assistant who will gather information from multiple sources and then publish reports, key skills might include synthesizing data and writing clearly. You might also look for specific knowledge of the subject matter the research assistant will cover. As for general qualities, consider the specific job and your organization as a whole. What traits do the most successful people with whom you work share? Does your organization have explicit or implicit "core values" that the person must hold? For example, your organization might place a high value on being able to operate in a fast-paced environment. If that quality is important, it should go on your list.

## Separate "must-haves" from "nice-to-haves"

As you make your list, distinguish between what is a "must-have" for the role and what is a "nice-to-have." In doing this, you should consider what qualities tend to be inherent (you either have it or you don't) versus what can be taught or developed. Underlying skills like strong critical thinking, effective writing, work ethic, meticulousness, or an ability to build strong interpersonal relationships are difficult to teach, so if they are important to the job, they should go on your "must have" list. More specific skills or knowledge – like mastery of a particular type of software, industry knowledge, or experience writing fundraising letters – can more easily be picked up along the way, particularly when more essential traits (in these cases, critical thinking and strong writing) are in place. There are, of course, times when prerequisite knowledge is essential – for instance,

> *Look for underlying qualities and skills, rather than specific knowledge or experience.*

your CFO needs to come in with an understanding of accounting principles – but *in many cases organizations overvalue specific skills or content knowledge and don't put enough weight on underlying skills or qualities that are harder to develop.* In the long (or even medium) term, underlying traits like critical thinking or initiative or assertiveness are much more likely to differentiate high performers than are things like specific experience in your sector.

*See page 136 for a sample worksheet on figuring out the role.*

### Create a job description

Once you are clear on your desired criteria, you should translate your list into a job description, listing responsibilities and qualifications. You want the people with the traits you desire to recognize themselves in your summary, so make clear what traits are essential and what traits are less important. For instance, in the case of the research assistant, many potential applicants will assume you want someone with experience in your particular field. If you value general skills like strong writing more than industry-specific knowledge, be sure that your job description makes this clear.

> *"The biggest thing I've learned about management is that the hiring process is absolutely crucial to everything else. Getting good people into important roles is the key to organizational success. My watershed, bell-went-off-in-the-head moment was when I realized that skills matter more than experience, and that finding someone with experience on paper isn't as important as finding someone with the right skills. Experience and knowledge are great, but they don't always transfer from position to position, and learning how someone handles a situation is more important than knowing what their job description was."*
>
> *- Alexandra Acker,*
> *Executive Director,*
> *Young Democrats of America*

You also should think about the profile of the ideal person who would fill the role well. For instance, if you're looking for an executive assistant, do you picture hiring a career "assistant" who has a great deal of experience or might a highly organized recent college graduate be well-suited to what you want? If the latter, you might make a point of saying that prior experience is less important than being extremely organized and attentive to detail.

The version of the job description that you turn into an ad or post publicly should also sell the position and organization. For instance, what are some of organization's recent successes? What exciting challenges are on the horizon? How will the person in this position help to address these issues?

*See page 139 for a sample job description.*

---

### What About Passion?

Contrary to conventional wisdom, exhibiting a great deal of passion for your organization's issue should generally not be a must-have quality for candidates. In fact, we've seen no correlation between visible passion and effectiveness. Passion is certainly not a bad thing, but we've seen far too many managers use passion as a substitute for talents, hiring highly passionate candidates (or at least candidates who talk as if they're passionate) who end up not being well suited for the job. So, beyond checking for a basic commitment to the objectives of the organization, don't let a candidate's enthusiasm about your work overly influence your thinking about her fit for the role. Ultimately, what you most want is a candidate who is passionate about *results*.

---

## DEVELOPING A STRONG POOL OF APPLICANTS

The most important variable in determining whether you hire a superstar is how strong a pool of candidates you have in the first place. As we noted in the opening to this chapter, most hiring mistakes occur not because managers select the wrong person, but rather because they don't have the right person to select to begin with. Given this, the more energy you spend on building your pool of candidates, the more likely you'll be to find high performers.

### Mass marketing

Perhaps the easiest part of recruitment, and certainly the most commonly practiced, is mass marketing – using techniques like newspaper ads that reach multiple people rather than specific individuals. In this category, most organizations think to hit the obvious sources, such as posting on

*Want to make the right hire? The most important place to put your energy is in building a strong pool of candidates.*

their own Web site, circulating announcements to e-mail lists, and posting on sites like www.idealist.org or www.craigslist.org.

In designing your advertising efforts, get creative and go beyond the obvious. For instance, if your ideal profile is someone with strong writing skills and you don't necessarily need prior experience in your specific field, post your job announcement at the English departments of local universities and on online job banks geared toward writers. If you're hiring an IT staffer, send notices to IT consulting firms in your community.

**Individual Headhunting**

The most successful managers go beyond mass channels and bring their searches down to an individual level, basically becoming headhunters. They consider the ideal profile of the person in the role, and they try to think of anyone they know who might fit that profile, including current members of their staff. Besides being candidates themselves, your current staff can also help think of people to target. When there are important openings at one organization we know, the executive director gathers a small group of staff members and in 30 minutes of brainstorming they inevitably come up with a list of 10-15 good possibilities.

Once you have a list of prospects, you should recruit them aggressively. Rather than simply e-mailing them a job description and asking whether they're interested, make it harder for them to say no. For instance, invite them out for a cup of coffee and talk to them about their future plans and the position you have open. This sort of personal interest is usually far more compelling than a quickly e-mailed job posting.

**Finding connector sources**

You should also think of "connector sources" – people who aren't right for the job themselves, but who might know others who are. Go through your

116

list of contacts and pick out people who might be good sources, whether they're connected to your organization or are social acquaintances.

Here too, once you have a good source, you should try to speak with the person directly rather than e-mailing an announcement. You will be surprised how many more names you get when you force someone to spend a few minutes on the phone with you. (This is why professional headhunters almost always want to speak to you on the phone rather than simply e-mailing you an announcement.)

## Striving for diversity

For a variety of reasons, including the fact that many nonprofits have missions connected to promoting social, racial, or economic justice, many organizations strive to have a staff that is diverse in different respects. At a minimum, organizations should aim to have a workforce that reflects the relevant population in their community. The best way of reaching this aim is to try to ensure through both mass marketing and individual headhunting that your applicant pool is diverse. For instance, at the mass marketing level, if you are looking for strong African-American

---

### The Permanent Campaign

Whether or not you have a current opening, you should always be looking for strong potential staffers, noting interesting prospects you come across – and encourage your staff members to do the same. To ensure that good candidates readily come to mind when the time comes to hire, keep a running list of prospects. A simple Word document listing names, contact information, and one sentence of context about the person to trigger your memory works well.

And don't just passively track these potential stars – actively reach out and cultivate them. Send the occasional e-mail with updates on your work, take them out for coffee and talk about their career goals and how your organization might fit in, or drop them a periodic e-mail to see how they're doing.

---

candidates, you might try to get your position posted on e-mail lists for black professionals in the area. On the personal headhunting level, if you

---

### Ideas for Building a Strong Pool

Most hiring mistakes occur not because managers select the wrong person, but rather because they don't have the right person to select to begin with. Here are a few tips to help you build a strong pool and avoid that trap.

Mass-marketing:

- Post ads on your Web site and those of other friendly organizations
- Send a message out to e-mail lists
- Contact friends, colleagues, and staff members and ask them to circulate the announcement
- Submit posts to job sites (including www.idealist.org and www.craigslist.org)
- Use industry-specific online job banks
- Get on social networking Web sites
- Contact the alumni/career-service offices of undergraduate or graduate schools
- Reach out to professional societies
- Advertise in local newspapers

Individual headhunting:

- Go through your contact list and note potential candidates or sources
- Hold a meeting of strong members of your staff and brainstorm ideas for candidates or sources (set a target: "We will not leave until we think of six good candidates and 20 good sources to call")
- Keep a running list of staff prospects and review it when you have openings
- Review your own staff list for candidates
- Call peers at allied organizations and ask them to brainstorm with you
- Identify "pipeline" organizations for your staff and call contacts there (could be service organizations, government agencies, private sector companies, etc.)
- Call former staffers and interns who were strong (either as candidates or sources)
- Hire an actual headhunter

don't have diverse networks of your own, reach out to others who do, finding sources who might be more likely to know of diverse candidates. The personal headhunting piece is key here; of the many organizations we know that have wrestled with how they can build a more diverse staff, the ones that have made the most progress are those that made a serious, proactive effort to build and cultivate a strong pool of diverse candidates over time.

*See page 140 for a worksheet on building the applicant pool.*

## SELECTING THE RIGHT PERSON

Once you've started building a strong pool of candidates, you'll begin the selection process, which typically consists of successive stages with cuts at each step along the way. The details will vary depending on the position, your organization, and the quality of applications you receive, but typically you'll begin by making a first cut after simply reading through candidates' resumes and cover letters, rejecting the ones who clearly aren't a strong match. You'll then do interviews on the phone or in person, often of greater length as the process goes on. Interspersed along the way – sometimes even before the first interview – you should ask candidates to complete exercises that assess the qualities you'll need them to demonstrate on the job. Finally, as you get more serious about a candidate, you should check with people who know her to find out their opinion about her fit with your role.

Let's take a look at the main steps: initial screening, interviews and exercises, and checking references.

### Initial screening of candidates

To make your job easier at the initial screening stage, think carefully about what you ask applicants to submit. A resume and cover letter are fairly typical, of course, but you can also ask for more. If a position involves writing, save yourself the trouble of interviewing poor writers by asking for a three-page writing sample along with the resume. If you're looking for a Web designer, ask applicants to submit links to several sites they created. As applications begin coming in, you'll know immediately that some aren't right and you can reject these immediately (see sidebar below). For others, you'll need to scrutinize the materials more closely, looking for evidence of the must-have qualities you want in a role. For instance, if you need a go-getter who will take initiative even without close supervision, look at how the candidate describes her accomplishments in prior jobs to see if there's evidence of going above and beyond. If you need a good writer, scrutinize the cover letter or writing sample.

---

### Rejecting Candidates

Make sure to inform candidates when they are no longer under consideration, even if all they have done is to submit an application online. These candidates could be your future donors or supporters (or could be perfect for a job opening you have in the future), and how you handle rejections will give them an impression, good or bad, of your organization.

The fastest way to send a rejection is by having a standard e-mail template that you can easily adapt, depending on how much interaction you have had with a candidate *(see page 159 for a sample).* Managers (including your authors) differ on whether or not a phone call is more appropriate for candidates who have gone through an extensive process. If you do make a call, you can be direct without being insulting – tell them the ways in which you thought they were strong, and the ways in which they might not have been the right fit for your position. For instance, you might say, "You clearly have a tremendous amount of knowledge about the industry. For this position, we were putting even more emphasis on the ability to network and bring in new supporters, and while I'm sure you could do that, it didn't strike me as your primary strength. I have no doubt, though, that you'll be a real asset to someone in the right position."

## Interviews and exercises

Once you've chosen the candidates who seem promising enough to pursue further, you'll proceed to the "get to know you" stage. In the typical process, a candidate who makes it all the way through might have undergone two or more rounds of interviews, with a shorter first interview and a longer second (and perhaps third or more) round. During the later rounds, the candidate might meet others in the organization – such as the hiring manager's boss, prospective subordinates if the person would be managing others, and/or a would-be peer who would be working closely with the person. By getting others' perspectives, the hiring manager often surfaces underlying issues that she might be missing, and she also gives candidates a better sense of the work they might be responsible for and the culture of the organization.

However many rounds of interviews you do, your primary goal in an interview is to find out how well the candidate matches up with the list of "must-have" traits you developed earlier. If there's one thing to keep in mind as you try to glean this information, it's this:

*Focus on the actual rather than the hypothetical.*

In other words, the best way to gauge how people will act in the future is to find out how they have *actually* acted in the past or to observe how they *actually* act in the present. Too often, though, managers ask about the hypothetical – that is, they ask how a candidate might hypothetically handle a difficult situation. For instance, if you want to figure out whether an assistant will be able to handle multiple tasks efficiently and without losing track of things, asking, "How do you think you would stay on top of everything?" or worse yet, "Do you think you could handle the volume?" gets you little useful information (the first question tests more for critical thinking than efficiency, and the second tests whether the candidate is awake). Instead, ask, "How much volume did you have to handle in your last job? How did you stay on top of it all? Tell me about a time when the volume was at its peak. What did you do?" These questions probe the *actual* by looking at what the candidate did in her past. Alternatively, you can say, "Here's a pile of tasks to complete – I'd like you to figure out which order to do them in and then do them. I'll come back in 20 minutes," which probes the candidate's actual ability to do tasks quickly.

With this principle in mind, here are three ways to gather useful information during the interview process:

1. <u>Probe prior experiences deeply</u>. Focus on depth over breadth in your questions, because you will learn more by getting into the details of a few experiences than by covering each and every job listed on a resume. In discussing a particular experience, start with general questions but then probe for the specific traits you are interested in. Along the way, your main challenge will be to get beneath the surface of general descriptions and to get into the nitty-gritty of how a candidate actually operated. For example, if one of the key traits you are seeking is an ability to stay on top of a large volume of work, your line of questioning might look like this:

   - Tell me about X – what did you do there?
   - What was the project on which you spent the most time?
   - That sounds interesting. How did you approach that?
   - Was it successful?
   - What was the biggest challenge?
   - How did you deal with that challenge?
   - I would think one challenge must have been staying on top of everything at once – did you ever get overwhelmed?
   - How did you stay organized?
   - I know this is pretty nitpicky, but walk me through the organizational system you used. When you came in in the morning, how did you decide what to start working on? As items came up during the day, where would you capture those so you didn't forget?

If your probing of specific experiences does not yield information about the traits you are looking for, you can also ask directly:

- Tell me about a time when you had to stay on top of a lot of work.
- How did you do it?
- What was hardest about that?

Be sure that you don't allow your desire to be nice to the candidate prevent you from digging until you have a really clear sense of her strengths and weaknesses. Pushing as much as it takes to get into the details is key to making an accurate assessment, and good candidates actually appreciate challenging questions.

*See page 141 for a full outline.*

2. <u>Simulate real job activities</u>. If you've hired even a few people before, you may know the terrible feeling of realizing after just a few days with a new hire that she is not going to cut it. Having candidates complete activities similar to what they'd be doing on the job *before* they get hired can give you that insight before it's too late. For instance, if you are hiring a marketing director and you want a candidate who can internalize your desired branding and help choose collateral that fits your image, you could have candidates read your brand positioning statement and look at your Web site, and then ask for their opinions on whether the site fits your brand and how it might be improved. If you want someone who can write quickly under pressure, you might give a candidate a set of talking points and give her 30 minutes to draft a press release for you. Or if you want a CFO who can explain financial matters to other executives in simple terms, you might send candidates your financial statements ahead of time and ask them to explain them back to you in plain English during the interview.

You can ask candidates to engage in these sorts of exercises at a variety of stages in the process. Even before granting first interviews for an assistant position, for instance, you could cull your pool further by having applicants read a scenario about an upcoming meeting and draft a mock e-mail to a hypothetical executive at another organization. Once you're at the interview stage, you can weave activities

*Get candidates to do what they'll do on the job.*

into the course of the interview (by asking for a role-play of a funder meeting, say), or you can have candidates complete them while they are on-site, or you can have them complete the tasks off-site and then send them back to you. You can also send background materials to candidates in advance of interviews so they can come prepared. However you do it, finding ways to see the candidates demonstrate the "must-have" qualities you're looking for in some kind of real-life situation can be of tremendous help in informing your decision.

*See page 150 for a worksheet on job simulation exercises and page 152 for a sample e-mail to candidates asking them to prepare for job-related activities.*

3. <u>Get to know the candidate</u>. Many organizations focus almost their whole interview process on general "get to know you" questions. You will find out more from exploring prior experiences and having candidates perform actual tasks for you, but don't neglect this category entirely, as it will sometimes elicit useful information.

In this category, you might ask general questions about motivation and commitment (such as, "What are you looking for at this point in your career?" and "How does this role fit into your path?"). You might also explore more specific questions about work preferences to help you understand a candidate's fit with your organization's culture, which is often one of your "must-have" criteria. (Try questions like, "What drives you crazy at work?" and "What was your favorite work environment and why?")

Keeping in mind the "actual vs. hypothetical" rule, ask candidates to tie their answers back to specific experiences. ("You mentioned that you like having autonomy. Can you give me an example of a time you had that and how it worked?")

Pulling it all together, a good one-hour interview might go something like this:

- Introductions and small talk (3 minutes)
- Getting to know the candidate/general questions (5 minutes)
- Probing prior experiences (20 minutes)
- Simulating activities (15 minutes)
- Description of the job, culture, and organization, from you (5 minutes), followed by questions from the candidate (5 minutes) and questions about their questions – "You asked about a collaborative environment. How important is that to you?" (5 minutes)
- Wrap-up – thank the candidate and tell her when she should expect to hear from you next (2 minutes)

*See page 148 for a full list of interview questions and page 145 for a worksheet on conducting interviews.*

---

### Don't See 'Em Sweat

Throughout the interview process, do everything you can to put candidates at ease so that you get a better sense of who they really are. What you want to find out is what candidates are like day-to-day, not what they're like in an interview. So be warm and friendly, and try to help candidates who seem nervous or tense to relax (unless of course "calm under pressure" is a key trait you're looking for).

---

**Speaking with References**

As you go through your interviews, hopefully you have some idea of who you want to hire. But complete one more step first: talking to references about the candidate. When done well, checking references can save you from a bad hire or help you choose between two strong candidates.

Managers often find checking references to be the most frustrating part of the selection process, since it can be hard to get useful information out of what is usually a carefully selected set of people. But there are ways to increase your chances of getting helpful information from these conversations.

- <u>Don't limit yourself to the candidate's list of references.</u> You don't need to confine your reference calls to the references provided by the candidate, especially since these people have likely been selected for their willingness to speak glowingly about her. Most obviously, if you know people in the candidate's circle, reach out and ask them about her. You can also ask candidates to put you in touch with specific people from their past. For instance, you can simply say something like, "I'd love to speak to your supervisor from that job you held from 2003 to 2006 – can you put me in touch with her?"

- <u>Make it easy to tell the full story.</u> Whether or not a reference is selected by the candidate, in most cases the reference will have a stronger relationship with the candidate than with you. Since references may feel disloyal or guilty providing negative information, your job is to make it easier for them to tell you what you need to hear. You can do this by making it easy for the reference to tell you negative things as well as positives. For instance, you might pair positives and negatives by asking questions like, "What type of job would you hire X for? What type of job would X be less suited for?" or "What do you think X will excel in? What do you think we'd want to focus X's professional development on?"

*Make it easy for references to tell you the downsides.*

Particularly when asking for downsides about a candidate, try to force the reference to give you something. Instead of asking, "Is there anything X could improve in?" (to which references might respond, "Nothing comes to mind") ask, "If you had to pick two ways X could improve, what would they be?" You can also provide options where there is no "bad" choice and ask the reference to select the choice that sounds most like the candidate – for instance, "Some people thrive in fast-paced environments but might err on the side of losing precision, whereas others are incredibly precise but do better when there's more time to focus on their work – which sounds more like X?"

You can also simply ask the reference to describe the candidate's greatest strengths or the words that most come to mind in describing the candidate, and listen for whether the key criteria you are interested in make the top of the list.

*See page 153 for a sample outline on checking references and page 156 for a full list of sample questions.*

> ### No Phone Tag
>
> If you're having trouble getting in touch with references, put the burden on the candidate. Tell her, "I can't move forward until I speak with your old boss but she's not calling me back. Do you think you'd be able to get her to return my call?" Often when the candidate hears this, she'll make sure you receive a call that day.

## MAKING YOUR DECISION

Once you have gone through the stages above, there's no magic to making the right decision. In general, you want to assess the candidates against the criteria you established at the beginning of the process. If you have a clear sense of what you are looking for and a sufficiently strong and diverse pool of candidates and you have effectively gathered information about them, your decision might be straightforward.

In making your decision, listen to your gut: would you be thrilled if this person came on board? If you have concerns or aren't excited about bringing the person into your staff, pay attention to your instincts! We've both ignored our guts and ended up regretting it. It's also a good idea to involve other people in the process so that you have multiple guts to check (especially if you don't have much experience in hiring). Listen to the opinion of others involved in the process, and take seriously any warning signs noted by multiple people.

If you're uncertain and think more information would help, feel free to modify the process to gather what you need. For instance, it is perfectly acceptable to explain to a candidate that you view this as a big decision, that you know she has already been through an extensive process, but that you realized it would be helpful for her to meet with your board chair so that you could get one more opinion, or that you'd like the candidate to give you one additional writing sample. At the end of the day, you may never be 100% certain, but you should gather the information you feel you need to make the best decision possible.

At times, after you have gathered all of your information, you may realize that you are not excited enough about any of the candidates. *No matter how desperately you need to fill a vacancy, rather than hiring someone*

---

### Keep People Posted

At every stage in the hiring process, make getting back to people quickly a priority. Not only do you risk losing good candidates by moving too slowly or not sharing information about your timeline, but you also send the wrong messages about your culture. You want whoever you end up hiring to have begun picking up messages about "how we do things here" – meaning being responsive and moving with a sense of urgency. Even when things don't go as planned, don't underestimate the power of sending a quick e-mail simply saying, "Although I told you last week that I would be scheduling interviews this week, I've had to push that back to next week. I'll be in touch by Monday."

*who you think might not be right, you will almost always be better off keeping the position open and searching for short-term solutions.* You might consider shifting responsibilities among your existing staff members to meet your highest priority needs, bringing in temporary help to fill gaps, or as a last resort simply putting work on hold. In the long run, you will spend far more time and energy dealing with the consequences of a bad hiring decision than you will save by filling a vacancy with the wrong person.

*See page 158 for a worksheet on making your decision.*

> ### Try Before You Buy
>
> Since the best way to know whether someone is likely to succeed at a job is to actually see them do it, in an ideal world you'd be able to do that before you commit to hiring them. Think about whether your organization has ways to try people out more extensively than in a normal hiring process without actually offering them a staff position – for instance, by bringing people on to do short-term pieces of work or creating an internship program.

## SELLING THE POSITION AND MAKING THE OFFER

All along, you have been evaluating candidates, but once you're ready to make an offer, the focus shifts to the candidate's evaluation of you and the offer you will make. After all, two things need to happen to make a hire: you must choose the candidate, and *the candidate must choose you.*

### Selling the position throughout the hiring process

The best way to ensure that things go smoothly at this stage is to have been selling the position throughout the entire process, not just once you are ready to make an offer. This doesn't mean convincing someone at all costs to join you, but rather painting an authentic picture of the benefits of working with you so that the candidate can make a wise decision. (In fact, you want to paint a very accurate picture, so that candidates who will not thrive can self-select out.)

Some of this work occurs through the interview process itself. For instance, by meeting some of the staff you have involved in the process, the candidate will see what types of people work for you. In addition, one of the benefits of having the candidate complete activities that mimic the actual challenges of the position is that often the right candidate will be intrigued by the possibility of taking on that kind of work.

You can also talk about potentially enticing culture factors directly. For instance, Alison tells candidates during phone interviews, "One thing about our culture is that we hold ourselves to high standards. We strive for excellence in everything we do, the work ethic here is higher than anywhere else I've worked, and we're direct about addressing it when things aren't working out. Some people absolutely love that, but it's definitely not for everyone." Candidates who will fit in well with that culture become excited and more invested in the job prospect at this point, and candidates who aren't good matches tend to reveal that through their responses or drop out on their own.

Beyond the interview process, you want to ensure that working at your organization is in fact an attractive proposition. Be aware that word of mouth about what it is like to work at the organization, and for you as a manager, may be the most important determinant of people's interest. In addition, you want to make strategic decisions about your benefits package, knowing that building an organization of strong performers is generally the most important investment you can make. Among other things, you should consider salary levels (finances permitting, seek to have salaries that at a minimum are not a barrier to someone taking the job, but that ideally might be an active selling point for the position), other benefits (including things like vacation time, which might be slightly more affordable than salary or other perks), and titles (which are cheap).

Perhaps most fundamentally, you need to be able to communicate a clear story about your organization, the position, and the impact that the right person in the position can make. For people in the nonprofit sector, the most important "benefit" is often the opportunity to make a difference in the world, and you should communicate that opportunity to candidates throughout the process.

**Making a great offer**

Having sold the position throughout the hiring process, don't let it fall apart when you make the offer. Put yourself in the candidate's shoes: making the decision to join a new organization and team of people is anxiety-producing, and having an offer conversation that is enthusiastic, organized, and thorough versus mechanical, unprepared, and uncommunicative can have a real impact on whether the candidate accepts.

- <u>Create a sense of excitement</u>. Let your enthusiasm show when you call. Tell the person how excited you are to have her come on board, why you think she will do a great job, and why you think she'll enjoy the position and organization.

- <u>Lead with a strong, clear offer</u>. Don't lowball people on salary. Open with your strongest or close-to-strongest salary offer to show the candidate that you really want her. And if your budget allows it, be prepared to negotiate, within reason, so that you don't lose the right person over a small amount of money. You should also be specific about benefits and other details so that the candidate has all the info she'll need in order to make a decision.

- <u>Give the candidate time to think it over</u>. Many candidates will ask for time to think it over before giving you a decision (usually a few days but sometimes longer). While you don't want to rush your best candidate into saying no and you should always be willing to give at least a few days, your circumstances should inform your judgment about how much total time you can give. If a top-notch candidate says she needs several weeks because her partner is waiting to find out if his company will transfer him to your city, that's a reasonable request that likely makes sense to accommodate. However, if you have an excellent second-choice candidate whom you might lose if you wait too long, you'll have to decide how much risk you're willing to tolerate in order to wait on the first candidate. A good rule of thumb is to be as flexible as you can while protecting your own interests.

- <u>Get a sense of the candidate's thought process</u>. Ask directly what factors she's considering, so you can better respond to them. For instance, when making the offer, you can say, "So, do you have any initial reaction?" and if you sense the candidate isn't sold, you can ask, "What, if anything, might make you hesitate?" This will help you understand the candidate's thought process so that you can tailor your discussions to address her concerns.

- <u>Make it clear you really want her to say yes</u>! If you really want to get the best people, you can't make an offer and then sit passively by waiting for the candidate to respond. While you don't want to harass your potential new employee, you do want to make sure she feels valued. Call periodically to check in, to offer to answer any questions, to ask whether she has any hesitations, and to reiterate your excitement. Find others to call and do the same as well. Calls from future peers, other senior managers, or the head of your organization or board chair can be remarkably persuasive. You can make it more comfortable to do all this by letting the candidate know up-front that you might, saying something like, "Unless you object, I might pester you before the deadline we set just to hear any new thoughts you've had, and I might ask my board chair to give you a call because I'd love for you to hear her thoughts about your potential role here."

132

- Wrapping it up. Ideally, the candidate will accept your offer and you will set a start date. But if she turns you down, try to find out why and suggest that you keep in touch in case other opportunities arise.

---

### Legal Issues

Hiring can raise a host of legal issues that go well beyond the scope of this book. If you are at all uncertain about the legality of something you are doing in the hiring process, you should consider checking with a lawyer. That said, here are a few specific issues that you should be careful about:

- Record keeping. If a rejected job applicant sues you, you will need to be able to articulate why the person was not selected (and general statements such as "not the best qualified candidate" may not suffice). You should have a record keeping system in place that allows you to capture that rationale at the time you make your decision (in practice, at a minimum a file to put your interview notes in where you jot your quick rationale) and should take steps to preserve such records for the length of the local statute of limitations period.

- Diversity considerations. If you are taking race or sex or other similar factors into account in the actual selection (as opposed to recruitment) process, there may be significant legal concerns. You should consult with counsel before you engage in this kind of a program.

- Interview questions. This area of the law has many gray areas, but the bottom line is that you should not ask questions that might create a suspicion that you are going to make your hiring decision based on an illegal criterion, such as the applicant's race, religion, marital status, sex, or national origin. In addition, you should not ask any questions that may elicit information about a disability that is protected under the Americans with Disabilities Act. If you are not sure what is acceptable, check with a lawyer.

- Disparate impact. If you're using employment tests or selection criteria that might have a disparate impact on a protected category of applicants (such as members of a particular racial or ethnic group or applicants of a particular sex), you should consult with legal counsel about the possible applicability of the "disparate impact" doctrine.

---

## Key Points

- Managers often overvalue specific knowledge or prior experience and don't put enough weight on underlying skills or qualities that are harder to develop and which in the long run are much more likely to differentiate high performers.

- The key to success in hiring is to build a strong pool of candidates in the first place. View yourself as a headhunter, and go after the people you want.

- The best way to gauge how people will act in the future is to find out how they have actually acted in the past or to observe how they actually act in the present – *not* to ask them how they might act in the future. Make your selection process about the actual, not the hypothetical.

- In making your decision, listen to your gut. Would you be thrilled if this person came on board? If you have concerns, pay attention to your instincts. If more information would help, modify the process to gather the facts you need. If you don't have the right person, find short-term solutions rather than making the wrong hire.

## 📖 Additional Reading

- Marcus Buckingham and Curt Coffman, "Skills, Knowledge, and Talents," "The World According to Talent," and "Talent: How Great Managers Find It" in *First, Break All the Rules: What the World's Greatest Managers Do Differently* (Simon & Schuster 1999), pages 83-104.

- Jim Collins, "First Who… Then What" in *Good to Great: Why Some Companies Make the Leap… and Others Don't* (Harper Collins 2001), pages 41-64.

# ✎ <u>Tools</u>

- Figuring out the role sample

- Figuring out the role worksheet

- Sample job description

- Building the pool worksheet

- Sample interview outline

- Interview worksheet

- Sample interview questions

- Job-simulation exercises

- Sample interview cover letter

- Sample reference check outline

- Reference check worksheet

- Sample reference questions

- Making your decision

- Sample rejection e-mails

## *Figuring Out the Role Sample*

### State Health Care Now
### State Policy Director

Core responsibilities
- Build and maintain relationships with key actors in state – policy makers, NGOs, industry execs, leading experts on the issue, and constituents
- Lead implementation of state advocacy agenda—current activities include three major programs and one annual conference
- Supervise 3 state-based project staff, 2-4 consultants and volunteers
- Monitor legislative proposals and trends
- Serve as a member of the organization's leadership team

Specific things this person would be doing now
- Call Joan at Citizens United and convince her ED should speak at their state conference
- Manage development of c4 voter guide – get input from national team members and from allies, oversee communications team process to make sure on track
- Let lobbyist know we're not renewing contract, without burning bridges
- Sit in on health care caucus retreat and give input on legislative strategy

> Getting concrete about this person's day-to-day actions will help pinpoint what skills and qualities he or she really needs.

One-sentence profile
Relentless, results-oriented person who excels at building relationships and at managing complicated projects.

*This person is like: Joe from NGA.*

> Thinking of a specific person who embodies your ideal candidate gives you a concrete picture of the kind of person you are looking for (even if this person isn't available for the job).

| Must-haves | Nice-to-haves | Not-haves |
|---|---|---|
| ▪ **Relationship-building:** able to connect with individuals and build alliances among wide range of players in the state<br><br>▪ **Results-orientation:** has a track record of achievement and a bias for producing results (rather than getting immersed in process), perseveres despite obstacles<br><br>▪ **Project management skills:** stays on top of multiple projects without dropping any balls, plans backwards and anticipates obstacles, identifies and involves stakeholders appropriately, uses resources wisely | ▪ Background: prior knowledge of or experience in healthcare policy<br><br>▪ Legislative experience: this would be good to have, but we've seen that we can teach the general approach<br><br>▪ Writing: should be good enough to send e-mails on our behalf, but doesn't need to be stellar – policy papers and testimony will be drafted by national team, will work with communications department on reports and media/outreach products<br><br>▪ Strategic thinking: will be an important helper in spotting opportunities and thinking of smart ways to move our issue forward, but ED will drive Policy Director's work in setting strategic direction<br><br>▪ Belief in promoting social justice issues (obviously important, but won't differentiate the best) | ▪ Public speaking/charisma: we will use ED and/or allies for most major public appearances<br><br>▪ Research skills: should become able to monitor trends and be fluent in healthcare policy and related issues, but can rely on research and reports from our analysts and outside sources<br><br>┄┄┄ Not-haves are skills and qualities that are not relevant to this role and that you won't test for. Articulating the not-haves often helps clarify who you **do** need in this role. |

## *Figuring Out the Role Worksheet*

Getting top talent into the right roles is key to getting great results. Use this worksheet to develop a clear idea of who you are looking for. This list can also be translated into a job description *(see sample on page 139).*

**1. Define the role**

I am hiring for the following position: _____

The core responsibilities of this role include:

- 
- 
- 

Specific things this person would be doing now:

- 
- 

**2. List your must-haves, nice-to-haves, and not-haves**

Think about what skills, knowledge, and general qualities this person needs to have. Keeping in mind the distinction between "underlying" or "inherent" traits (such as critical thinking or work ethic) and "teachable traits" (such as how to use a particular software program or write a specific type of article), separate your list into must-haves, nice-to-haves, and not-haves. Note that not-haves aren't negative qualities or "deal-breakers," but rather skills that aren't essential to this role and that you don't need to test for.

| **Must-haves**<br>*Skills and qualities you will not compromise on and must test for* | **Nice-to-haves**<br>*Skills and qualities that are a plus but not a requirement* | **Not-haves**<br>*Skills and qualities that you will not actively screen for* |
|---|---|---|
| ▪<br>▪<br>▪ | ▪<br>▪<br>▪ | ▪<br>▪<br>▪ |

**3. Draft a one sentence profile of your ideal candidate.**

_____

(Optional) My ideal candidate is someone like:

_____

## Sample Job Description

### State Health Care Now – State Policy Director

#### Overview
State Health Care Now seeks a full-time State Policy Director to lead our state advocacy activities, primarily by building and maintaining alliances among key actors throughout the state. The ideal candidate has a proven ability to foster coordination and cooperation among diverse – and even competing – groups. He or she will be committed to getting results in a fast-paced environment and able to handle a heavy workload without dropping the ball. This position is an excellent opportunity to engage with policy makers, NGOs, industry executives, and constituents to help bring about real legislative change. The position will be based in X state and report to the ED.

#### About State Health Care Now
State Health Care Now is a fast-paced nonprofit organization whose mission is to bring about affordable, meaningful health insurance for every state resident. We work to achieve our mission through educating and organizing policymakers, advocates, business leaders, and the general public. As chair of the Coalition for Universal Coverage, we plan to add 24 partners over the next two years and achieve universal coverage for all children in our state by 2012.

#### Job Responsibilities
The State Policy Director will be responsible for the following:

- Building and maintaining strategic relationships with policy makers, NGOs, industry executives, leading experts on the issue, and constituents
- Implementing our state advocacy agenda – current activities include three major programs and one annual conference
- Supervising 3 state-based project staff, 2-4 consultants and volunteers
- Monitoring legislative proposals and trends
- Serving as a member of the organization's leadership team

#### Qualifications
State Health Care Now seeks candidates who excel in **relationship-building**, are **results-oriented,** and have strong **project management skills.** The Policy Director will have:

- A track record of developing and maintaining strong working relationships with and among a diverse group of actors
- A demonstrated commitment to meeting a high bar and a history of getting things done even in the face of obstacles
- Experience managing multiple projects and ability to oversee a cadre of staff, consultants and volunteers

The following are a plus but not requirements:

- Knowledge of health care policy issues
- Prior experience in a legislative environment

State Health Care Now is an equal opportunity employer and to apply. Compensation depends on experience and is highly competitive.

#### How to apply
Please send a cover letter and resume to Pat Rodriguez, VP of Advocacy, at pat@statehealthcarenow.org.

## Building the Pool Worksheet

Most hiring mistakes occur not simply because managers select the wrong person, but because they don't have the right pool to select from. Use this worksheet to build a strong pool of applicants.

**Job title:** _____

1. Identify potential candidates and "connector sources," or people who can put you in touch with other good applicants.

| Draw from... | Potential Candidates | Connector Sources |
|---|---|---|
| Your contact list | Sarah Smith (RJ) | |
| | | |
| | | |
| Your current staff | | |
| | | |
| | | |
| Former staff | | Jesse Lee (SK) |
| | | |
| | | |
| Peer or pipeline orgs | | |
| | | |
| | | |
| Other | | |
| | | |
| | | |

> Assign someone to pursue each lead and put their initials in the parentheses.

> Tip: Try conducting a brainstorm session with a set target: "We won't leave until we have 6 good candidates and 20 good sources to call."

2. Next, brainstorm ways to mass market the job posting.

| Mass marketing category | Places to post job listing |
|---|---|
| Your own organization (Web site, newsletter) | |
| Allied organizations' Web sites | |
| Community or industry-specific listservs (idealist.org, indeed.com) | |
| Professional societies or associations (Assoc. of Fundraising Professionals) | |
| Alumni/career services offices | |
| Other? | |

## Sample Interview Outline

Interview for ___State Policy Director___

Candidate _Susan Smith_____          Date/location  _9/18/2008,_
                                                                  _DC office_
Interviewed by _Tracy Brown, ED____          Interview round # ___1___

Key Must-Haves:
Relationship-building, results-orientation, project management skills
(Joe from NGA)

Nice-to-haves:  Knowledge/experience related to our issue or legislative
environment, writing, strategic thinking, belief in social issues

Not-haves:  Public speaking, research skills

---

### I.  Introduction
I thought we'd start by having you share a bit more about your interest in
the position and then dig into your background by discussing some of
your past experiences. I'll then share with you more about where we're
headed as an organization and what we're looking for in this role. At the
end, we'll talk next steps. Sound good?

### II.  Warm-up questions
1.  What led you to apply for this position?
2.  What kind of role are you looking for at
    this point in your career?

> Start off with one or two quick
> questions as a warm-up; then dive
> into the meat of the interview –
> probing prior experiences.

### III.  Prior experiences
*General (seeking useful information keeping in mind all the must-have
qualities)*
1.  I see from your resume that you worked with Neighbors in Action.
    Tell me more about that.
    -  What was the project on which you spent the most time?
       *(Candidate answers "Neighborhood Safety Campaign")*
    -  What were you trying to achieve?
    -  How did you approach the development of the campaign? Walk
       me through your process: What did you do first? Why? What did
       you do next? What other options did you consider? Why did you
       end up pursuing that route? What happened after that?
       What was the result?

- Who else was directly involved with you in designing that campaign? What were some of the challenges in working together? How did you approach them?
- What other challenges did you face during the course of this campaign? How did you deal with them?
- What were the major victories? Would you say you met your original goals?
- How did the campaign conclude? Lesson learned?

- - - - - - - | Delve deeply into three or more prior experiences. Don't be shy about pressing for details and concrete evidence. |

2. What other job or project has been significant in your prior professional experience? Tell me about that.

*Direct (probing for evidence of specific must-have qualities)*

1. Relationship building: More than anything else, this position involves a lot of relationship-building. You mentioned partnering with a couple other organizations when you worked on the Neighborhood Safety Campaign. Can we talk about another time when you had to build relationships with other actors?
    - How did you go about pursuing that relationship?
    - How did you gain access to their top level of management? Who else in that organization did you speak to? How often would you meet?
    - What were the major outcomes of that partnership? Is there a particular success in this area we could discuss? A challenge?

- - - - - | Stick to real examples and avoid the hypothetical. |

2. Project management: As the State Policy Director, you would be managing several projects at the same time, from our advocacy campaigns to monitoring legislation to building the state-wide coalition.
    - Can you tell me about a project you managed that went well? What do you think made it successful? How did you plan it and how did you manage to the plan?
    - What about a time when things didn't go so well? Was there ever a "dropped ball" on a project you were managing? What happened and how did you handle it?
    - Have you ever had to manage multiple projects at once? How did you keep track of what was on your plate and what other people were doing?

- In general, how do you stay on top of so many details? When you get into work in the morning, how do you decide what to do that day and where to begin?

## IV. Exercises

1. We sent you a project plan before this meeting and would love to turn to that now.
    - What did you think of the plan? Anything you would change or add to it?
    - What do you think the likelihood of success is for this project, as it's currently laid out?
    - How would you manage to this plan if you were the owner of the project? What about if you were managing the owner of the project to this plan? How would you know things are on track?

## V. General information/fit

General information on organization and role

- Outgoing director moving to Iowa to oversee an expansion of our operations.
- Time of growth for us and this position is key to our success: building alliances among a range of state players, conceiving and managing campaigns and other projects that move our issue forward, valuing results over process (public speaking nice-to-have but relationship building is key).
- Would work with national team and communications team and be part of the organization's leadership, reporting directly to me.
- Perhaps biggest selling point for our organization = our core values—continuous learning, excellence, integrity—means good people who like their work and are very good at it.

Questions about personal goals/fit

1. If you could design the position, how would you prioritize each of the areas of responsibility? What would be your favorite part of the job? Least favorite?
2. At the beginning of this interview, you said your next position would ideally help you to develop "grasstops" advocacy skills. How do you see our organization and this particular position fitting into that goal?
3. What are your concerns about this position? What questions do you have for me?

## VI.  Next steps

*Assuming the interview went well and you are interested in continuing the process, you might assign homework.*

We find it useful to simulate part of the job in the interview process so that you get a taste of the role and we get to see you in action a bit. Assuming you're interested in continuing in the process, I'd like to start by giving you a "homework" assignment.

1.  <u>Homework assignment</u>: Create a project plan for our spring advocacy day. Ideally, it would include goals as well as a timeline and key steps along the way. Here's a description of the campaign, the actors involved and what we're aiming to achieve (hand-out memo). Ideally, you'd create a plan that would specify the path we'd take to get to April 15. Major constraints are a budget of $10,000 and a commitment to include all major stakeholders in key roles (see the overview for more detail). Would it be possible to send me a draft by next Tuesday? Also, if you have a project plan you've used for a past project I'd love to see that as well.

> Exercises can take place during and/or outside of the actual interview. Starting with a "homework" assignment is a good first step if you know you want to advance the person to the next round and/or if you want more information.

I'll look forward to reviewing your project plan next week. Next round interviews (and exercises) with me and our COO will be held the last week in September. I'll let you know about next steps either way by next Friday.

> Specify by when you'll follow-up whether or not you're advancing the candidate to the next round.

### Other exercises:

*If the homework assignment goes well, you might bring the candidate back for a second round interview and have them conduct additional on- or off-site exercises.*

1.  <u>Relationship building</u>: Participate in a meeting between our outgoing director and the advocacy officer from Small Business Owners' Health Forum. Give input/feedback on how/whether to partner with them.

## Interview Worksheet

Interview for _____

Candidate _____    Date/location _____
Interviewed by _____    Interview round # _____

Key Must-Haves:


Nice-to-haves:

Not-haves:

_____

### I. Introduction
I thought we'd start by having you share your interest in the position, then digging into your background by discussing some of your past experiences in-depth and then sharing a bit more about the role and where we're headed as an organization. At the end, we'll talk next steps. Sound good?

### II.  Warm-up questions
1. What led you to apply for this position?
2. What kind of role are you looking for at this point in your career?

### III.  Probing prior experiences
*Using the candidate's resume as a guide, ask questions about what this person has done and how he or she has done it. Delve into at least three prior experiences and listen for concrete demonstration of must-have qualities – no hypotheticals! This section is the "meat" of the interview and should take the majority of the time available.*

General
1.  I see on your resume that you worked with
    _____. Tell me more about that.
    - What was the project on which you spent the most time?
    - What were you trying to achieve?
    - How did you approach it?
    - Was it successful?
    - What was the biggest challenge? How did you deal with that challenge?

2. What other job or project was significant? Tell me about that.
   *(Repeat)*

*Direct*
*If your questions about the candidate's prior experiences have not surfaced strong evidence of the must-have qualities, ask direct questions about the ones that you still have questions about. List the trait you are probing for on the left and structure the question to elicit specific examples. See page 148 for sample questions.*

| Quality | | Question |
|---------|---|----------|
| _____ | 1. | _____ |
| _____ | 2. | _____ |
| _____ | 3. | _____ |
| _____ | 4. | _____ |

### IV. Exercises

*Job-simulation activities give you a chance to see the candidate in action. They may be woven into the interview or conducted separately. For example, you may test for critical thinking skills by sending a report to the candidate ahead of the interview and discussing it during the meeting. Exercises such as observing or participating in a meeting may be scheduled for after the interview. List the quality you'd like to test for on the left and the exercise you'd like to conduct on the right. See page 150 for more sample activities.*

| Quality | | Exercise |
|---------|---|----------|
| _____ | 1. | _____ |
| _____ | 2. | _____ |
| _____ | 3. | _____ |
| _____ | 4. | _____ |

### V. General information/fit
General information on organization and role
*Tell the candidate about your mission, approach, current circumstances, and future direction. Give a brief overview of the position and be prepared to talk about why it's open. Remember, you're "selling" the position and organization, so include a couple notes on what you would say to capture the interest of strong candidates.*

_____
_____
_____

<u>Questions about personal goals/fit</u>
*Ask questions to determine if this person would be a good fit for the position, considering his or her enthusiasm for the position/organization and fit with the organization's culture. See page 149 for sample questions.*

1. If you could design the position, how would you prioritize each of the areas of responsibility? What would be your favorite part of the job? Least favorite?
2. At the beginning of this interview, you said your next position would ideally teach you/help you to _____. How do you see our organization and this particular position fitting into that goal?
3. What are your concerns about this position? What questions do you have for us?

## VI.  Next steps
*Will there be another round of interviews or more exercises? If so, when and with whom? What samples would you like to see? What are the next steps of the process?*

_____

_____

## Sample Interview Questions

The overarching key to each category is to listen carefully, to probe to get beneath the surface, and to focus the questions or activities around the key traits that you are most interested in. Use this list with the Interview Worksheet.

### Probing prior experiences

- Of your prior jobs, which do you think was the most significant?
- What was the part of your role you spent the most time doing (or what was the most significant project)?
- What were you trying to achieve?
- How did you approach it?
- Walk me through your process: What did you do first? Why? What did you do next? What happened after that? What was the result?
- What was the biggest challenge there?
- What was your biggest achievement? What was something you accomplished that you think someone else in your role might not have gotten done (or where you approached it differently from how others might have, or where you went above and beyond)?
- It must have been hard to do Y. How did you approach that?
- On your resume you mentioned that you accomplished ABC. How did that come about? What was your specific role in it?
- Why did you leave X job?
- Tell me about Z job. What led you to work there? What was your role?...

### Direct questions about specific qualities

Tell me about a time at X when _____. What did you do? What did you do next? What happened after that? What was the result? Would you do anything differently? Did you ever face another similar situation? How did you handle that one?

- you were faced with a really difficult challenge
- you went above and beyond to get a result
- you persisted despite obstacles
- you gave up or almost gave up
- you had to put your ideas into writing
- you had to deliver an important speech
- you had to motivate someone to do something

- you came up with a new approach for tackling a problem
- you had to come up with a strategy for how to get to a particular outcome

- you had to move a group to action (within or outside the organization)
- you had to stay on top of a large volume of work/had to multi-task
- you had to explain complex ideas in a simple way

**Personal goals/general fit**

- What makes you want to work here?
- What leads to your interest in X issue?
- Where does that desire to improve things come from?
- What do you think is the most important problem facing our society today?
- Where do you see X (our issue) fitting in?
- What are you looking for in your next job? If you could design the perfect job, what would it look like? Why?
- Some people are at a point in their career where work is their top priority and they're dying to immerse themselves fully in their work. Others are at a point where they want to do interesting work but it may not be the most important thing for them. Both are legitimate – where would you put yourself on that spectrum right now?

> Note: Be careful not to ask about marital status, family, etc. here, though the interviewee might bring those things up. You are trying to figure out whether the person is looking for a job that might require going above and beyond, or whether they are looking for a 9-5 job, regardless of their external circumstances.

- What was your favorite job and why? What was your least favorite and why? How do those things compare to what you're looking for now?
- *A number of the following can be followed-up by probing prior specific experiences. You can ask, "So tell me about a time when that happened/when you demonstrated that/when that came up? What did you do next/how did you handle that?"*
  - What really frustrates you at work?
  - What do you think it is that makes you outstanding at what you do? What do you think you need to get better at?
  - If I were to talk to your colleagues – or your managers – what would they say are the things you're best at? What would they say you need to improve in?
  - What works for you in a manager? What doesn't work for you?

## *Job-Simulation Exercises*

Having candidates complete exercises similar to what they'd be doing on the job can give you a good idea of how they would perform if hired. Below is a list of sample exercises that test for specific qualities.

| Position | Must-have | Sample Exercise |
| --- | --- | --- |
| COO | Critical thinking, writing | Observe the organization in action (delivering a training session, staging a rally, holding a hearing, etc.) and propose recommendations for improvement in a 2-3 page memo |
| Manager of programs | Strategic thinking | Read and analyze a set of goals and objectives and come up with recommendations on which to pursue |
| Director of communications | Public speaking, judgment | Rehearse a press conference or a call with a reporter about a controversial program we support |
| Manager of a small- or medium-sized department | General management, staff supervision | Simulate giving positive and corrective feedback to a supervisee |
| Fundraising associate | Persistence, interpersonal skills | Simulate a meeting with a funder |
| Special events associate | Organization/project management | Develop a project plan for an annual conference |
| Director of policy and advocacy | Strategic thinking, interpersonal skills | Sit in on a meeting with a potential partner organization. Afterwards, give feedback including a recommendation on whether and how to engage with them |
| Senior associate for policy and advocacy | Explain complex ideas in a simple way | Produce a visual outlining key players in the healthcare industry and the relationships among them |
| Research associate | Strategic thinking, writing | Write a memo on how a specific change in legislation might affect state support for low-income families |
| Trainer | Presentation and teaching skills | Make a short presentation teaching a skill of your choice (how to write a grant, how to create a work plan, how to plan a conference, etc.) |
| Executive assistant | Writing and communication skills | Write an e-mail to a potential client requesting a meeting with our ED |

Brainstorm activities for your candidates below.

| Position | Must-have | Exercise |
|----------|-----------|----------|
|          |           |          |
|          |           |          |
|          |           |          |
|          |           |          |
|          |           |          |
|          |           |          |

## Sample Interview Cover Letter

*This is a sample e-mail to a job applicant prior to a second interview.*

Subject: Meeting on Tuesday

Susan,

I'm looking forward to speaking with you again next week about the State Policy Director position here at State Health Care Now.

As I mentioned on the phone, in addition to talking more about your prior experiences, I'm also hoping we can spend a portion of our time focusing on materials related to the position. Enclosed, you will find:

- Monthly and quarterly goals. During our discussion, I'd love to get your feedback on these goals and hear how you might approach them.
- A newsletter and informational brochure from the Small Business Owners' Health Forum. As we discussed, you will be sitting in on Daniel's meeting with their Advocacy Officer next week. I look forward to hearing about your conversation and getting your thoughts on whether and how you would structure a partnership with them.
- A list of our core values, a statement of expectations for managers, and a one-page version of our annual objectives to give you more background about our organization and where we are headed.

Thanks again for your interest, and I look forward to seeing you on Tuesday at 2:00.

Best,
Tracy Brown
Executive Director

## Sample Reference Check Outline

### Introduction

I'm the Legislative Director at State Health Care Now. Thanks for agreeing to speak with me about your experience working with Susan. Before we start, I'd like to give you a quick overview of our organization and the position we are considering Susan for. We're a 20-person advocacy organization committed to enacting universal health coverage legislation in the state. The organization is growing, and Susan is a finalist for our new State Policy Director position. This director must be a pro at working with a diverse group of actors and building alliances among them, have a demonstrated track record of getting results in a fast-paced environment, and be capable of managing multiple projects tightly without dropping any balls.

### Overall strengths and weaknesses

➤ What parts of this job sound most like something Susan might succeed in?

➤ Can you describe Susan's greatest strengths? What words come to mind in describing her?

➤ If you had to pick out two pieces of the job where you think Susan might not be as strong or might need some development, what would those be?

### Specific traits and skills

➤ What was Susan's greatest achievement in the time you worked together?

➤ Tell me about a time when you were not entirely thrilled with her performance.

➤ Tell me about a time when Susan...

- was faced with a really difficult challenge
- went above and beyond to get a result
- gave up or almost gave up      - - - - - - - -   Ask about specific examples to get at your must-haves to get under the surface of broad generalizations.
- had to stay on top of a large volume of work/had to multi-task
- had to move a group to action (within the organization or outside the organization)
- had to find partners for a particular project

➤ In my experience, I've seen some people who are more uptight and organized, if a little prickly, and some who are more laid-back and friendly, though maybe not always hitting deadlines – which sounds most like Susan?

### General/other relevant information

➤ What kind of job would you hire Susan for? What kind of job would you not hire her for?

➤ If you were thinking of hiring again for Susan's position, how would you describe your reaction if she applied: would not hire, would consider hiring, would strongly consider hiring, would definitely hire, would move earth and moon to lure her back?

➢ How would Susan rank compared to people in similar positions – would you say about average, a little better than average, top quarter, top 10%, top 1%, or the best ever? What makes you say that?

➢ What should I know about Susan if I'm going to manage her effectively?

**Wrap-up**

➢ Overall, how would you rate Susan's likelihood of success in this role?

➢ Is there anything else you would want to know about Susan if you were in my shoes?

## *Reference Check Worksheet*

### 1. Identify outstanding must-haves

List the must-haves for the position you're filling below. Cross off the qualities you're convinced the candidate has demonstrated through interviews and application exercises. Focus your reference checks on the remaining qualities.

☐ _____ ☐ _____

☐ _____ ☐ _____

### 2. Prepare an introduction

Prepare a description of the position you're filling and its key "must-have" traits. Give the reference a sense of the job's responsibilities, level of seniority, and place in the organization to allow her to see the candidate in relation to the position.

_____

_____

_____

### 3. Brainstorm questions

For each category below, list a few questions you could ask to help determine if your candidate has what you're looking for. References may feel disloyal or guilty providing negative information, so ask bounded questions or pose neutral options where there is no "bad" choice. *See page 156 for more sample questions.*

*Overall strengths and weaknesses*

Example: In my experience, I've seen some people who are more uptight and organized, if a little prickly, and some who are more laid-back and friendly, though maybe not always hitting deadlines – which sounds most like Susan?

_____

_____

_____

*Specific traits and skills*

_____

_____

_____

> **Tip:** You don't have to limit your calls to the list of people provided by the candidate. If you know people in the candidate's circle, reach out to them directly. If not, ask to be put in touch with specific supervisors or co-workers.

*General/other relevant information*

_____

_____

*Wrap-up*

_____

_____

## Sample Reference Questions

Draw from the following list to brainstorm questions for references. In addition to discussing their overall impressions of the candidate, talk about specific must-have qualities you're not sure the candidate has demonstrated. Make it easier for references to talk about the candidate's downsides by asking bounded questions or posing neutral options where there is no "bad" choice.

- *(Describe the position you're filling and the key traits you need.)* What parts of that sound most like something Y might succeed at? If you had to pick out two pieces of that where you think Y might not be as strong or might need some development, what would those be?

- What do you think Y's co-workers would say were Y's greatest strengths? What would they say Y might need to work on?

- What was Y's greatest achievement?

- Tell me about a time when you were not entirely thrilled with Y's performance.

- In my experience, I've seen some people who are more like A, and some who are more like B – which would you say Y is? *(For example, "In my experience, I've seen some people who are more uptight and organized, if a little prickly, and some who are more laid-back and friendly, though maybe not always hitting deadlines – which sounds most like Susan?")*

> Questions that force a reference to choose between two alternative profiles can give people a face-saving way to share useful information.

- Tell me about a time when Y...

  - was faced with a really difficult challenge
  - went above and beyond to get a result
  - persisted despite obstacles
  - gave up or almost gave up
  - had to put her ideas into writing
  - had to deliver an important speech
  - had to motivate someone to do something
  - had to move a group to action (within the organization or outside the organization)
  - had to explain complex ideas in a simple way
  - came up with a new approach for tackling a problem
  - had to come up with a strategy for how to get to a particular outcome
  - had to stay on top of a large volume of work/had to multi-task

- What should I know about Y if I'm going to manage Y effectively? What should I get Y to do a lot because she's really good at it? In what area might I need to get Y to most develop?

- What kind of job would you hire Y for? What kind of job would you not hire Y for?

- What would Y's co-workers say is her greatest strength? Her greatest weakness?

- Overall, how would you rate Y's performance?

- If you were thinking of hiring again for Y's position, how would you describe your reaction if Y applied: would not hire, would consider hiring, would strongly consider hiring, would definitely hire, would move earth and moon to lure Y back?

- How would Y rank compared to people in similar positions – would you say about average, a little better than average, top quarter, top 10%, top 1%, or the best ever? What makes you say that?

- Is there anything else you would want to know if you were in my shoes?

  > Note that references rarely give you anything in response to this, so do a thorough job before you ask this question!

- Can I come back to you if I think of other questions?

## Making Your Decision

Candidate _____

Must-haves                                    Notes

☐
☐
☐
☐
☐

Nice-to-haves                                 Notes

☐
☐
☐

**Yes!** What to say to convince her to take the position:

- This is an excellent opportunity to...

- The position is a great fit with your talent for/interest in...

- Our organizational culture...

**Need more info.** Will ask for (reference, exercise, or interview) by
_____ (date).

**No.** ☐ Send rejection e-mail (or delegate to _____) by
_____ (date).

☐ Call (or delegate to _____) by _____ (date).

Sample talking points:
- <u>Strengths</u>: You clearly have a tremendous amount of knowledge about the industry and strong writing skills.
- <u>Why the fit isn't right</u>: For this position, we are putting more emphasis on the ability to ramp up our advocacy efforts by building alliances among different groups than on expertise in health care. While I'm sure you could do that, it didn't strike me as your primary strength.
- <u>Encouragement</u>: I have no doubt, though, that you'll be a real asset to an organization in the right position. Please keep us posted on your next steps and best of luck.

## Sample Rejection E-mails

*This first sample e-mail is to a candidate who didn't make it to the interview stage.*

From: Barry Ruiz
Subject: State Health Care Now State Policy Director position
To: Josephine Jones

Dear Josephine,

Thank you for applying for the state policy director position with State Health Care Now. We appreciate your interest in our organization and your commitment to sensible health care policy reform.

We received more than 200 applications for the position , and the hiring process has been a very competitive one. Although we were impressed with your qualifications, we have decided not to move your application forward. However, we greatly appreciate your interest in working with us and wish you the best of luck with your job search.

Sincerely,
Barry Ruiz
Chief of Staff

---

*This sample is to a candidate who did have an in-person interview.*

From: Barry Ruiz
Subject: State Health Care Now State Policy Director position
To: Dan Miller

Dear Dan,

Thanks so much for talking with Tracy and me last week about our state policy director position. We really enjoyed the meeting, especially hearing about your work with United Way, and we were impressed with your qualifications.

We've had a very competitive pool and have had to make hard decisions, and unfortunately I won't be able to advance you into the next round of interviews. However, I very much appreciate the time you devoted to the process, and I wish you the best of luck with your job search.

Best,
Barry Ruiz
Chief of Staff

## Chapter 6
# Developing People

Contrary to popular belief, you don't need fancy professional development programs, formal mentorships, or large investments in staff training in order to develop your staff's skills and performance. In fact, in our experience, the results of these programs rarely justify the amount of energy that goes into them. Rather, the best staff development stems naturally from strong, hands-on management – because learning and development happen by pursuing ambitious goals, being held to high standards, and receiving candid and direct feedback about what is and is not working as you pursue your goals.

In this chapter, we'll discuss how to most effectively help your staff develop. We'll start by talking about when to develop people and when not to, then look at specific methods to use.

> *The best staff development comes from good management, not formal programs.*

### WHEN TO DEVELOP PEOPLE – AND WHEN NOT TO

From a purely practical perspective, you should spend time developing people because it will get you better results: it will make your staff more effective in both the short-term and the long-term, and it will make your organization a more attractive place to work. But because it's also a nice thing to do for your staff, sometimes managers forget that it's not an end in itself – and that because it's a means but not an end, you should be strategic about when and how you spend time on staff development, balancing it with other priorities that need your time and selecting staff development opportunities judiciously.

You should keep three principles in mind when deciding when to invest time in staff development:

1. Invest in your best.
2. Know what you can change and what you can't.
3. Distinguish between development needs and serious performance issues.

**Invest in your best**

Paradoxically, your best staff members are usually the ones who will grow the most. Strong performers are often more driven, and so their desire to take advantage of development opportunities is higher. They also tend to be generally skilled people who are able to take a small amount of assistance and put it into practice, whereas others may struggle to apply the help. Because of this, the pay-off from spending energy on your strongest performers will greatly exceed the results from energy you spend on your lowest performers.

For instance, in the introduction to this section we mentioned the new regional director with whom Jerry worked who increased fundraising in her area from $43,000 annually when she took over the position to almost $300,000 just one year later. Recognizing a star in its midst, the organization sent several senior staffers to spend a few days with her. An average employee might have leveraged the coaching into gains of 10% of so – but with just that bit of input, two years later she raised $1 million.

162

## Know what you can change and what you can't

As we discussed in the "Hiring Superstars" chapter, you can build staff members' knowledge and improve very specific skills, but you generally can't change talents and basic inclinations. You might teach someone to use a particular software program or to deliver an effective Powerpoint presentation, but talents (like writing, critical thinking, or being able to connect well with other people) and inclinations (like having a strong sense of responsibility or pursuing goals relentlessly) build up over a lifetime and tend to be deep-rooted and difficult to develop.

As an example, you might have a regional director who frequently gives presentations about your program to external audiences. She is enthusiastic and knowledgeable but lacks polish and tends to read directly from the slides on her Powerpoint. In her other work, she is very strong and, among other things, has raised significantly more money than her peers. This is a case where public speaking training – whether a formal program like Toastmasters or informal role-playing with you – could pay off, helping her become a more confident and skilled speaker.

In contrast, if you have a legislative analyst who is shy and uncomfortable interacting with others, you might be able to get her to speak up a bit more, but she's probably never going to excel at networking and building coalitions.

## Distinguish between development needs and serious performance issues

Fortunately, the meat of the shy legislative analyst's job is analyzing legislation and writing briefs – activities that don't require a lot of interaction with others. While it might be nice if she were more outgoing, her shyness doesn't interfere with her ability to do her job well. But in other cases, the behavior in question will impact the staff member's ability to do her job at the level you need. In situations where the employee's basic talents and inclinations are at odds with the requirements of the job, don't allow development to become a distraction that prevents you from dealing with core performance issues.

*Don't allow development to become a distraction from dealing with serious performance issues.*

For example, a media director needs to have good judgment when talking to reporters and needs to be able to represent the organization's positions clearly and compellingly. Perhaps your media director has been on the job for five months and has shown poor judgment in several cases – in one, speaking to a reporter calling about a delicate public issue without first consulting anyone and making comments that inflamed the situation, and in two others, confusing reporters to the point that they called the executive director asking for clarification. You have also noticed that she still doesn't give the standard "spiel" when describing your organization's work to reporters. These problems go to the heart of the media director's fit for the role. You might eventually succeed in drilling the basic spiel into her, but she lacks judgment, the ability to think on her feet, and perhaps even basic critical thinking skills. Development efforts might produce small improvements with her, but she will probably never perform at the high level you need.

In determining whether the problem goes beyond a simple development need, watch for the following signs:

- You've tried developing the person some but have not seen significant improvement.
- The issue is something fundamental to the job.
- You're busy and are simply unable to invest the amount of time that would be needed to guide the staff member to where you need her to be.

If any of this is the case, see Chapter 8 on dealing with serious performance issues and letting lower performers go.

## HOW TO DEVELOP PEOPLE

When it does make sense to invest in developing your people, how do you do it? While formal training programs can help when they are aimed at very specific, concrete skills, generally the best learning comes when employees stretch themselves in the pursuit of meaningful goals and when managers coach them through the process. So next we'll talk about specific methods you can use, including stretch assignments, introducing new areas gradually, modeling, feedback, performance evaluations, and promoting from within.

### Stretch assignments

People learn most by doing. You'll see the most growth by assigning a staff member a responsibility that requires her to apply new skills or old skills at a higher level (such as going from managing two people to managing eight).

Since the staff member is learning a new area and might not master it immediately, you can create an atmosphere of controlled learning by using a more structured approach of "plan, do, reflect." First, you and the staff member discuss what she is going to do, then she does it (perhaps with you observing her in action, where appropriate), and finally she reflects with you on how it went and how to improve in the future. For instance, if your assistant already screens job applicants' resumes, you might ask her to go further and begin conducting initial phone interviews with internship candidates. In the planning stage, you'd meet with her to discuss interview techniques, and perhaps role-play several interview situations. In the doing stage, you might observe her conducting one or two of the phone interviews. And in the reflecting stage, you'd discuss her results, identify what she found most difficult, and brainstorm alternate ways of responding in the future.

**Introducing one piece at a time**

Rather than expecting a staff member to master a whole new area all at once, you can structure it so that she starts with easier pieces and gradually adds others. For example, in grooming someone to become a manager, you might first have her manage others on a particular project, without giving her overall responsibility for managing all their work.

**Modeling the skill for the staffer**

Often people need to see a skill or approach applied before they can do it themselves. For instance, if you want a staff member to get better at conducting external meetings, you might have her accompany you and watch while you do one yourself. In modeling the skill, be explicit with your staff member about what you are doing and why – for instance, in modeling an external meeting, point out to the staff member how you were careful to agree to an informal agenda at the beginning of the meeting.

Modeling is also the best way to transmit cultural values and approaches you want your staff to demonstrate, such as "always follow up on things," "treat constituents with respect," and "be nice to your co-workers."

---

### Train People Right From the Start

If you've ever started a new job and discovered your new employer wasn't prepared for you from the moment you walked in the door, you know that the impression you make on an employee's first day can send messages about culture and expectations right from the start. By being prepared and organized when new employees start, you can send the message from day one that you're organized, efficient, running a tight ship, and care about using employees' time effectively.

One concrete way for you to prepare is to create in advance an agenda for a series of meetings that lays out everything that you'll cover with the new employee early in her tenure. See the sample on page 197 for suggestions on the types of topics you might cover.

---

## Additional resources

Particularly for help in developing very specific skills or knowledge, you can steer staff members to books or articles, workshops, or other people you have found helpful.

## Direct feedback

One of the most powerful tools managers have for developing staff is providing direct feedback. Simply articulating areas in which you'd like to see a staff member develop can go a long way.

Because managers often struggle with this area, let's delve into it in greater depth.

## PROVIDING EFFECTIVE FEEDBACK

You should provide feedback on a constant, ongoing basis, in order to reinforce behavior you want to see more of, prevent bad habits from becoming ingrained, and foster an atmosphere of open communication. Providing feedback regularly can also allow you to address potential problems while they're still small, rather than telling a staffer that something she has been doing for months is wrong.

Feedback generally falls into three broad categories: positive feedback, developmental suggestions for growth, and corrective feedback. Some managers do a great job with praise but are more reticent when it comes to talking about problems areas. Other managers are direct about problems but forget to balance their feedback with praise. And many don't give enough of either.

**Positive feedback**

One of the best ways to shape your staff's behavior is to give positive feedback. Telling a staff member, "I loved the way you organized that spreadsheet; the categories made sense and you made sure it was easy to read on the screen" almost guarantees you'll be seeing more well-organized spreadsheets in the future. In addition, positive feedback is a form of creating accountability. If your staff member consistently does a good job but never hears from you about it, she may wonder why no one appears to have noticed.

At the same time, most people can see through sugarcoating, so you shouldn't give positive feedback when you don't really mean it… but with good employees around, you should be able to find plenty of actions that warrant praise!

**Developmental suggestions for growth**

When you spot ways that a good employee could do even better, sharing these suggestions can help her take her performance to an even higher level. This type of feedback isn't about serious concerns. Likely, the employee would continue to do a fine job even if she for some reason didn't implement your suggestion. For instance, if you notice that your webmaster isn't at her most effective when explaining technical topics to non-technical staff, you might say something like, "I wanted to talk about our meeting with the campaign team and share some thoughts about how you might get your points across to them better." You could then explain that while her agenda was well-structured and her points strong ones, non-IT people don't know some of the terms she uses, and that using simpler language and stopping to check for understanding might help her communicate better with her audience.

## Corrective feedback

Unlike developmental suggestions for growth, where the staff member would still be doing a good job even if she didn't implement your suggestions, corrective feedback is about things that must change in order for the staff member to meet expectations.

Most managers find this type of feedback the hardest to give, and some will put it off out of discomfort. Don't fall into that trap! The longer you wait to give corrective feedback, the more the problem will take root – so get in the habit of giving this sort of feedback as immediately as you can. Additionally, be direct. Don't get so caught up in trying to be tactful that your message gets diluted or lost.

For instance, if you're disappointed in your communications director's poorly-written press release, simply say, "I'd like to talk about this recent press release – when would be a good time to do that?" Then, tell your director that the release did not meet your expectations. Point out specific ways in which the press release fell short and suggest concrete ways she might improve it.

You might also use the example as a vehicle for delving into other issues that might be at play. For instance, you might say, "What's strange to me is that I know you are a better writer than

*"Earlier in my career, I hired someone and it quickly became clear to me that he was so disorganized that we had made the wrong decision.*

*"In trying to reverse that decision, which is very difficult to do, I learned the limitations of trying to do things in a covert way. It doesn't work; it just backfires completely. I should have said, 'Here are the things you need to do to be more effective,' and had a rigorous process to evaluate against those things. Since then, I've realized that in that situation, you need to create extremely short-term goals that reflect the positive behaviors you want to see, things that are easy wins. If you do that in very short cycles, it clarifies whether the change is possible in a lower-stakes way than if you let the problems build."*

*- David Bennahum,
President and CEO,
Center for Independent
Media*

this. Do you have a sense of why you didn't apply your skills as well as you might have here?" The employee might reply that she forgot to schedule time to write the release and wrote it at the last minute (an opening to delve into issues of time management), or that she didn't think it was important to get it right because reporters rarely copy text straight from releases (responsibility), or that she honestly did give it her best shot and is frustrated that it didn't come out better (writing skills).

If the problem persists after talking about it directly, you may need to consider the employee's fundamental fit for the role. Chapter 8 has an in-depth discussion about what factors to consider in such a situation and how to have more serious performance warning conversations.

---

### Tips for giving feedback

- Describe the behavior you've observed in a short sentence: "I've noticed recently that when running meetings you sometimes have trouble keeping the group focused on the agenda."
- Provide two or three specific, concrete, relevant examples to support your feedback: "First in our meeting with X, and then with Y…"
- State the impact of the behavior on you, and as appropriate on your team, department, or organization: "We ended up not having time to reach conclusions and had to schedule a follow-up later, and we lost the attention of a couple people when the topic we veered into wasn't relevant to them."
- Suggest an alternative or recommendation for change: "Try allotting specific amounts of time to each item on your agenda to keep the meeting on track."

Note that the same structure applies for positive feedback as well (with the recommendation at the end amounting to "keep it up!")

---

### PERFORMANCE EVALUATIONS

In addition to giving feedback on a regular, ongoing basis throughout the year, you should also conduct more formal performance evaluations.

Formal performance evaluations give you a vehicle to assess an employee's performance and progress against goals, provide suggestions for growth and improvement, let you find out how the employee is feeling about her job, and, in the case of lower performers, send clear messages about the consequences of failing to improve.

## Effective performance review processes

Organizations vary in how they structure performance review processes, but typically a manager will provide a written evaluation to the employee and then the two will meet to discuss it in person. Managers often ask employees to fill out self-assessments ahead of time as well, ideally using the same form that the manager will use for the assessment.

Most organizations conduct evaluations annually, sometimes with a second mid-year review. As we noted in the chapter on goals, if you want your staff members to take their goals seriously, set the cycle for your evaluations so that you can assess whether or not the staff member achieved her goals for the relevant time period (as opposed to reviewing performance on staff members' anniversaries of employment). In addition, you should also conduct an evaluation with new employees two or three months into their tenure, in order to reflect on fit for the position and to identify areas for growth. These can also include questions about how the employee is adjusting and what additional help she may need to feel fully transitioned into her role.

## What should a performance evaluation form include?

To be truly effective, a performance evaluation should focus primarily on 1) the employee's results, 2) how she got those results, and 3) an overall summary and tenure considerations. A common mistake organizations make is focusing on how the employee did her work, to the exclusion of the actual outcomes she achieved – but in a results-oriented organization, the evaluation should start with outcomes.

1. <u>Results</u>. List the employee's objectives for the year and assess how well she met each of them. Take the context into account. For instance, if your development director didn't meet her fundraising goal for the year but it's because the stock market dropped 20%, acknowledge that. Conversely, if she met her goal but only because of an unexpected large bequest that she had little to do with, point out that she should have been able to vastly exceed the goal.

2. <u>Performance factors</u>. In the next section, assess how the employee approached her work. You might divide this section in two, first addressing organizational values that you expect all staff members to demonstrate (integrity, continuous improvement, etc.), and then assessing skills that are specific to this employee's role (public speaking, writing compelling briefing papers, etc.).

   *Completing evaluations is rarely urgent, but it is important. Putting off your employees' evaluations sends a bad message to them about the importance of their performance.*

3. <u>Summary and tenure considerations</u>. In the final section, discuss how the staff member is performing overall. Are there any next steps for improvement she should take? In order to send clear, unambiguous signals about the staff member's performance, we strongly recommend using a rating system of some sort.

In the summary section, you might also discuss the extent to which continued tenure in the role make sense. For higher performing employees, the tenure question can be a quick sentence or two in which you flag the topic to be raised in your in-person discussion ("I'm excited to talk about what you're thinking about your future when we meet"). But if you have concerns about the staffer's fit for the role, you should put that in writing here, noting that if she does not improve, she may face dismissal. (Chapter 8 covers performance warnings and coaching out in more detail.)

*See page 178 for an evaluation form template.*

## Elements of an effective performance evaluation

- Ideally, nothing in a performance evaluation should be a surprise, because you've been giving the staff member feedback throughout the year. (But if that's not the case, don't let that prevent you from being direct now. You have to start somewhere!)

- Be specific and use examples to illustrate your points, both when praising and when identifying areas for improvement. For instance, you could say, "You did a great job with the new inventory system," but it's more effective to say, "Your revamping of the inventory system has saved the organization money, and I've heard several people comment about how much easier you've made it to find the supplies they need."

- Be honest and direct about problem areas. As this is the definitive word on the staff member's performance, you should include concerns you have.

- Pay attention to the overall picture you're painting. We've seen managers inadvertently write lukewarm evaluations for stellar employees who they would be devastated to lose. Likewise, if the employee needs to make major improvements, make sure that comes through in the overall message. Think of the evaluation as a mini-essay, where you want to make sure that your thesis statement ("You're doing great!" or "I need you to reach the next level quickly") comes through. *See pages 185-196 for samples of completed evaluation forms.*

- Resist the temptation to be overly influenced by recent events. If an employee has struggled with something all year but recently improved, or if she has done well all year but recently had a major error, be sure the evaluation reflects the whole year, not just the last few months. At the same time, if someone has struggled all year but improved recently, be sure to note that so the person doesn't feel her efforts went unnoticed.

- Consider getting feedback in confidence from others who work closely with the employee. You may find out aspects of the person's performance, both good and bad, that you didn't know about.

## Promoting From Within

The last development method we'll discuss is promoting from within. Promotions can be a great way to recognize when a staffer has developed and is ready for new challenges, and promoting from within lets you avoid the uncertainties of hiring a relative unknown from the outside. At the same time, even when your staffer is outstanding in her current role, there are many cases in which a promotion isn't the right move.

When contemplating promoting someone, the most important factor to consider is not what sort of job the staffer is doing in her current position, but instead how strongly matched she is with the skills you need in the *new* position. Organizations often do the opposite of this: we have frequently seen outstanding staffers get promoted and then flounder because the skills that made them so fantastic in the first position aren't the same skills needed for the new position. Most commonly we see this with promotions to managerial positions, since the skills needed to get

174

results *through others* are often very different than the skills needed to get results on your own. For instance, a grant writer might excel at writing winning grant applications, but when promoted to development director, she might need very different skills, such as the ability to articulate expectations, help people solve their problems, and judge talent.

We do encourage you to create opportunities for promotion when they make sense for the employee and the organization. But don't feel you need to promote employees in order to retain them. There are many other ways to keep good employees on your staff, and we'll talk about those in the next chapter.

## Key Points

- The best staff development stems naturally from strong, hands-on management – pursuing ambitious goals, being held to high standards, and being given candid and direct feedback about what is and is not leading staff members to reach their goals.

- Invest in your best, because your best staff members are usually the ones who will grow the most.

- Know what you can change (skills and knowledge) and what you can't (talents and basic inclinations).

- Distinguish between development needs and serious performance issues, and don't allow development to distract you from dealing with underlying performance issues.

- Provide feedback on a constant, ongoing basis, in order to reinforce behavior you want to see more of, prevent bad habits from becoming ingrained, and foster an atmosphere of open communication.

- In addition to giving feedback on a regular, ongoing basis through the year, you should also conduct formal performance evaluations each year. To be truly effective, a performance evaluation should focus primarily on the employee's results, how she got those results, and an overall summary and tenure considerations.

- Promotions can be a great way to recognize when a staffer has developed and is ready for new challenges, but the key consideration must be how well matched the employee is with the skills needed in the *new* position, not how well she has done in the previous position.

## 📖 Additional Reading

- Marcus Buckingham and Curt Coffman, "Spend the Most Time with Your Best People" in *First, Break All the Rules: What the World's Greatest Managers Do Differently* (Simon & Schuster 1999), pages 153-163.

## ✏️ Tools

- Sample performance evaluation system

- Sample completed evaluation form – corrective assessment

- Sample completed evaluation form – strong assessment

- Sample orientation agenda

## Sample Performance Evaluation System

### Americans for All that is Decent and Good
### Performance Evaluation System

#### OVERVIEW

AADG is committed to continuous improvement. We hold ourselves accountable for the impact and quality of our work, including through regular conversations between managers and staff members. Frequent check-ins allow us to reflect on progress and on what is working or could be improved.

We also have an official performance evaluation system through which staff members receive formal performance assessments. In addition to ensuring that managers and staff members reflect on progress against goals, the process helps staff members understand their strengths, weaknesses, and overall performance. These conversations are also opportunities to clarify expectations and discuss a staff member's role and tenure.

Our performance evaluation consists of three main sections.

I.  **Results (what you got done)**
    This section reviews progress in reaching key objectives. Each objective has a measure (or measures) of success against which results are compared. Objectives or measures of success that are particularly important for the position should be marked **bold**.

II. **Performance Factors (how you got it done)**
    This section assesses demonstration of our core values and mastery of skills essential to the position.

III. **Assessment (overall, how well you did + next steps)**
    This section provides a summary rating and identifies next steps for improvement. Implications for tenure are also considered.

#### ASSESSMENT RATINGS

The following scale is used for all ratings in the review.

**Exemplary** – regularly exceeds expectations, is a model for others to follow, makes significant contributions to the organization, exceptional, rare

**Good** – almost always meets expectations and sometimes exceeds them
**Fair** – sometimes meet expectations but needs improvement to fully satisfy them
**Poor** – does not meet expectations, needs significant improvement quickly

## PROCESS

Performance reviews normally occur in December so we can reflect on results against annual objectives. For new staff, we also conduct an "Initial Assessment" at or before three months to reflect on fit, clarify the goals and objectives of the role, and identify areas for growth.

During the evaluation process, managers may review a staff member's work products and the results of relevant projects or engagements. Managers may also reach out to the staff member's team, colleagues from other departments, and/or people outside the organization for additional feedback.

The evaluation process consists of three main steps.

1.  The staff member completes a self-review and sends it to the manager. The manager then drafts his or her review and sends it to the staff member.

2.  The staff member and manager meet to review each section of the evaluation, highlighting key points, discussing questions, and summarizing conclusions. At the end of the meeting, the manager summarizes any overarching conclusions and next steps.

3.  The manager's evaluation is placed in the employee's personnel file (in rare cases, the manager may wish to edit the evaluation to reflect new conclusions that have emerged during the evaluation discussion). If there are specific areas where quick improvement is needed, the manager and staff member will agree on a plan, track progress against it, and take any other appropriate actions.

As noted above, while this formal evaluation system ensures managers and staff members engage in summary discussions about performance at least once a year, this process should not substitute for regular check-ins and discussions about performance between staff members and their managers throughout the year.

*CUSTOMIZING THIS TOOL*

*As you customize this tool for your organization, please pay attention to the following parts of Section II (Performance Factors).*

- ***Core values*** *and their descriptions should be drawn from the values agreed upon by your organization. Core values may reflect the organization's beliefs and principles, as well as its behavioral norms.*

- *Both the **organization-wide skills** and the **position-specific skills** should be tailored to reflect the needs and expectations of your organization. For example, you may require some or all staff members to be fluent in a foreign language or certain computer programs.*

# Evaluation Form

| | |
|---|---|
| Employee Name, Position | |
| Manager Name, Position | |
| Review Period | |
| Date of Review | |
| Reviewed by | Self ☐   Manager ☐ |

## SECTION I.  GETTING RESULTS
(Mark important objectives and/or measures of success in bold)

| Objective | Measure(s) of Success | Result(s) | Rating (E, G, F, or P) |
|---|---|---|---|
| | | | |
| | | | |
| | | | |

The evaluation should start with an assessment of whether the person achieved his goals from the previous evaluation period (usually one year).

**Comments:** To what extent did the staff member achieve objectives for the position this past period? Did the staff member complete the key steps necessary to reach objectives?

## SECTION II. DEMONSTRATING PERFORMANCE FACTORS

*A. To what degree did this person demonstrate each of the Core Values?*

| Core Value | Description | Rating (E, G, F, P, or N/A) |
|---|---|---|
| Relentless Pursuit of Results | We are determined to achieve ambitious, measurable results in working toward our vision. As a result, we continue pursuing our end goals despite the constraints or obstacles we encounter along the way, and we work towards those goals with a sense of urgency. | *Core values should apply broadly to all members of your organization.* |
| Good Thinking | We push ourselves to think critically about all that we do, approaching each issue and decision with rigor and always searching for the best idea. | |
| Collective Impact | We assume responsibility for the success of our broader movement and contribute toward increasing our collective impact. | |
| Constant Learning | We reflect on and draw lessons from previous experiences and apply them to do even better in future endeavors. We also seek out feedback and resources to help meet our goals. | |
| Respect and Humility | We approach others in a way that demonstrates that we value them and their contributions and have high expectations of what they can contribute. We are cognizant of the limitations of our own experience and value others' perspectives. | |

| | Description | Rating (E, G, F, P, or N/A) |
|---|---|---|
| Personal Responsibility | We do our best in all that we take on and assume ownership for producing the best possible result in our area of work. | |
| Positive Outlook | We establish big goals and greet new ideas with a sense of possibility. We assume the best in others and treat them with a generosity of spirit. | |

*B. To what degree did this person demonstrate each of the skills key to success in the position? (Select "Not Applicable" for skills rarely used in a particular position.)*

| Organization-wide skills | Description | Rating (E, G, F, P, or N/A) |
|---|---|---|
| Problem-solving | Identifies issues, effectively structures problems, analyzes data to produce insights, and generates wise, actionable recommendations. | |
| Communication | Produces strong written documents, edits documents effectively, engages in effective verbal communication – 1-on-1 and small group – and conducts effective large group presentations. | |
| Organization | Prioritizes tasks effectively, accomplishes tasks efficiently, follows through on all commitments, breaks down large projects to make them manageable, effectively manages complex projects involving multiple actors. | |
| **Position-specific skills** | Description | Rating (E, G, F, P, or N/A) |
| Management | Builds a team of high-performing staff members, appropriately structures jobs so that staff members can succeed, develops and motivates staff members, acts from the perspective of an organizational leader, manages other managers effectively to accomplish goals. | |
| External relations | Serves as an effective ambassador, builds connections, and maintains relationships with outside constituents. | |

*Organization-wide skills are those all staff members should have.*

*Position-specific skills are those important for the person in this position to demonstrate, but not broadly relevant for other staff members.*

183

**Comments:** In what priority areas of performance (values and skills) did the staff member excel? In what areas is improvement needed?

## SECTION III. SUMMARY ASSESSMENT, NEXT STEPS, AND TENURE CONSIDERATIONS

Overall performance rating

Exemplary ☐    Good ☐    Fair ☐    Poor ☐

**Comments:** How is the staff member performing overall? Are there any next steps for improvement or other implications? To what extent does continued tenure in this role make sense?

*Sample Completed Evaluation Form – Corrective Assessment*

**Americans for All that is Decent and Good**
*STAFF EVALUATION FORM*

| | |
|---|---|
| Employee Name, Position | Eric Bardwell, Technology Director |
| Manager Name, Position | Julia Torres, Managing Director |
| Review Period | January – December 2008 |
| Date of Review | December 5, 2008 |
| Reviewed by | Self ☐   Manager ☑ |

**SECTION I. GETTING RESULTS**
(Mark important objectives and/or measures of success in bold)

| Objective | Measure(s) of Success | This Year's Result(s) | Rating (E, G, F, or P) |
|---|---|---|---|
| Achieve high level of internal customer satisfaction | 75% "Highly satisfied" on year-end survey | 62% Highly satisfied | Fair |
| **Complete Web site build-out and redesign on-time and bug-free** | **New site is online, complete, and bug-free by July 1** | **Site launched three weeks late and there were four bugs reported over the first month** | Fair |
| Complete online application system on-time and bug-free | System is online, fully-functional, and bug-free by October 1 | Launched on October 3, three bugs reported and fixed in first week | Fair |

**Comments:** To what extent did the staff member achieve objectives for the position this past period? Did the staff member complete the key steps necessary to reach objectives?

In terms of overall results, I think you achieved at a fair-to-good level in your realm. Positive highlights include completing a number of the priority items we identified through the quarterly plans: getting the online application system up and running well and missing an aggressive deadline by just two days; building reporting tools for a number of teams; and meeting a large number of recruitment and admissions needs (including enhanced reporting and helping trainings function at a higher level). In several other areas, the results were not what we would have wanted. Satisfaction is the most notable one. You'll need to improve those numbers by doing more around some of the specific levers we've identified, including building tech capabilities for the regions more quickly and taking on regional connectivity and remote access issues more aggressively. The Web site result was mixed. It was an aggressive goal and you worked extremely hard in May and June to meet it, but it might have been reachable if you'd prioritized hiring JS earlier in the year.

> Use a clear initial sentence to present the overall picture, then focus on specifics within that context.

> Be honest and straightforward with negative feedback.

## SECTION II. DEMONSTRATING PERFORMANCE FACTORS

*A. To what degree did this person demonstrate each of the Core Values?*

| Core Value | Description | Rating (E, G, F, P, or N/A) |
| --- | --- | --- |
| Relentless Pursuit of Results | We are determined to achieve ambitious, measurable results in working toward our vision. As a result, we continue pursuing our end goals despite the constraints or obstacles we encounter along the way, and we work towards those goals with a sense of urgency. | Good |
| Good Thinking | We push ourselves to think critically about all that we do, approaching each issue and decision with rigor and always searching for the best idea. | Good |
| Collective Impact | We assume responsibility for the success of our broader movement and contribute toward increasing our collective impact. | Good/Fair |

186

| | Description | Rating (E, G, F, P, or N/A) |
|---|---|---|
| Constant Learning | We reflect on and draw lessons from previous experiences and apply them to do even better in future endeavors. We also seek out feedback and resources to help meet our goals. | Good/Fair |
| Respect and Humility | We approach others in a way that demonstrates that we value them and their contributions and have high expectations of what they can contribute. We are cognizant of the limitations of our own experience and value others' perspectives. | Good |
| Personal Responsibility | We do our best in all that we take on and assume ownership for producing the best possible result in our area of work. | Fair |
| Positive Outlook | We establish big goals and greet new ideas with a sense of possibility. We assume the best in others and treat them with a generosity of spirit. | Good |

*B. To what degree did this person demonstrate each of the skills key to success in the position? (Select "Not Applicable" for skills rarely used in a particular position.)*

| **Organization-wide skills** | **Description** | **Rating** (E, G, F, P, or N/A) |
|---|---|---|
| Problem-solving | Identifies issues, effectively structures problems, analyzes data to produce insights, and generates wise, actionable recommendations. | Good |
| Communication | Produces strong written documents, edits documents effectively, engages in effective verbal communication – 1-on-1 and small group – and conducts effective large group presentations. | Good/Fair |
| Organization | Prioritizes tasks effectively, accomplishes tasks efficiently, follows through on all commitments, breaks down large projects to make them manageable, effectively manages complex projects involving multiple actors. | Good/Fair |
| **Position-specific skills** | **Description** | **Rating** (E, G, F, P, or N/A) |
| Management | Builds a team of high-performing staff members, appropriately structures jobs so that staff members can succeed, develops and motivates staff members, acts from the perspective of an organizational leader, manages other managers effectively to accomplish goals. | Good |

| | |
|---|---|
| External relations | Serves as an effective ambassador, builds connections, and maintains relationships with outside constituents. | Good |
| Staying current on latest technology | Stays up-to-date on latest technological developments and how companies can use them to improve performance, and draws on this base of knowledge to address organizational challenges. | Good/Fair |

**Comments:** In what priority areas of performance (values and skills) did the staff member excel? In what areas is improvement needed?

I want to start by recognizing your improvement on Respect and Humility and Positive Outlook. Beginning with our discussion at this time last year, we've talked about these at several points and you have made significant progress on both. I know you've been more conscious of how you approach others – including showing people that you respect what they bring to the table, and making sure that you address problems head-on instead of leaving them to simmer, and I think your efforts have borne fruit.

A related area is Constant Learning, where I put a mixed rating. On the positive side, you were open to feedback in the areas I just mentioned, and you applied the lessons to change your approach, which is impressive. You have the potential to be exemplary on this score by being more proactive in regularly reaching out and requesting feedback in areas where you can improve. For instance, on organization I still think there's room for improvement but I haven't seen you trying new things and adapting your game as quickly as you might.

Of all our core values, the area where I think you have the most potential for improvement is Personal Responsibility. You are sometimes good on this score, like last year when you got the servers up and running quickly. But there are other situations, like with the Web site, where you seem content to have circumstances determine project outcomes. What I want to see – and the online regional reporting system will be a good test – is for you to take full responsibility for making it a success. At the start, this means when people are vague about what they want, you ask lots of questions, show them examples of other systems, and insist on figuring out what they will and won't like so the end product works well. Then, you'd need to plan backwards to figure out what needs to happen by when in order to bring it in by the deadline. And in that plan, you should build in enough of a cushion so when hurdles inevitably emerge you have time to deal with them, rather than allowing circumstance to determine whether you succeed or not. If you do that, I think you can get to where I'd like to see you get, which is making our technology work at an exemplary level.

> Be as specific as possible about what success looks like.

188

On skills, a few areas to highlight: On management, you are doing a good job overall. Your team has clear project goals and a sense of what's expected of them, you're a helpful resource to them, and a number of your team members mentioned getting good

constructive feedback from you along the way. They also feel that their efforts are valued and that when you give praise it's genuine. You also lured BR to the team, which was a big catch.

On organization, things seem to have improved, but there's still room for improvement. Personally, I'm still not 100% confident you'll follow through when you tell me you'll do something. To flag a recent example, we had agreed you would send me your evaluation of ST before you conducted the meeting so we could touch base about the overall message, and that did not happen.

> Where relevant, cite specific examples.

On communication, there's still room for improvement in creating documents and plans, and running meetings that clearly and concisely communicate to others (especially your key clients) what your team is going to produce by when. For instance, at the management team meeting in November your presentation left several people confused about how highly you were prioritizing their projects and when they could expect delivery.

## SECTION III. SUMMARY ASSESSMENT, NEXT STEPS, AND TENURE CONSIDERATIONS

Overall performance rating

Exemplary ☐   Good ☐   Fair ☑   Poor ☐

**Comments:** How is the staff member performing overall? To what extent does continued tenure in this role make sense? Are there any next steps for improvement or other implications?

> Put the headline assessment up front and, again, be straightforward and honest.

As I said initially, your performance this year was fair and we need it to continue to improve in order for you to reach your goals and for us to reach our goals as an organization.

On the positive side, you have built a technology infrastructure that works well overall and helps people do their jobs much more effectively than they were able to before. You have also instilled a strong ethic in your team of responding to "client" needs and have adjusted your style to fit our culture, which has led to smoother communication all around.

We need more from you, however, in order to maximize our effectiveness as an organization. What I'd like you focus on next year is the Personal Responsibility piece I mentioned in the previous section. Probably the best place to start is with the online regional reporting system. Taking personal responsibility for that process would mean talking in the next month to the regional directors who tend to have the most to say about technology, and getting their thoughts on what they would like to see. Then, draw up a blueprint of a proposed system and get them on board early in terms of functionality, output data, interface design, etc. Then, if things shift along the way, make sure the regional directors have a chance to weigh in on the options. Doing all the little things to ensure that you build a reporting system people love won't be easy, but you have the skill so it really will come down to taking personal responsibility for making it happen. If you commit yourself to taking this to the next level, I strongly believe that you can.

> Be specific about next steps where appropriate.

## *Sample Completed Evaluation Form – Strong Assessment*

### Americans for All that is Decent and Good
### *STAFF EVALUATION FORM*

| | |
|---|---|
| Employee Name, Position | Jesse Souweine, Development Director |
| Manager Name, Position | Julia Torres, Managing Director |
| Review Period | January – December 2008 |
| Date of Review | December 8, 2008 |
| Reviewed by | Self ☐   Manager ☑ |

#### SECTION I.  GETTING RESULTS
(Mark important objectives and/or measures of success in bold)

| Objective | Measure(s) of Success | This Year's Result(s) | Rating<br>(E, G, F, or P) |
|---|---|---|---|
| Raise operating funding | **$12.5 million raised** | **$12.8 million** | Exemplary |
| Secure federal funding for following FY (2009) | $2 million | $1.8 million | Good |
| Increase number of individual donors giving at least $5K | 150 donors | 170 | Exemplary |

**Comments:** To what extent did the staff member achieve objectives for the position this past period? Did the staff member complete the key steps necessary to reach objectives?

In short, I think your results were pretty spectacular. Even in a year when the economy was only so-so, we're on track to exceed our funding goal by roughly $300K. Not too shabby! We did this by focusing on key areas within regions, maximizing contributions from numerous national funders, and turning things around from the previous year in terms of ongoing funding at the federal level.

As I said, you had a tremendous year. Going forward, in addition to just generally keeping up the great work and doing what you're doing, the main area I think you should focus on more is being out in the regions (physically and virtually), proactively engaging with and serving as a resource to RDs. (To be clear, the RDs all report that you're incredibly helpful, but in several cases it's also clear that deeper engagement would be valuable, especially for newer folks who are still learning.) Identifying the key levers that can take things to a higher level in particular regions will be valuable, particularly as our growth rate slows in more well-developed regions.

> Even in a strong evaluation, identify the path for the person to get to the next level.

## SECTION II. DEMONSTRATING PERFORMANCE FACTORS

*A. To what degree did this person demonstrate each of the Core Values?*

| Core Value | Description | Rating (E, G, F, P, or N/A) |
|---|---|---|
| Relentless Pursuit of Results | We are determined to achieve ambitious, measurable results in working toward our vision. As a result, we continue pursuing our end goals despite the constraints or obstacles we encounter along the way, and we work towards those goals with a sense of urgency. | Exemplary |
| Good Thinking | We push ourselves to think critically about all that we do, approaching each issue and decision with rigor and always searching for the best idea. | Exemplary |
| Collective Impact | We assume responsibility for the success of our broader movement and contribute toward increasing our collective impact. | Exemplary |

| | Description | Rating (E, G, F, P, or N/A) |
|---|---|---|
| Constant Learning | We reflect on and draw lessons from previous experiences and apply them to do even better in future endeavors. We also seek out feedback and resources to help meet our goals. | Exemplary |
| Respect and Humility | We approach others in a way that demonstrates that we value them and their contributions and have high expectations of what they can contribute. We are cognizant of the limitations of our own experience and value others' perspectives. | Exemplary |
| Personal Responsibility | We do our best in all that we take on and assume ownership for producing the best possible result in our area of work. | Exemplary |
| Positive Outlook | We establish big goals and greet new ideas with a sense of possibility. We assume the best in others and treat them with a generosity of spirit. | Exemplary |

*B. To what degree did this person demonstrate each of the skills key to success in the position? (Select "Not Applicable" for skills rarely used in a particular position.)*

| Organization-wide skills | Description | Rating (E, G, F, P, or N/A) |
|---|---|---|
| Problem-solving | Identifies issues, effectively structures problems, analyzes data to produce insights, and generates wise, actionable recommendations. | Exemplary |
| Communication | Produces strong written documents, edits documents effectively, engages in effective verbal communication – 1-on-1 and small group – and conducts effective large group presentations. | Exemplary |
| Organization | Prioritizes tasks effectively, accomplishes tasks efficiently, follows through on all commitments, breaks down large projects to make them manageable, effectively manages complex projects involving multiple actors. | Good |

| Position-specific skills | Description | Rating (E, G, F, P, or N/A) |
|---|---|---|
| Management | Builds a team of high-performing staff members, appropriately structures jobs so that staff members can succeed, develops and motivates staff members, acts from the perspective of an organizational leader, manages other managers effectively to accomplish goals. | Exemplary |

| External relations | Serves as an effective ambassador, builds connections, and maintains relationships with outside constituents. | Exemplary |
|---|---|---|

**Comments:** In what priority areas of performance (values and skills) did the staff member excel? In what areas is improvement needed?

As your exemplary ratings indicate, you embody our core values as well as anyone in the organization. Below I've made comments on particularly noteworthy areas:

Relentless Pursuit of Results – You continued pursuing every last channel relentlessly, turned around applications for funds at the last minute, etc.

Good Thinking – Your recent engagement around the "Significant Positive Impact" issue, beyond being a good example of pursuing collective impact, also nicely illustrates your truly wrestling with issues and wanting to ensure we get to the right answer, which is the essence of this value.

Collective Impact – HG said it well in her recent e-mail to you on this, where she alluded to your pushing us to pursue the additional channels "even though you knew it would create an added burden for the development team and despite the fact that it had nothing to do with your overall funding goal."

Positive Outlook – The best illustration of this may be the fact that you got two kudos for your humor from RDs ["Fun to work with (and really funny)"; "Makes me laugh."]

As with core values, you're operating at an exceptionally high level when it comes to skills:

Problem Solving – It's hard to overstate your strengths as a thinker. On so many occasions over the past year, you've exercised great judgment about which levers we should pursue and how we should pursue them. One great example is the 2006-10 funding memo you wrote, which I think does a great job of recognizing where we stand and what our realistic opportunities and constraints going forward may be.

> Be detailed even in a strong review – it's a great opportunity to let a high performer know he or she is valued, which will be a big factor in retention.

194

Organization – I'd be interested to hear whether you think this has improved. My sense is that you have gotten better in terms of prioritizing work and that this area may come down to management and hiring the right people. The fact that things like end-of-year giving are rolling forward speaks well of your ability to take big projects and break them down. At the same time, you might think about whether there are any systems you could put in place to help guarantee that a big project (like the fund initiative) meets its deadline and stays on track, perhaps by setting up additional "padding" around deadlines.

Management – Your greatest management achievement this year was doing an outstanding job managing the make-up of your team, notably around transitioning out SH, bringing on LF and HW, and retaining MK. Your team feels that you're an incredibly helpful, accessible resource. This is not a big deal, but just so I don't lose it: one person wrote that "it'd be helpful if he could provide more feedback, good and bad, on a regular basis."

## SECTION III. SUMMARY ASSESSMENT, NEXT STEPS, AND TENURE CONSIDERATIONS

Overall performance rating

Exemplary ☑    Good ☐    Fair ☐    Poor ☐

**Comments:** How is the staff member performing overall? Are there any next steps for improvement or other implications? To what extent does continued tenure in this role make sense?

This should be pretty clear by now, but I think you had an outstanding year and that you're operating at an amazingly high level. You led us to spectacular results on overall funding and awards, you've made progress in areas for development that we talked about last year (management most prominent among them), and you've done even more to be an essential contributor to the broader discussions around the future of our organization.

In terms of areas to focus on going forward, the one thing I'd flag is what I mentioned in the goals section – i.e. engaging with RDs to identify key levers. I think that will be essential for us to continue meeting our considerable funding needs.

In terms of tenure, are you ready to sign the 2010 contract? ☺ Seriously, I know we'll be having lots of discussions re: your future plans as part of our planning around organizational capacity for the long-term plan, and I'm assuming we'll talk about this then.

With your superstar performers, use the evaluation process as a retention tool and an entry point into discussions about their future with your organization.

**Sample Orientation Agenda**

### Orientation Agenda
### (Executive Assistant)

**Desired outcomes:**
- You understand your overarching role and my expectations
- We're aligned about logistics
- You know which projects to get started on

I.    **Your role**
  - A.    **Overarching aim: free up as much of my time as possible**
  - B.    How you'll do that:
    1.    Coordinate office functions by handling meeting scheduling, conference room reservations, travel booking, and other administrative tasks as needed.
    2.    Provide support on a range of other projects as needs arise.
    3.    Serve as point person for tech vendor and others as appropriate.
  - C.    Potential impact of your role = huge! (I'm a major bottleneck now.)

II.    **Working Together/Expectations**
  - A.    Some ideas on keys to success:
    1.    100% follow-through – no dropped balls.
    2.    "Customer service" orientation – our field staff are busy people doing amazing work. Our job is to make their lives easier.
    3.    Attention to detail – everything going out (i.e., other than internal e-mail communication) should be polished, though it's fine to be casual when the situation calls for it. In general, have our organizational "look and feel."
    4.    Take good notes so you remember the subtleties of what we discuss.
    5.    Repeat back what you've heard so we're aligned upfront.
    6.    Model a positive attitude and flexibility – makes a huge difference.

7. Open door policy (i.e., come to me for help without hesitating). Ask questions and let me know when your load is light or heavy so we can balance it out.

8. Take initiative and be proactive – if you see ways we could do things better, let me know. We are constantly learning and growing and we see you as part of that effort.

B. What you can expect from me/us:

1. 100% follow-through.

2. Good communication on expectations, priorities, and specific projects.

3. Engaging you in projects and practice as much as possible and where appropriate.

4. Interest in hearing your ideas and welcoming your contributions.

5. Interest in your professional development.

C. Comments/questions/thoughts on above?

D. Logistics/Communications

1. Hours – 9:30 – 6:30, may extend beyond, be available for on-call items, typically no weekends.

2. Meetings – regular weekly check-ins to review previous week and week ahead and discuss other topics (you create agenda, bring any challenges/topics I can help with and have suggested solutions – but don't feel obligated to "save up" items for our check-in) – proposed time Monday at 11:00?

3. Communication – early and often!

a) Phone/voice mail: cell phone for most urgent if I'm out of the office; if leaving a message, let me know if it's urgent/non-urgent up-front. Double call if super urgent. You can always leave me messages or e-mail and I will be responsive (unless I'm on a plane).

b) E-mail: for slightly less urgent and less nuanced items. Most urgent stuff e-mail together with double call.

c) Calendars and scheduling: give as much information as needed when scheduling information (e.g., time, location, who's at meeting, etc.) so I have it at fingertips (come back to this).

  4. Office tour: supplies, front desk, conference rooms, copier, fax, etc.

 E. Your goals/preferences/thoughts/quirks/questions?

## III. Orientation/Background Info

 A. Review of mission (why we exist and what we do) and core values (how we do it).

 B. Review annual plan: priorities and goals for this year.

 C. Confidentiality policy.

 D. Employee handbook – any questions?

 E. Financial policies and procedures.

 F. Recent history to be aware of, tips for working with other departments, relevant dynamics to be sensitive to inside and outside office.

## IV. Getting Started

 A. Keys, phone/vmail, internet/e-mail, and calendar (set up to be shared)

 B. Timesheet basics: what and how to track

 C. Upcoming meetings for you:

  1. Today: lunch with staff at 1:00

  2. Payroll, benefits, 403b, etc: meet with Jim today at 2:00

  3. Wednesday: continue this meeting at 12:00

  4. Friday: lessons learned with staff on Fridays at 4:00

## V. Specific Initial Topics

 A. Short-term scheduling requests

 B. Server: need to back-up our information automatically and share files

 C. Office space: need to figure out longer-term arrangement. Add this to next week's check-in list

 D. Office supplies: copy paper, printer, large paper clips, other?

 E. Reimbursement forms: see receipts

## VI. Background readings for you

 A. Organizational plan and latest quarterly update

 B. Management manual

 C. Monkey article

 D. Web site

## Chapter 7
# Retaining Your Best

So now that you have great staffers, you're set for life, right? Wrong. As it turns out, people leave jobs. And there's nothing worse for a manager than having a stellar employee tell you that she has accepted another offer.

As a manager, retaining your best people is a critically important part of your job. Since you're trying to get great results, and you know the right people are key to great results, you need to make sure that your best employees stay. You can't lock them to their desks, but you can create a situation that they won't want to leave.

You do this by being strategic about retention, in the same way you'd be strategic about anything else you don't want to leave to chance, like fundraising or lobbying. Treat your retention efforts like as much of a priority as anything else you care about, and include retention on your to-do lists or in your quarterly plans. Even just writing, "Do everything I can to keep Miguel" on your plan for the quarter can help keep the goal on your radar screen. We'll talk below about what you do once you have the aim in mind.

But first, one note of caution: as you're hatching strategies for keeping great staff members on board, make sure that you're strategic about *who* you focus those efforts on. You don't actually want to retain

*Across-the-board retention is not your goal. Retention of your best is.*

*everyone*. You want to retain your high performers, but not the mediocre or low performers. Focus your efforts accordingly.

## METHODS FOR RETAINING HIGH PERFORMERS

Contrary to conventional wisdom, retention isn't just about salaries and benefits packages, although these things do matter. Retention most often comes from ensuring that high-performing staff members feel valued, understand how their role fits into the bigger picture, and have a manager who helps them focus on meeting ambitious, meaningful, and challenging goals.

However, as with most of management, you should adapt your approach to fit the context. Different staffers are motivated by different things, so you should develop an individualized strategy tailored to each specific staffer you're trying to retain. Here are some of the potential levers you might incorporate in your retention strategy:

- Direct discussion. The single best way to retain a good staff member is to discuss the subject directly. Take the staff member out to lunch or for coffee to talk about her future and ask her directly, "How can we make sure you stay for the next two years?" Even if you don't get an immediate commitment, having an explicit discussion and showing that you care enough to talk about it can go a long way.

- Sense of purpose and personal indispensability. Give the staffer a strong sense of where the organization or her part of it is headed and why her role is essential to that larger picture. Show her that *she* is a key lynchpin in your plan for moving forward. For instance, you might emphasize how crucial your lobbyist's work is to ultimately passing your legislation, how her relationship-building skills and legislative savvy are paying off, and how unlikely someone else would be to get the results she is generating.

202

- <u>Employee-manager relationship</u>. One of the factors that most strongly influences job satisfaction is an employee's relationship with her direct supervisor, because a manager has such a pervasive impact on the day-to-day work environment. No matter how much a staff member likes her job or the organization, if she has a bad relationship with her manager, it will seep into her quality of life every day. Therefore, it's important to care about your staffers as people and to treat them with respect and kindness – in other words, to treat them as you would want to be treated.

> *"An employee may join [an organization] because she is lured by their generous benefits package and their reputation for valuing employees. But it is her relationship with her immediate manager that will determine how long she stays and how productive she is while she is there.... Managers trump companies."*
>
> *- Marcus Buckingham and Curt Coffman in First, Break All the Rules: What the World's Greatest Managers Do Differently, page 36*

- <u>Growth</u>. Don't let your best employees get bored, and don't make them go elsewhere to continue to grow in their careers. Three ways to avoid those pitfalls are:

  1. *New challenges*. As great employees master an area, increase the bar so they are challenged to do better and better within that area. For instance, once your fundraising director hits her $5 million annual goal, you might agree on a new, higher goal for next year or even for three years down the road (tied, of course, to what the organization needs to accomplish in order to fulfill its mission).

  2. *Increased responsibility*. Aside from new challenges within existing areas of responsibility, you can also add entirely new responsibilities to the plate of an employee who has proven she's ready for them. That said, be sure your strategy here is tailored to the individual. Some staff members see increased responsibilities as an affirmation of trust and a chance to develop new skills, while others, depending on where they are in life and what factors

they're contending with outside of work (such as a new baby or an ailing relative), might see them as a burden rather than a reward.

3. *Grooming*. As we noted in the last chapter, sometimes your best performers may not thrive in a more advanced role. Some, though, will have the talents to move on to the next level, so give these staff members an idea of what their career development plan might look like if they stay with you. Think about what they can do in their current role to prepare them for the next rung on the ladder, and then talk to them explicitly about that. For instance, if you are a communications director with a phenomenal marketing associate, you might have her shadow you at higher level meetings and explain that you want her to get exposed to the issues discussed there. You might also ask her to begin drafting some of the press releases you normally draft and give her feedback on them, again explaining that you want to help her prepare for the next step in her career. And you might even tell her explicitly, "In two years, I could see you taking on this role."

- <u>Ongoing positive reinforcement</u>. Don't underestimate the impact of regularly making sure great staff members know you think they're great. Let employees know that you notice their accomplishments and that you value their role in the organization.

- <u>Salaries</u>. We said earlier that retention isn't just about money. It's not, but money can help. Your best staff members are probably not motivated by money, but they're probably not blind to it either. Your best people will also have many opportunities to make an impact in the world, and the reality is that money can sometimes sway their decisions about where they apply their talents.

Unfortunately, most nonprofits radically under-invest in salaries for their best people. Instead, they might pour as much money as possible into direct program work. While well-intentioned, this can end up having the opposite of the desired effect – actually harming program activities by making it harder to attract and keep the people who will execute those activities most effectively. After all, as we talked about in the introduction to this section, your best performers get dramatically better results than the average – not just a bit better, but often five or more times better. If one high performer will get better results than several mediocre performers combined, paying your best staff members quite well can actually be an extremely economical move.

At a minimum, your salaries should not be a reason people leave. Beyond that, though, ideally your salaries would be high enough that your best people know that while they might make more money elsewhere, they'll never make this much money *and* do work this interesting *and* contribute as much as they do with you.

*Don't be penny-wise and pound-foolish: pay your best staff members well!*

Keep in mind, too, that salary offers can be game-changing, convincing employees who might otherwise have moved on to stay. For instance, at Teach For America Jerry had a staff member he desperately wanted to retain, but who was considering graduate school. He knew that a small salary increase would not change her mind. Instead, he offered her a 50% increase, which amounted to tens of thousands of dollars. She stayed, and the dramatically higher-than-expected salary increase changed her entire way of thinking about her position with the organization. She is still there, and the investment in her salary continues to pay enormous dividends.

- Titles. Titles cost nothing and can be an effective way to recognize employees' development. For instance, your outstanding membership assistant might be rewarded for her achievements with the title of development officer, or you might recognize your superb communications coordinator's work by changing her title to assistant communications manager. You want titles to be accurate, of course, and as an organization grows there is often an overall structure with which titles must be consistent, but there is often room to be creative in this area.

Now that you're on the road to keeping your high performers, we'll turn to one of the hardest realities managers face: the unavoidable fact that you won't want to retain everyone. Just as you shouldn't leave retention to chance, chance shouldn't come into play when it comes to moving people out either. In the next chapter, we'll discuss how to transition out employees who aren't helping to propel you forward.

## Key Points

- If you want great results, retain your great (and only your great) employees.

- Retention most often comes from ensuring that high-performing staff members feel valued, understand how their role fits into the bigger picture, and have a manager who helps them focus on meeting ambitious, meaningful, and challenging goals.

- Different staffers are motivated by different things, so you should develop an individualized strategy tailored to each specific staffer you're trying to retain.

- Retention strategies can include direct discussion; giving the staffers a sense of purpose and indispensability; having a strong, positive employee-manager relationship; providing opportunities to take on new challenges and increased responsibilities; regularly providing positive feedback; and ensuring that titles reflect growth.

- Most nonprofits radically under-invest in staff salaries, which can harm program activities by making it harder to attract and keep the people who will execute those activities most effectively. Since one high performer may get better results than several mediocre performers combined, paying your best staff members quite well can end up being extremely economical.

## 📖 Additional Reading

- Marcus Buckingham and Curt Coffman, "The Art of Tough Love" in *First, Break All the Rules: What the World's Greatest Managers Do Differently* (Simon & Schuster 1999), pages 182-205.

# Chapter 8
# Addressing Performance Problems and Letting People Go

Even with the best efforts to hire well and develop your people, the reality is that you are going to have some staff members who simply don't perform at the level that you need. This is an unavoidable reality of managing, and one of the most important things you can do as a manager is to address it head-on.

By addressing these situations forthrightly and matter-of-factly, you can sometimes help an employee get to the level you need. And when that doesn't work, you can lay the groundwork for transitioning the employee out in a way that is fair and compassionate.

In this chapter, we'll talk about how you can move employees "up or out" – successfully, fairly, and quickly.

A word about the "out" part of this: we know letting someone go is difficult. We've both been guilty on multiple occasions of waiting too long to move out lower performers. It's especially tough when the staff member isn't flagrantly underperforming (or lying, stealing, or committing other ethical violations), but rather does contribute somewhat but isn't getting you the results that you need. Because we are human, because we like to give people additional chances, and because we don't like telling people they can't meet our needs, too often managers shy away from firing when they should. As a result, most managers do not remove low or mediocre performers anywhere near quickly enough or frequently enough.

Letting people go is hard, but it's also critically important. We've both been fairly shocked after we let people go and brought in new staff by just how much more the new people accomplished. And of course, not being assertive in this area has particularly dire consequences in the nonprofit world, where having a "weak link" directly harms our ability to deliver on our missions to the communities we serve.

If you're serious about getting results, you will have to fire people. You can do everything else right – setting goals and expectations, delegating effectively, giving feedback, and so forth – but if you aren't willing to fire people who aren't performing at the level you need, you will never accomplish what you could.

In this chapter, we'll cover:

*If you're serious about getting results, you'll have to fire people.*

- How to determine if a performance issue is a serious problem

- Two methods for dealing with the issue:

  1. The "textbook" approach of progressive discipline – informal warnings, formal warnings, and letting people go

  2. The less traditional method of coaching out, in which you and the employee mutually agree that continued tenure in the role doesn't make sense and agree on a transition plan that leaves you both better off than progressive discipline might

---

**Ask the Right Question**

Imagine that you're in a relationship with someone who isn't quite what you're looking for. You like the person but know deep down that it isn't the right match for you. Most people would agree that it's kinder to be honest and end things than to continue stringing the person along. The question you ask yourself isn't, "Do I have enough reasons to break up with this person?" but rather, "Is this person so great that I want to stay with them long-term?"

But when it comes to employee fit, the picture gets much fuzzier for most managers. Managers tend to look at mediocre performers and ask, "Is this person really performing so badly that he should be fired?" when the question to ask instead should be, "Is this person performing so well that I should retain her?"

---

## HOW TO DETERMINE IF YOU HAVE A SERIOUS PERFORMANCE PROBLEM

Sometimes it's clear you have a problem: your accountant is chronically making serious errors on financial statements, or your membership coordinator isn't sending out renewal notices. Other times it's not as clear-cut: your lobbyist seems up-to-date on legislation but hasn't actually moved any. Or your communications director has creative ideas for generating media coverage but doesn't always follow through on the plans she forms.

Maybe there are good reasons why your lobbyist hasn't delivered any results. After all, legislators have their own priorities and outside factors can derail the best of plans. And perhaps your communications director's workload is so high that no one in her shoes could carry out all the plans.

Perhaps. But perhaps these things are true and you still have a problem. How can you decide?

**Rule #1: Keep the focus on what the ideal staffer would do in a similar context**

Managers often tailor their expectations for the position to the person who happens to be inhabiting it. While it's sound management to play to your team members' strengths and weaknesses, this should not mean lowering your expectations about core results. The bar you use to assess performance should not be "the best this particular person could do," but rather a vision of what a truly high-performing staff member would be doing in the role.

For instance, maybe your vision of a star lobbyist tells you that although she wouldn't necessarily be able to pass your model legislation quickly, she would still be able to build relationships that would allow you to tweak related bills and advance your agenda in less direct ways. In the case of the communications director, maybe you can't be sure that the workload isn't too great for one person. But you do know that an outstanding employee would handle a high workload differently – keeping the work organized, proactively updating you about what isn't getting done, and not forgetting about projects entirely.

*Keep a high bar for performance by asking what the ideal staff member would do.*

**Rule #2: Determine if the problem is one of fundamental fit for the position or one that could quickly be resolved through more guidance**

Once you have a clear vision of what you expect from the position and how the person in it is falling short, you'll want to determine whether the problem is one of fit for the position or an issue that you could address through more feedback and guidance.

Begin by considering the employee's talents and key traits and how well matched they are with the needs of the position. For instance, you want an assistant to be uptight about details and organization. If you have an assistant whose nature is simply more laid back, while she could improve, she'll likely never be one to obsess about the details of your travel schedule at the level you need.

Be careful to avoid the trap of sinking too much of your own time or the organization's resources into remedial training. For example, you might believe that if you were able to spend several hours each week with a staff member working on her writing, you could get her to an acceptable level, but that might not be a good use of organizational resources.

Another area to consider is the extent to which you have clearly communicated your expectations to the employee. If you haven't already, you should talk explicitly about those expectations now to try to get into alignment. That said, even when you have not communicated your expectations as well as you could have, sometimes there's still a question of fit. You're never going to have done absolutely everything you could have done to create the optimal environment for every staff member. Think about what top performers would have done in similar contexts: would they have found a way to succeed with the same amount of resources and guidance?

An extreme example of this is a client we worked with who hesitated to hold a staff member accountable after the staff member twice missed planes and trains intended to get him to important meetings. The manager worried that perhaps they hadn't set clear enough expectations for the staffer: after all, he had never spelled out that the staffer needed to be on time for such things. But clearly, a great performer (or even merely a reasonable person, in this case) wouldn't need that guidance.

**Rule #3: Trust your gut**

In some cases, you may not be sure if your concerns are valid. Perhaps the employee's work is in a field far outside your expertise, like technology, or perhaps the position is a new one and so you haven't seen anyone else tackle the work.

In such cases, listen to your gut, because it's likely reacting to a larger body of knowledge than you realize. For instance, you may not feel equipped to judge much of your technology director's work because of its technical nature, but your gut is reacting to the fact that your e-mail network has more downtime than feels reasonable, the director doesn't react with a sense of urgency when things go wrong, and you're often told that problems "can't" be fixed.

If the small amount you do feel competent to judge is not good, it's very likely representative of the rest. Don't be afraid to generalize from what you *do* know, and keep in mind that you don't need to "prove" your case with courtroom accuracy. The question for you is whether or not you're getting what you need from the employee, not whether you could convince a jury.

**Rule #4: Pretend it would be easy**

Make your assessment independent of how difficult the next step may be to execute. Don't focus on the discomfort of having to tell someone she isn't meeting your expectations or the hassles of interviewing and training someone new. The main question before you is, "Is this the best person for the job?"

*Pretend that you have a red button which, if pushed, would lead to your staff member being replaced. Would you push it?*

Time and time again, we see managers who know deep down that they should replace an employee but want to avoid the discomfort of addressing it head-on.

Here's a revealing test. Pretend that you have a red button which, if pushed, would lead to your staff member being replaced instantaneously. Would you push it?

Another way to look at it – would you feel relieved if the person told you she was leaving?

### What About High Performers Who Aren't a Culture Fit?

What if you have a high performer who delivers when it comes to the meat of her job but who is difficult to work with in other ways? An employee who is abrasive, unable to get along with others, or otherwise culturally "off" can be as disruptive as one who isn't meeting a performance bar.

Alison once worked with a research director who was highly skilled when it came to knowledge, research, and writing. His many years in the field had given him an almost unparalleled body of knowledge, and he had a unique talent for making highly complex subjects easily understandable by laypeople.

However, he increasingly wanted to focus solely on his own interests and began swatting away ideas that weren't his own. Frequently when staff members inquired about getting research done to support a project another department was working on, the research director would cite a minor obstacle and respond that it couldn't be done. Only after much coaxing would he agree to do the work requested of him. He also scoffed at and shot down other people's ideas in meetings, something that was particularly corrosive on less experienced staffers who weren't confident in their ability to push back.

Staff members like this can be poisonous to both your culture and your results. Yet when the employee is producing good work, a manager may be hesitant to consider transitioning him out.

Rarely are such cases just a bad cultural fit. The results usually can be seen as performance issues as well. The research director's nay-saying prevented the research department from tackling projects as vigorously as it otherwise would have, ate up time of other employees when they had to convince him that it was worth doing assigned work, and corroded the willingness of other staffers to contribute. Therefore, it would have been reasonable to decide that a can-do attitude and a willingness to explore new ideas rather than jumping to conclusions were key requirements for a successful research director, and to hold him to that bar.

When faced with a staffer who doesn't fit with your culture, try viewing the troubling behavior through the lens of performance and see if it might be about performance after all.

**OVERVIEW: PROGRESSIVE DISCIPLINE AND COACHING OUT**

Once you've determined that the performance issue is a serious one, you have two paths for addressing it:

1. the more traditional path of progressive discipline; and
2. a less traditional – but sometimes kinder and more effective – path that we'll call "coaching out."

## Progressive discipline

Progressive discipline consists of a brief series of increasingly serious warnings, culminating in dismissal if an employee fails to improve sufficiently. Typically there are three stages: an informal verbal warning, followed by a formal warning with a written improvement plan, followed by termination if sufficient improvements aren't made. At each point, the employee can make the necessary corrections. If she doesn't, you move to the next stage.

---

**The Three Stages of Progressive Discipline**

1. Informal warning
2. Formal warning
3. Termination

---

Note that each step foreshadows the next ("If this doesn't get better, we're going to have talk about a more formal plan"), so that the staffer is very clear about where she stands and isn't surprised by negative consequences. We've seen numerous situations where a manager gives lots of negative feedback to a struggling staff member but never explicitly says that the person's job is in jeopardy – and the staffer ends up shocked when she is ultimately fired. This is unfair to the staffer, who deserves to know the severity of the concerns. As importantly, it can create significant anxiety and a culture of fear among *other* staff members, who may begin to worry they're on the verge of being fired every time they receive negative feedback. A progressive discipline system lets your staff know that they won't be fired without first knowing that their job is in jeopardy and having time to improve.[1] *See page 240 for a sample progressive discipline policy.*

### *Step One: Informal Warning*

So you've considered what a high performer would be doing in a given situation and have realized that you have a serious performance problem – i.e., a staff member whose performance does not reach the level you need it to. You need to see significant improvement in order for her to ultimately stay in the job.

The first step is to deliver an "informal warning," by having an honest talk with the employee. Your goal is to let the employee know that her performance must improve, to be specific about what improvements are needed, and to be clear about potential consequences if improvements aren't made.

This is different from the sort of corrective feedback we talked about in Chapter 6, in that you're making it very clear that this isn't routine feedback. You're talking about a more severe problem that is holding the employee back and has the potential to become an even more serious problem if not fixed. In other words, the conversation has an "or else" attached this time.

In some situations, the staff member will already have recognized the problem and will feel relieved to discuss it openly. In others, the staff member may not have realized that the problems rose to this level – which, of course, makes the conversation even more important to have.

No matter what the outcome is, you will be doing the employee a significant service by speaking honestly about where her performance is

---

[1] Nonetheless, from a legal perspective your progressive discipline procedures should be guidelines, not promises. You need to be able to act more quickly in unusual situations. Note the language in the sample policy on page 240.

falling short. Too many managers never put aside their discomfort about such conversations, and as a result, many employees never have the opportunity to learn how they could do better.

Let's walk through the process step by step:

- You may want to give your employee advance warning that you need to have a serious conversation about her performance. Consider, though, how much advance notice you want to give. While you don't want the staff member to be caught entirely off-guard, too much advance warning can make your staff member go through days of worry in anticipation of the meeting. Whether it happens a day in advance or just at the start of the meeting, raise the subject by saying something like, "I want to have a step-back conversation about your performance."

- At the start of the meeting, explain that you want to talk about changes you want to see from her. You might say something like, "As I mentioned in my e-mail, I'd like to talk about your performance lately. To be honest, your work is falling short of what I need from you."

- Explain your general categories of concern, and offer specific instances to support your points. This could sound something like, "I'm concerned about the quality of your recent grant applications, as well as the fact that you've been missing deadlines lately. Your last several grant applications were disjointed, confusing in places, and didn't make a compelling case for funding our work. And you've missed three deadlines this month, including one that caused an important mailing to be held up."

- Ask the employee to tell you how she perceives the issues. Say something like, "I'd like to hear your thoughts about what's causing these issues. What's your sense of what might be going on?"

- As you would with corrective feedback, probe to understand what the root of the problem might be. Pick a few specific instances where the staffer didn't perform as you would have liked and delve into what happened. For instance, if you're concerned about poorly-written grant applications, it might be that the employee just isn't a strong writer, but before you conclude this, probe for other factors that could be at work. Is she a poor time manager and writing at the last minute? Have you and she agreed on what a good grant application should look like? Is the fundamental issue one of responsibility, in that she isn't assuming ownership for ensuring that grant applications are as strong as possible?

- If you're able to identify factors contributing to the problem, make any suggestions you have about how the employee might do things differently. For instance, if she has a time management issue, you might suggest she begin planning projects backwards and set interim deadlines for herself to better structure her work.

  In some cases, you might decide it's worth it to make a one-time, up-front investment in trying to help the person improve. With a chronic deadline misser, you might spend time suggesting organizational systems and walking her through the basics of how to track projects and deadlines. At other times, you may decide that it's not reasonable for you to spend your time on this sort of intensive development. (If you do decide to offer such help, be sure it's not unlimited. You can't afford to spend significant amounts of time hand-holding an employee who shouldn't need that level of help.)

- Regardless of the cause, be explicit about the standard you need the person to meet – and hold firm. For instance, say something like, "I need you to begin producing grant applications that are clearer and more compelling, using the samples I showed you as the standard, and which don't require more than brief editing from me. And I need you to start meeting deadlines right away. In the rare case that you do need to miss a deadline, I need to be informed ahead of time, not after the fact."

- If you sense that the staff member believes that your expectations are too high or that she is doing the best that can be done, a good response is to acknowledge that the bar is high while holding firm about your needs. For instance, you might say, "I know that the bar is high, but we need someone who can do this work and keep track of deadlines without a lot of supervision. I hear you that it's hard and I know it's a challenge, but in this context we need someone who can handle a large workload and get the very difficult done with limited staff resources."

- Most importantly, clearly state the consequences if performance does not improve, by explaining that the next step would be a formal improvement plan. You might say something like, "Assuming your performance improves and you sustain that level, then we'll just move forward. But if we're still seeing these issues in three weeks, I'll need to put you on a formal improvement plan and after that, if it doesn't improve, I'd need to let you go. So my concerns here are serious ones – I think you have a great deal of potential, but I also need you to be performing at a higher level."

- As we describe later in the chapter, you might consider using the coaching out option here, by asking the employee if she feels the role is the right one for her and seeing where the conversation leads. You might jointly agree to a solution that works better for both of you, giving the staff member time to search for a new job and you to look for a replacement without having a vacancy.

In some cases, the staff member will make the improvements needed after an informal warning. If she does, congratulate her, be specific about what's better and why, and make clear that she needs to sustain the improvement.

*See page 241 for a sample script of an informal performance warning.*

---

**Four Tips for Progressive Discipline Conversations**

1. Discuss the situation with your own manager ahead of time, so that she is in the loop on the problems and your approach.

2. Prepare talking points. Treat the conversation the way you would an important presentation, outlining your points and how you will make them. Having a "script" to fall back on will make you more comfortable and make the conversation go more smoothly.

3. Use your manager, a friend, or a colleague to practice the meeting. Identify and repeatedly practice the hardest part – i.e., whatever it is that you find yourself most reluctant to say. Whatever you do, don't wing it!

4. Keep in mind that you are engaging in this conversation because you are acting in the organization's best interest. For you to be effective in your job, you have to develop a high-performing team.

---

### Step Two: Formal Warning

When sufficient improvement doesn't happen, the next step is to move to a formal warning. Your goal here is to give the staff member a final chance to make the improvements and also to be explicit about the fact that dismissal is now a very real possibility.

- At the start of the meeting, explain that you haven't seen the changes you discussed earlier and now you need to put her on a formal written improvement plan, setting areas for improvement and a timeline.

- Be explicit about the standard you need the staffer to meet and the timeline for meeting it. Long, drawn-out probationary periods generally aren't necessary, since you should look for improvement in weeks, not months.

- Clearly state the consequences if performance does not improve – explain that the staffer will lose her job if she does not improve to the level you are specifying. We cannot overstate the importance of this step! Managers often find these words hard to say, and you may worry about damaging the person's morale with this warning. But however difficult it may be to raise the possibility of termination, it's far worse for the employee not to know that she risks being fired.

> *Make sure the employee knows her job is in jeopardy.*

Sometimes managers think, "Surely she knows her job is in danger, given the serious talks we've been having and the level of my concern." Yet many people have a startling inability to hear negative input. In addition, if the employee has struggled professionally in the past, she may think negative feedback is normal and not realize that you, unlike her previous bosses, actually plan to do something about it. So fairness demands that you be explicit and never assume that an employee will figure out the severity or possible consequences on her own.

- Establish the next steps. For instance, you might say something like, "I'd like you to come up with a system for better tracking deadlines right away. Let's check back in two weeks to see how it's going, and we'll do the final review four weeks from today. If you've met and continue to sustain the level we just discussed, we'll just move forward. If you don't improve, though, then we would have to dismiss you."

- Follow up with a written summary of your conversation, laying out your expectations and the consequences for not meeting them. This is essential, so that there can be no doubt that the staff member heard the message and understands the key points, and so that the consequences of not improving are in writing. As part of the document, include clear criteria for how you'll judge success. For instance, on an improvement plan for a struggling assistant, you might specify that success means no dropped balls over a three week period and no more than one instance of inaccuracy (such as a meeting listed on the calendar at the wrong time).

*See page 244 for a sample of a short, formal performance warning and page 245 for a more in-depth example.*

---

### What About Moving People to Different Roles?

Sometimes a manager, in a last-ditch attempt to salvage an employee, will move the person into another role in the organization. In our experience, this is rarely successful if it's done in order to address a problem. Someone who has failed to meet a bar for performance in one role within an organization often lacks the requisite talent or values to excel in other roles within the same organization. She may be able to "survive" in a new role better than in the old, but rarely will she be so strong that she will become the type of high performer you ultimately need.

Usually when managers try this, it's because they are uncomfortable making a decision that feels as difficult as letting someone go, so they take a less drastic course – and in doing so, stretch out the problem.

That said, we have seen a limited number of cases where shifting roles has worked. In these cases, the staffer was a very strong culture fit and brought strong talents, but those talents were better suited to a different role. For instance, in one case, a regional director lacked the assertiveness necessary to move his region forward as quickly as was needed, but he was a great culture fit and an outstanding writer, so he was switched to a role where he could apply that talent, and he thrived.

---

### *Step Three: Assessing Where to Go Next*

You should expect to either see improvement quickly or know that it's not going to work out. As you watch for improvement, don't get sidetracked by incremental improvements. While small improvements can feel promising, hold out for your ultimate goal of outstanding performance. The staff member doesn't need to become great overnight, but you should see a steep climb in that direction. A climb to "barely acceptable" isn't what you're looking for here.

In some cases, the staff member will be able to make the improvements needed. When this happens, as at the informal warning step, be sure you recognize it – tell her explicitly what you've noticed and what an improvement she's made. At the same time, the improvement must be sustained over time, so make sure she understands that if the problems recur, you will not go through the entire process all over again.

In other cases, you will not see the improvement you need. When that happens, it's time to move the person out.

**Letting People Go**

If you have followed the progressive discipline process, the employee has been clearly told about the problems and what needs to change, warned that the progress isn't what it needs to be, and explicitly told that her job is in jeopardy if specific changes don't occur. When the termination conversation happens, it's more of a wrap-up than anything else; it shouldn't be a surprise. (As we note below, there are some offenses so egregious that they warrant firing on the spot, like, say, embezzlement or punching someone, but such situations are rare.)

- Decide ahead of time about logistics, such as whether or not you will offer severance and how much, and whether the person will be expected to leave the office immediately or will have until the end of the day.

- Some organizations have a third person in the room during a firing to corroborate what was said in case the employee later sues. Generally this would be an HR staffer or another manager above you. However, if your staff is small, consider that it may be impossible to find a third party who could sit in without violating the employee's privacy and dignity.

## Will a Firing Lower Morale Among the Rest of the Staff?

Just the opposite! Keeping low or mediocre performers on staff is in almost every case an enormous morale drain for high performers.

If you've ever worked somewhere where shoddy work was tolerated, you know how frustrating and demoralizing it can be when a manager doesn't do anything about poor performers. It's likely that your staff has spotted the problems and will be relieved when they are resolved. Good people want to work with other good people, and they want to know that their employer is discerning when it comes to results. Their quality of life goes up when they work in environments where standards are high, accountability is clear, and they can count on their co-workers to pull their own weight.

Even when employees are friendly with the staff member being let go, most people can separate personal affection from professional assessments. In fact, one client we worked with managed a man and a woman who were romantically involved. When he had to fire the man, he obviously worried about how the girlfriend would react. Would she continue working for a boss who had fired her boyfriend? Would her morale take a hit? But after the firing, the female employee approached the manager in confidence and told him that she agreed with the decision to fire her boyfriend.

As long as you are open with your staff about how you address performance problems so that they understand you don't make arbitrary personnel decisions, you will have a confident, motivated staff. But do keep in mind that that understanding is key. If firings occur without a general understanding on staff that employees are clearly warned and given a chance to improve before being let go, you risk creating a climate of fear where employees worry that they could be terminated at any point. So it's important to be open and honest with your staff about how problems are handled. *See page 240 for an example of a progressive discipline policy.*

- Begin the conversation itself with a statement like, "I want to have a conversation about your progress in the areas of concern we've discussed."

- Be direct and to the point. You should announce your decision at the start of the conversation, because you don't want the employee to think she's supposed to be defending herself or thinking of an improvement plan when your decision has already been made. Say something like, "We talked last month about the fact that if these issues didn't change, I would need to look for a replacement. Unfortunately, while you have made some progress, it hasn't been enough, so we're now at the point where we're going to have to let you go, and today is going to be your last day."

- Be honest about the reason for the firing. Sometimes a manager will come up with a cover story for the firing, thinking the real reason will hurt the employee's feelings. (Often managers use a cover story because they haven't been direct enough about the problems earlier. You, of course, have followed the steps above and won't find yourself in this situation.) Not being honest can come back to haunt you – see the Legal Issues sidebar on pages 236-237.

- Be compassionate. It's okay to say, "I know this is hard" or, "I really do appreciate your efforts." Even if you've been incredibly frustrated with the employee, you can allow yourself to feel and express genuine compassion. When at all feasible, try to truly believe this is a case of a bad fit, rather than that the employee is incompetent, lazy, or difficult. If you go into the meeting with this mindset, it will change the way you come across, helping to defuse the situation and helping the employee keep his or her dignity.

- Make it clear your decision is final. If the employee tries to change your mind, don't enter into prolonged discussion, which can make the employee think the decision is up for debate. Instead, say something like, "I realize that we see this differently, but the decision is final." Additionally, ask for input only where you mean it. Don't ask questions like, "What do you think about this?" or "Does this make sense?" unless you really mean to start a conversation. Present options only where there is a real choice (for instance, a staff member might be able to choose between different forms of a severance package, but not about whether or not you are firing her).

- Consider a communications plan. Depending on the circumstances, you and the staff member might agree on a plan for explaining the change to the rest of the organization in a way that fairly reflects the situation and respects the staff member's privacy.

- Cover all the details the employee may be wondering about, such as the effective date of the termination, COBRA (which gives employees the right to continue health benefits at their own cost), the final paycheck, etc.

- When it's all over, debrief with your manager or a trusted advisor. As part of your commitment to continuous improvement, we recommend asking whether there's anything you can learn from the situation. While some number of terminations will always be unavoidable, it's worth asking some hard questions. Are there ways to improve your interview process to ferret out these sorts of problems before making a hire? Did the choice result from making the hire under pressure? Use terminations as a trigger for reflection and see if you might be able to strengthen your processes for the future.

### Firing without using progressive discipline

There are some situations so egregious that they warrant firing without moving through the stages of progressive discipline or attempting to coach the person out. Obviously, if an employee embezzles, physically accosts someone, or commits intentional sabotage or another grossly egregious offense, going through a progressive discipline process would be silly. Some things are so serious that they don't deserve a second chance. In these cases, you would move straight to termination.

*See page 251 for a sample firing script.*

---

### Reasons Managers Resist Letting Employees Go

The vast majority of managers err on the side of not firing when they should. Let's take a look at some of the most common reasons managers tend to resist letting low performers go:

- <u>Believing that everyone deserves another chance (and another... and another)</u>. This belief is especially common in nonprofits, which are often staffed by people who highly value compassion and who believe in giving people chances to develop. But as tempted as you may be to be lenient with struggling performers, don't lose sight of the fact that your donors are paying you to advance your mission – and, no matter how personally kind it may be, a commitment to providing a job for someone mediocre is contrary to that mission.

- <u>Believing that you haven't invested enough in helping the person</u>. Yes, you should help people succeed – but within reason. You're never going to have done absolutely everything you could have done to create the optimal environment for every staff member to excel in. Take a look at what top performers have done in similar contexts. Would they have found a way to succeed with the same amount of resources and guidance?

- <u>Feeling overwhelmed by the amount of time it would take to bring a new person up to speed</u>. Managers tend to overestimate how much time it will take a new employee to become trained and start delivering value compared to the person currently in the role. Strong performers will get up to speed far faster than you realize. Besides, even if this weren't true, wouldn't you rather have a short period of downtime followed by an all-out stellar performance, as opposed to years of mediocrity (or worse)?

---

---

**(Reasons Managers Resist… continued)**

- <u>Hoping that the employee will leave on her own</u>. A bad situation rarely gets better without direct intervention. You don't leave your fundraising or lobbying to wishful thinking; you make decisions and take action. Why would you leave something as crucial as having the right staff to chance?

- <u>Feeling bad and/or feeling sorry for the staff member</u>. It's okay to feel sorry for the staff member: after all, getting fired is no one's ideal outcome. But if you handle the situation directly and honestly, she'll know that it's coming, she'll have had the chance to improve, and you can be kind as you help her transition out of a job that she'll never thrive in (and you can even help her brainstorm about other jobs she might be more suited for). After all, not only are you doing a disservice to your mission by keeping a low performer on staff, but you're also doing a disservice to the employee herself, by keeping her in a job that doesn't fit her well.

- <u>Feeling nonprofits should be different/more egalitarian</u>. Sure, nonprofits have different missions than the private sector, but we're not different in our need for high performance. In fact, we should be *more* committed to high performance, because so much more is at stake. Let the corporate sector absorb the low or mediocre performers – we can't afford it!

- <u>Wimping out</u>. Let's be honest – these are all excuses. Ultimately, the most common reason people wait too long in these situations is about avoiding discomfort or hassle for *ourselves*. Just like with dating, putting off the day of reckoning (or trying to avoid it altogether, by ignoring the problem or hoping the other person acts so you don't have to) is unfair to the person, who could be using this time to find something that *is* right. Unlike with dating, at least as managers we get paid to handle difficult situations.

---

### *Logistics*

Organizations vary widely in how much time they give a dismissed employee to leave. Some expect employees to leave immediately, while others allow more time. Generally employees who have been coached out may stay for weeks or even several months, while employees who have been fired outright would be expected to leave that same day.

If you have any cause to worry about an employee's reaction, you may prefer to err on the side of caution and have the person leave immediately.

In all cases, you'll also want to consider logistics such as disabling the person's access to e-mail and computer networks. You'll also need to arrange for the return of keys and any company property (such as a laptop, cell phone, or credit card), as well as establish with other staffers how the person's e-mail, voice mail, and computer files will be handled.

---

### Should You Give Severance Pay?

A generous severance package can save the organization money if it gives you mental "permission" to move aggressively rather than spending several months going through a performance warning process with a foregone conclusion.

If you offer severance pay, tie it to a smooth transition. This gives you some leverage to prevent the employee from wreaking havoc before leaving. And in all cases, severance should be contingent on the employee signing a general release agreement, forfeiting any future legal claims.

---

## Coaching out

An approach that can be a very effective supplement to a progressive discipline policy is "coaching out." A coaching out conversation is aimed at convincing the employee that continued tenure in the role doesn't make sense and agreeing on a smooth transition plan.

Coaching out is often the right choice for mediocre performers. These are people whose performance is not terrible – i.e., you may not be able to document many egregious instances of poor performance – but whose performance doesn't reach the high bar you need in the role. It's also a good choice for a long-term, loyal employee whom the organization has simply outgrown. In cases like these, rather than dragging an employee through a formal improvement process, it can be far kinder to simply move straight to an honest conversation about the employee's fundamental fitness for the role.

These conversations can turn difficult situations into truly productive ones and can work out with all parties satisfied. The key is to talk honestly and recognize that the employee may simply be "miscast" in the role – stealing a phrase from Marcus Buckingham in his book *First, Break All the Rules: What the World's Greatest Managers Do Differently*. Buckingham points out that poor performers often aren't poor performers because they're lazy, obstinate, or insubordinate but rather because they are placed in a role that is a fundamental mismatch with their true talents.

Buckingham suggests thinking of it as "tough love" – you're not going to compromise on your standards and what the organization needs, but you care about the employee and want to see her in a role where she'll blossom. You want to help her move out of a situation that is holding her back from true success and toward opportunities where her talents will be better utilized.

Here's an example of how this can work in real life. A few years ago, Alison had an employee whose work was good, but not stellar. The employee frequently got frustrated and resentful over several demands of the job, snapped at people, and constantly needed to be talked down. Numerous conversations hadn't improved things, so Alison tried a different approach. She sat down with him and acknowledged that he was frustrated by these particular things but that they simply weren't going to change, that they were inherent parts of the job, and that they couldn't be constantly battling over them – and that rather than trying to force himself into a job that obviously was making him frustrated and stressed, she wanted to see him figure out if he could really be happy in the position, knowing that the things he was complaining about weren't going to change. She asked him to take a few days and think about whether he wanted the job in its current form, as opposed to the job he kept trying to change it into, and she told him that if he decided it just wasn't for him, there was no shame in that and she would help him in the transition out.

> *Coaching out can ultimately leave your organization and your staff member better off.*

Several days later, the employee told Alison that he realized he should move on. During the next month, he worked on organizing his files and leaving his work in good order, he trained his replacement, and Alison helped him brainstorm about jobs he'd be happy in. On his last day, he confessed that he was shocked that such a potentially awful conversation had actually been pleasant. And since then, he's stayed in touch, periodically sending helpful leads and information.

In other words, coaching out can turn a potentially difficult and unpleasant situation into one that ends with all parties happy. Here are some keys to doing it well:

- Begin a coaching out conversation itself with a statement like, "I want to talk with you about your fit for this role and some of our options for moving forward."

- Try to make the tone of the conversation as collaborative as possible. The overall feel of the meeting should be that you want to jointly figure out a way forward that will be best for both the employee and the organization.

- Focus on the high bar for performance you're setting rather than ways in which the staff member has truly "messed up" (because in the case of a merely mediocre performer, instances of a true "screw up" may be rare). Frame the conversation by laying out what the ideal performer in the role would do, and then focus on the gap between the staff member's performance and that bar. Use a format similar to, "What we need is someone who can do ____. I see your strengths as being more ____."

- In some cases, the bar may be higher than it once was because of changed circumstances, such as organizational growth or changing demands of the job. Prepare to "tell the story" of why that is the case.

- Depending on the circumstances, you might offer the staff member two different options: she can pursue an improvement plan under your progressive discipline policy and try to meet the bar you're describing, with the understanding that she could be let go if she doesn't improve, or you can jointly form a transition plan that will give her time to search for another job while giving you time to look for a successor.

- Make clear why the joint agreement would be an attractive option. For instance, you might give the person more time to look for her next job than she would have otherwise, and she might be able to say that she's still employed at your organization while she's looking. Be honest about your self-interest as well. It's

### The Right Kind of Turnover

*Good to Great* author Jim Collins notes that top performing companies don't have any more or less turnover than other companies do. What differs is when the turnover occurs. He found that at top performing companies, people either left very soon after starting or stayed for a long time. The best companies "did not churn more, they churned *better*," he writes. Great leaders "adopted the following approach: 'Let's take the time to make rigorous A+ selections right upfront. If we get it right, we'll do everything we can to try to keep them on board for a long time. If we make a mistake, then we'll confront that fact so that we can get on with our work and they can get on with their lives.'"

okay to explain that this helps you because it prevents a vacancy in the role.

- In the case of a long-time, once valued employee who the organization has outgrown, it could be appropriate to soften this approach and steer the person away from the improvement process option altogether, if you believe it's unlikely to be successful. For instance, you might still offer the two options, but say something like, "To be honest, I'm happy to give you a chance to pursue the improvement plan option if you want to, but I would hate for it to turn your experience here sour. I would much rather work together on a transition that meets your needs and ours."

- Give the staff member an appropriate amount of time to reflect and to come back to you with her decision. Set a deadline for when you would like an answer (no longer than a week, since you want to make moving forward a priority).

- If the staff member chooses to pursue an improvement plan under your progressive discipline policy rather than to agree to a transition plan, be sincere in your willingness to give her a chance to improve.

*See the sample "coaching out" script on page 253.*

**Progressive Discipline and Coaching Out Combined**

Often, you won't necessarily pick one path at the beginning but rather will pursue both in parallel. That is, you might be clear with a staff member about your concerns and try to steer her toward a "coaching out" approach rather than going down the progressive discipline road in the first place. If the employee chooses to, though, she can pursue the progressive discipline process, beginning with the informal warning. At the end of that stage, you can again offer the negotiated agreement.

As we noted above, whatever stage you're at, you should be sincere in your willingness to give the staff member a chance to improve if she chooses that course. You might say something like this:

> "To be honest, I'm just not sure that this role as we're now conceiving of it is a good fit for your skills. We need someone who's going to be highly effective at networking and building external relationships. While I'm sure you could do that at some level, I see your real strengths lying in analysis and working one-on-one with others inside the organization. We've given you a chance to improve over the past month, and I haven't seen much change. At this point, we can go one of two routes. We can put you on a formal improvement plan for the next month, which means I would write up my concerns, and we would agree on what success looks like. At the end of that month, if you delivered on what we had outlined and then were able to sustain the improvement over time, we'd move forward with you in the role. If you didn't improve, we'd let you go, and you'd have two weeks of severance. I'm willing to go down that road, and I promise that if you choose that path, I'll be fair and will try my best to help you succeed. I do, though, wonder whether you're ever likely to thrive in that role, so I want you to think hard about this other path. Before we put you on a formal improvement plan, we could agree that this just isn't the right role for you. You'd then have six weeks to look for a job, and you'd be able to devote some of your time here to

---

**Unions**

In our experience, very few nonprofits are unionized. While working with unions is beyond the scope of this book, the same principles apply. Hold a high bar and address performance problems clearly and forthrightly, even when your ultimate authority to fire may be more difficult to exercise or employees may be entitled to more formal processes than what is discussed here.

that – I would just need you to keep the database updated during that period. Why don't you think about this, and let me know which way you want to go by Friday."

In other words, even if you have started through a progressive discipline process, keep in mind the possibility that employee may not improve and consider raising the idea with her that there might be a better path.

---

### Legal Issues

You don't generally need to speak to a lawyer before dismissing an employee, but there are a few specific situations where you should consider consulting a lawyer in advance.

For at-will employees (i.e., the vast majority of your employees – those without a specific employment contract), legal issues typically arise when there is evidence of illegal discrimination related to the employee being a member of a protected class (protected classes revolve around traits like age, gender, religion, race, or sexual orientation). When potential for such evidence exists, talk to a lawyer before taking action.

In particular, you should watch for situations where the following could pose issues:

- <u>Direct comments related to a protected class</u>. Remarks about an employee's age, gender, race, religion, or other protected status, even when meant as a joke, can give rise to legal claims. For instance, a birthday card delivered to a 50-year-old employee about the horrors of aging could be used as evidence for an age discrimination claim.

- <u>Disparate treatment</u>. Evidence that "similarly situated" employees are treated differently can also give rise to claims. What "similarly situated" means is a complicated legal issue, but be careful if you are treating employees of comparable tenure, seniority, and performance level differently (particularly when they differ in race, gender, sexual orientation, disability, etc.).

---

*(Legal Issues continued)*

- <u>Pretext</u>. If you give false statements about why you are firing someone, a jury might infer that you were covering up real reasons that were actually discriminatory. Most commonly, this occurs when you have been giving someone positive feedback along the way (even if you didn't really mean it) and then – feeling that you don't have enough of a record to cite your real reasons – use a rationale that is not the actual cause for the person's dismissal. If the person argues that your true reasons were discriminatory ones, this sort of cover-up can make it much harder to defend yourself.

- <u>Retaliation</u>. If an employee has raised a complaint involving some kind of legal issue – such as a concern about sexual or racial harassment or about financial wrongdoing within the organization – the firing can look like retaliation, even if the firing is unrelated to the complaint.

In addition, situations that involve disabilities – including mental illness – and/or family or medical leave can raise tricky legal issues that managers may not find intuitive.

When one of the situations described here arises, it does not mean that you cannot dismiss an employee, but it does mean that you should proceed with caution and speak to a lawyer first. As a general rule, speak with a lawyer if you are in doubt.

Additionally, if you are concerned the employee you are firing may be litigious, be extra sure to document the reasons for the termination. This can be as simple as a detailed memo before or after the firing, laying out the reasons for the decision. The goal is to be able to demonstrate that you had performance-based reasons for the firing if the employee later alleges your reasons were discriminatory.

## Key Points

- Addressing performance problems and moving mediocre or low performers out of your organization is, at its core, about a fundamental commitment to having great people.

- Most managers don't remove low or mediocre performers quickly enough or frequently enough, and their organizations suffer as a result.

- The bar you use to assess performance should not be "the best this particular person could do," but rather a vision of what a truly high-performing staff member would be doing in the role.

- Make your assessment of an employee's performance independent of how difficult the next step may be to execute. Pretend that you have a red button which, if pushed, would lead to your staff member being replaced instantaneously. Would you push it?

- When you have a serious performance problem, you can address it through the more traditional path of progressive discipline, or you can "coach out" the employee through a direct conversation.

- Progressive discipline is a series of increasingly serious warnings, culminating in dismissal if the problems aren't fixed. Typically there are three stages: an informal verbal warning, followed by a formal warning, followed by termination if sufficient improvements aren't made. At each point, the employee can make the necessary corrections; if she doesn't, you move to the next stage. Each step foreshadows the next, so that the staffer is very clear about where she stands and isn't surprised by negative consequences.

- In "coaching out," the aim is to convince the employee that continued tenure in the role doesn't make sense and agree on a smooth transition plan. The key is to talk honestly and collaboratively and recognize that the employee may simply be "miscast" in the role.

## 📖 Additional Reading

- Marcus Buckingham and Curt Coffman, "The Art of Tough Love" in *First, Break All the Rules: What the World's Greatest Managers Do Differently* (Simon & Schuster 1999), pages 206-212.

## ✏️ Tools

- Sample progressive discipline policy

- Sample script – informal performance warning

- Sample formal performance warning in writing (short)

- Sample formal performance warning in writing (in-depth)

- Sample script – firing

- Sample script – coaching out

## Sample Progressive Discipline Policy

State Health Care Now is committed to a work environment in which employees receive clear messages when their performance needs to improve. We generally use a policy of progressive discipline to address performance concerns. Under this policy, employees who are not performing at the level they need to typically receive an informal verbal warning, followed by a formal warning and written improvement plan, followed by termination where sufficient improvement has not been made.

However, State Health Care Now is an at-will employer and while it will generally take disciplinary action in a progressive manner, it reserves the right, in its sole discretion, to decide what disciplinary action will be taken in a given situation, including termination without prior warnings.

*NOTE: We strongly advise having any written progressive discipline policy reviewed by a lawyer, so that you do not inadvertently create a legal commitment to following these steps in every situation. You want to retain the flexibility to act outside your progressive discipline policy in particularly egregious or unusual situations, so you should be careful not to create a binding commitment.*

## Sample Script – Informal Performance Warning

*In this sample, the employee is a staff attorney whose management of casework has been poor. This initial performance warning conversation would typically be the first step in the progressive discipline process. If your staff member's performance did not improve, this would be followed by a written performance warning and, lastly – if performance still did not reach the necessary level – firing.*

As I mentioned in my e-mail about our agenda, I wanted to talk about your performance lately.

To be frank, your performance has fallen short of what I need from you. I have concerns in two big areas: the quality of your written work, and your interactions with our activists.

> Frame big-picture concerns upfront so the employee knows what to expect.

In terms of written work, I've been having to re-write significant portions of your draft filings in order to get them to where they meet our standards. For instance, on last week's reply to the motion to dismiss, your summary of the argument section was at least a page too long and didn't mention of one of our three major points. In addition, the transitions from one section of the argument to another were abrupt and disjointed, and in at least two places your parentheticals summarizing holdings were inaccurate.

> Provide specific examples of where the person is falling short.

So that's the written work piece. On the activist front, we continue to hear feedback that you aren't responsive enough when they try to get in touch with you.

I'd love to get your perspective on what's causing these problems. On the writing, do you have any sense of why the product hasn't been strong?

> Probe for insight from the employee – it's possible there could be an outside factor affecting performance that you should know about.

[*We assume here that the attorney says that she has been too busy to devote enough time to ensuring a quality product.*]

I know what you mean about writing under pressure and without enough time.

> Be empathetic as appropriate, but hold firm on the standard needed.

241

Unfortunately, though, I don't think the workload is going to get any lighter, and others on staff are handling comparable amounts of work. I could see, though, how better planning in advance might lead to a better product. Should we talk about how you might do that, working backwards from the deadline to ensure you don't hit a time crunch?

[*The manager and staff member agree that better advance planning would indeed help and that the staff member will send the manager a quick e-mail after each new piece of writing is assigned in which she lays out her timeline for producing a draft.*]

So better planning may help, and I'm happy to be a resource by looking over your initial timeline. Over time, though, you'll need to be able to do that independently because I wouldn't be able to supervise everyone that closely in the long run.

> Offer help but make it clear that your staff member must be self-sufficient in the long run. Be specific about next steps where appropriate.

Stepping back from this, I want to be clear about my expectations, and I also want to make sure we're both on the same page about what needs to happen and what the potential consequences are.

Going forward, I expect you to begin producing drafts of written documents that are ready to file with minimal editing by me – and by that I mean 30 minutes or less. Among other things, the arguments need to be clear, concise, and well supported, and flow smoothly from one point to another.

> Lay out a clear, specific bar that must be met.

In terms of activist relations, as you know, we promise a response time of no longer than two days. I know that can be hard when you have a lot of work on your plate, but again, it's a bar we're committed to meeting and we can't have you continue to miss it.

In the short term, I want you to re-draft the brief you sent me last night and have a stronger version to me by tomorrow end-of-day. I'm also going to put it on my calendar for us to check in on your performance in three weeks. Assuming it improves and you sustain the higher level,

> Clearly identify next steps.

then we'll just roll forward. If it doesn't, though, then I'm going to have to put you on a formal written improvement plan.

A formal written plan lays out areas for improvement and a timeline – and as with this discussion, if you improve and sustain that level, things go forward. If you don't improve, though, then at that point we would have to dismiss you. So my concerns here are serious – I think you have a great deal of potential, but I need you to be performing at a higher level. Given our workload, I need someone in your position who can create strong written documents and respond to activists promptly and reliably, and if you can't meet that bar we would have to find someone who can.

> Be straightforward and clear about consequences.

Do you have any questions about how we're moving forward?

## Sample Formal Performance Warning in Writing (short)

Alice,

Per our discussion, I wanted to capture how we're moving forward. As I mentioned, I realize that you've been trying very hard, but unfortunately your performance isn't where I need it to be, and without significant improvement I will have to let you go. That improvement needs to happen in the next two weeks, and then it needs to be sustained going forward. Due to the holiday, we'll use Friday, December 5th, as our deadline.

The main areas in which I need to see improvement are:
1. Timeliness – All bills must be paid on time.
2. Accuracy/Oversight – You need to catch any errors in billing and/or any discrepancies with vendors, around benefits, etc.
3. Financial statements and budget – You need to give me financial statements for each month this year, with the agreed upon documents, through October and a draft through November. In addition, I need a calendar of when they will be finalized each month.
4. Personnel – All personnel files complete and a list of contractors with amounts and start and end dates.
5. Credit Card – We need a better system so credit card use is tracked and all receipts are in one place.
6. Systems – We need overall systems that work for budget monitoring for you, me, and each staff member who oversees a budget. We also need simple, easy-to-understand systems for the following: new staff and leaving staff, managing money in and out, contracts, accounts receivable, and paying invoices. These must be systems that make sense and leave behind a clear record that we can refer back to if necessary. By the 5th, I need to see at least three of these systems up and running.
7. Ownership – As the director of finance and administration, it is your job to meet your objectives. Highlighting problems and then expecting others (i.e., me) to solve them is not enough. You need to propose solutions, get input, and then fix the problems to ensure that our needs as an organization are met in a timely manner.

I will be happy to discuss this further if you have any questions, and I hope to make it work.

My best,
Ron

## Sample Formal Performance Warning in Writing (in-depth)

*This is a formal written performance warning for a low-performing executive assistant serving two managers (the warning comes from both). This follows an earlier informal performance warning where these same issues were discussed in-person, and the memo would coincide with and formalize the same message as a second in-person discussion.*

TO:       RK
FROM:   AW and BT
RE:       Performance Improvement Plan
DATE:   October 20, 2008

This memo reiterates our concerns about your performance, which we discussed in-person two weeks ago. At that time, we said if your performance did not improve you would be put on a formal improvement plan, and if you did not improve after that we would have to dismiss you. As we discussed yesterday, your performance has not improved over these two weeks.

This memo lays out the formal improvement plan we discussed and reiterates the areas in which you need to improve and the level of performance you need to reach.

> Be clear from the beginning about where things stand in the process and reiterate that if things don't improve the consequence will be dismissal.

Our hope is that you will meet the expectations laid out in this plan, and that BT and I will be fully satisfied with the job you are doing. We have tried to be clear and specific about what these expectations are; please let us know if you have any questions about what follows, so we can clarify.

Performance Concerns

As we discussed, our concerns stem primarily from issues we have seen arise in three key areas: timely follow-through, quality/accuracy, and volume:

> Be clear about where the person is falling short.

1.   Follow-through: Needs to be 100%, and needs to be timely (and where it can't be, at a minimum we need to know that it hasn't been dropped). Examples where you have fallen short on follow-through in the last month include:

- *Two of the three alumni meetings I e-mailed you about (OCCO meeting, lunch with Julie)*
- *Following up with HD on missing info for a data pull*
- *Replying to MB about a charge on AJ's budget*
- *Scheduling a check-in with JY (he had to e-mail you several times)*
- *Daniel orientation meeting*
- *Moving my check-ins scheduled for Columbus Day*

> Provide as many specifics as possible.

2. Quality/Accuracy: We need to be able to trust that when you do take something on, it will get done in the manner we have agreed to without a great deal of supervision (or that if it can't, you will let us know so we can brainstorm solutions or make choices about how we want to proceed). Examples where you have fallen short on quality/accuracy in the last month include:
   - *Program committee call (3 hours instead of 4, overlapped with MN call)*
   - *Alumni step-back meeting (2 hours instead of 3; scheduled after date I had asked for)*
   - *Sending Bulletin to AY without the communications piece in it*
   - *FedEx to M (not checking on the address, and not flagging that as the issue right away when it didn't show up)*

3. Volume: At a minimum, we need you to be able to handle the flow of the "ordinary course of business" work, and ideally you'd be taking on additional work as well. Examples of things I would ideally hand-off but am holding on to for now:
   - *Site visits for me for second half of the year*
   - *A series of step-back meetings with KC and MM to be scheduled*

Moving Ahead

Going forward, we need you to operate at a significantly higher level, and to demonstrate the performance of a high-performing executive assistant. This means executing your job responsibilities thoroughly and with accuracy, and handling all of the tasks that come your way. To be more specific, our expectations are that you will demonstrate:

> Describe what strong performance in the role would look like.

*100% follow-through, in a timely fashion*
We need you to take care of all of the items on your plate, including: meeting requests, issues raised via voice mail or e-mail, research requests, and other tasks that are part of the general course of business. As we discussed, this truly needs to be 100% because given the volume of issues neither BT nor I can check back in on every item, so we need to trust completely that when we hand you an item it is as good as done. Everyone is human and mistakes do happen from time to time, but over the next three weeks (and in general over any comparable time period) if more than one item slips through the cracks then we would deem that to be falling short of expectations.

> Where possible, explain why the performance needs to be high.

In terms of timeliness, it is hard to set an absolute rule, and the best guideline is that when you are in doubt you should ask. In general, though, we would assume that you would handle most issues that cross your plate that are not bigger projects – e.g. printing documents, reaching out to others around meeting requests, replying to e-mails and voice mails from us or from others, etc. – within one business day of receiving them, with many happening on the same business day. If for some reason you are not able to get to items that you normally would within this timeframe, at a minimum we assume you will let the relevant person know that you are still on top of the item.

> Be as specific as possible about the level of performance you're looking for (and how you'll know if it's being reached).

*Quality/Accuracy*
We need to be able to trust that when you do take something on, it will get done in the manner we have agreed to, or where that is not possible that you will brainstorm potential solutions and, where appropriate, communicate options or your recommendations back to us. For instance, this means that we should be able to assume that meetings will be scheduled for the length we ask for, with the participants we have identified, and within the window of time we have requested. Again, our expectation is that within a three-week

span there might be one instance of inaccuracy or one slip-up regarding quality, but not more.

*Volume*
Performing at a high level in this role means handling the large volume of items that come your way on an ongoing basis. BT and I will continue to put things on your plate, and our expectation is that over the next three weeks we will reach a "steady state" where there is no significant backlog of items that you are handling. This does not mean that at the end of the three weeks there will be no items left on your action plan, but it does mean that you will be dispensing of items within our agreed upon timelines and that items will be getting completed as quickly as they are being added.

*Other Dimensions*
Beyond operating at a high level in these three key areas (timely follow-through, quality/accuracy, and handling the volume of the job), there are several other general expectations that characterize high performers and that we need to see from you:

- *Systems* – As we discussed today, you need to have an organizational system that lets you efficiently track everything on your plate and ensure that nothing slips through the cracks (and this includes tracking follow-through of items where you are expecting some action from others).

  > Beyond areas of specific shortfall, it may be helpful to describe the kind of performance you're looking for.

- *Communication* – We also talked about the need to over-communicate so that you minimize the possibility of confusion or lack of clarity. This might mean ensuring that everyone involved in a process is clear on next steps or just assuring people that you are following-up on an item. Additionally, going forward when you are in doubt about how to proceed on something or when there is a choice to be made (for instance, whether to postpone a meeting or hold it without all the desired participants) you will reach out to us.
- *Responsibility (being "uptight")* – In other contexts being called uptight might be an insult, but in an executive assistant it is an essential quality. In a number of the incidents that caused us concern, uptightness – combined with better communication – might have led you to operate differently. For instance, when you left for vacation knowing there was still a stack of

unfinished items, being uptight would have meant ensuring that we knew which items were unfinished and ensuring that there was a plan for completing them.

- *Continuous improvement* – Finally, one quality that differentiates virtually every high performer in our organization is continuously improving – i.e., identifying areas for improvement, reaching out for resources, and then incorporating new ideas to improve your approach. In addition to applying the feedback incorporated here, we talked about other resources you might reach out to – for instance, you might talk to SN or others who may have found ways to schedule meetings more efficiently. You should also, of course, feel free to use both of us as resources, as you work to refine your systems and otherwise meet the expectations laid out above.

Consequences

As we discussed, we need to ensure that you quickly reach a high level of performance where you are satisfying the requirements of the Executive Assistant job. That means that this Improvement Plan will be in effect for the next two weeks (starting today, Monday, October 20th). The three of us will check in at the end of the week to review your performance against this plan (we will assume that you will set up a time on our calendars for this mid-point check-in). If you do not fulfill the requirements of this plan, then we will dismiss you, with one week of severance pay.

> Reiterate the consequences and be clear about the terms (severance pay) so there is no confusion about what's at stake or how it will happen.

Our hope is that you will fulfill the requirements of this plan. If you do, you will no longer be on an official Improvement Plan. You will, however, need to maintain that high level of performance over time.

We have tried to be direct in laying out our expectations going forward and the consequences of this plan. What this memo does not do justice to, however, is how much we both enjoy working with you on a personal level and how much we appreciate your commitment to this organization and all the hard work that you have put in up to this point. As we said today, we know that this is not a matter of your putting in more hours or trying harder.

> You should not hesitate to be kind; just be sure it doesn't blunt the substance of your message.

Again, please let us know if you have any questions about what is laid out in this plan.

## *Sample Script – Firing*

*In this sample, an administrative assistant has already been placed on a formal improvement plan and has not shown the necessary improvements. He was warned in his formal improvement plan letter that if he did not improve he would be dismissed.*

As I told you yesterday, I wanted to use our meeting today to reflect on your progress against the improvement plan. We talked two weeks ago about the fact that if you couldn't meet the expectations of the job, I would have to let you go. We're now at that point, so unfortunately today will be your last day.

> Refer back to the earlier agreement that you would need to replace him if sufficient improvements weren't made.

> Be clear upfront about what is happening.

When we met two weeks ago, I explained that I needed an assistant who could handle a high volume of tasks, follow through on everything, and convey a positive attitude toward the organization. We talked about how your performance needed to improve in each of those three areas – how you needed to be able to handle the daily flow of work from me, how there could be no dropped balls, and how people who interacted with you should be left with a positive impression.

I know you've tried hard, particularly in terms of the interactions with others. When I asked the rest of the team (as we had discussed that I would) I received a number of positive comments about your improvement.

> Acknowledge any improvement that has been made...

On the other two dimensions, though, your performance still doesn't meet my expectations. I know you've been trying, but there have been at least three items that I asked you to handle more than two days ago that are still not complete: scheduling the meeting with Melissa, printing background materials for my meeting next Thursday, and completing my expense report.

> ...but be clear that it hasn't been sufficient and specify in what areas it has fallen short.

You can use today to clean out your desk, say goodbye to people, and finish any other items. I would really appreciate it if you would go through your e-mails and send me an update on where each item stands – whether you haven't gotten to it yet, if it's partly or fully done, and anything else I should know. This afternoon you should talk to Erica in HR about exit procedures. She'll give you a list of other things – like returning keys – that you need to take care of by the end of the day.

Be clear about the logistics.

Assuming all of that happens before the end of the day, then we'll be in good shape and we'll be able to give you two weeks of severance pay.

Make severance pay contingent on a smooth exit.

I know that this has been a challenging experience for you and that particularly over these past two weeks you have been trying hard. On a personal level, I've enjoyed our interactions, and I really do wish you the best of luck.

Do you have any questions about the exit procedures or what you need to do?

Offer an opportunity for the employee to ask questions related to logistics, but not to argue the decision itself.

## Sample Script – Coaching-out

*In this sample, the staff member (a director of technology) has been a reasonably loyal, well-intentioned employee whose skills no longer make sense for the position. The ideal outcome is for the staff member to agree to begin looking for a better-fit job in another organization, but the manager wants to give the staff member the choice of going down the progressive discipline process path. Therefore, the core of the manager's message is:*

1. *The demands of the role have changed and you may not be a good fit for it anymore;*
2. *You can choose to pursue the progressive discipline process route; but*
3. *I think the alternative route makes the most sense.*

Manager: As I mentioned to you yesterday, I'd like to talk about how I see the director of technology role evolving. This is a tough conversation, because the bottom line is that I've started to have concerns about your fit for the role. I wanted to talk today about why that is and how we might move forward.

Let me start by saying that I know how much work you've put into this job over the past two years, and that on a number of occasions you've gone above and beyond.

> Be clear upfront why you're having the conversation so the employee understands the context for the conversation that follows.

For instance, last year when the servers shut down you cancelled your weekend plans at the last minute to get them running again quickly. You've been great at paying attention to every last detail, to fixing problems as they come up, and to watching the bottom-line. When we were starting up you were great at working with vendors and driving a hard bargain to get us good deals on what we needed. Your attention to detail, that ability to look at someone's computer and diagnose what's wrong and fix it quickly, and your understanding of finances are real strengths.

> Acknowledge your staff member's strengths and contributions to the organization.

As our organization has grown, though, what we need in our director of technology role has changed. We used to be a small, single-site shop, and now we have multiple locations. Also, as we've added new programs our database development needs have increased tremendously. We just have a huge demand for new

253

applications from the database, and those are things we have to do if we're going to maximize our impact as an organization.

As we entered this new stage, I realized we needed our director of technology to do a different set of things than we needed earlier in our evolution. When I realized that, I started to question whether you're the right person for the changed role, and whether in the long run this is the job that is going to make the best use of your skills.

> "Tell the story" of how and why the role has evolved.

What we need in the director of technology role now is someone whose strengths are things like big-picture conceptualization, communicating with the program staff about their needs, and project management. Take, for instance, the other day when the online advocacy team was meeting about their strategic plan. We need someone who can sit in that meeting, understand fully what the team is trying to accomplish, translate that into a set of technological solutions that they don't even know to ask for, and then explain their options to them in terms that they can understand so that they can make an informed choice. Once we've decided on an approach, we need someone who can handle all the complexities of managing the development process with our staff members, account for the inevitable setbacks, and deliver a product on time that works and meets everyone's needs.

> Explain the new bar that you now need.

Candidly, I don't think those are your strengths. For instance, when we tried to develop the new database of our subscribers, there were quite a few issues, including the teams misunderstanding what you were going to deliver, and delays in completing the final product. I realize that there were problems on both ends of that process, but I need someone who even when the other team isn't performing perfectly will communicate the issues, help the other team understand what they need to do, and manage them to the deadlines they need to meet. I think that's a high bar, but it's also critical that we meet it.

> Be clear in your assessment of the person's weaknesses as well as their strengths – this is the first step in steering them toward the mutually-beneficial process.

So where does this leave us? I think we have two options. As you know, we have a formal process in place for staff members who aren't meeting expectations, and if you want we can head down that road. This meeting would be the first step in that – it would be the informal performance warning, and we would talk concretely about how we would know over the next three weeks that your performance had improved. After that, if your performance didn't improve, there would be a written performance warning and improvement process, which would last another four weeks. At the end of all that, if your performance didn't meet expectations, we would have to let you go and look for someone else. If it did, then we would move ahead with you in this role as long as your performance stayed at the level we need. I want to be clear that this is a real option – if you choose to go this route, I promise that I'll work with you to set clear expectations and to give you the reasonable help I can in developing your skills, given the constraints on my time. This won't be a game of "gotcha" – I would give you a fair chance to meet what I see as the new bar for performance.

> Note that you're willing to follow progressive discipline steps.

All that said, from what I know of you and your strengths, I'm not convinced it would work. At the end of that process, we'd be giving you the standard two weeks of severance, and we'd be left with a vacancy in the tech role. I want to put forth another option for you to consider. If you agree that the role as I've described it isn't what you ideally want or think you're best at then we could set up an arrangement that might work better for both of us. Frankly, I think it would take me three months to hire a new head of technology from the time I started looking, and I'd rather not have the role vacant. I also know that you'd need time to conduct a job search, and I'd want to give you time to do that.

> Be straightforward and clear about how you see the situation in order to steer the staff member toward the best possible outcome.

> Offer a win-win path that would work for you both.

So what I'd propose is this: we could agree now that you'll leave the role at the end of April. In the meantime, you'll continue ensuring our basic tech needs are met, but we won't expect you to take on any new projects, which will allow you to focus on a job search. We'd continue to pay you your current salary through the end of April. (If you found a job sooner, then you could leave before that, but we'd stop paying you.) All of this would be contingent on your continuing to perform as you have been, which means having a good attitude at work, keeping our basic infrastructure running, etc. You'd also have to sign an agreement that our lawyers insist upon. Knowing what I know about you and how you've operated, my sense is that this would work out.

> Preemptively address the preconditions of the offer.

I know I've just thrown a lot at you, but I wanted to put it all on the table. We can talk more about this now, or I can give you some time to think about it and then we can talk in the next day or two about which way you'd like to go. I do feel urgency around figuring this out, so I'd like to meet no later than Thursday to hear your decision. Do you want to talk now, or would you rather wait?

> Give a clear deadline for deciding.

# Section III
# Managing Yourself

## BECOMING A MANAGER

As we've tried to make clear, management is how you get things done through other people.

In order to do that effectively – to do everything we've talked about in the previous two sections – you need to be effective yourself. If you're like many of our clients, you have a long history of being effective – as a solo practitioner. What you may need is to learn how to "manage yourself" now that you're in a new role, and practices that might have worked for you before may no longer suffice.

This section is all about what it means to manage yourself as a manager:

- In Chapter 9, we'll talk about how to exercise authority without being a wimp or a tyrant.

- In Chapter 10, we'll delve into how to figure out where your time should be focused, and we'll give some specific tips for staying organized and managing your time.

- In Chapter 11, we'll talk about your relationship with your own manager and how to work with her in a way that will maximize your results.

- And in the final chapter, which serves as a conclusion to the entire manual, we'll talk about the personal qualities exhibited by the best managers we've seen.

*Chapter 9*
# How to Exercise Authority... Without Being a Wimp or a Tyrant

Many new managers worry about something that sounds simple but can actually be the source of a lot of anxiety: how to act now that you have authority over others. And you may feel especially awkward if you're managing people who are older, wiser, or more experienced than you.

While getting your style of authority right isn't going to make you a great manager all on its own, getting it wrong can be ruinous. If you're too passive and shy away from using your authority, you'll end up a wimp. On the other end of the spectrum, if you use your authority too aggressively, you risk becoming a tyrant. Both wimps and tyrants drive away good employees and struggle to produce results.

The best managers we've seen aren't wimps or tyrants but are simply normal, assertive people. But simply saying "just be normal" would make this a pretty short chapter, so we'll go into more detail about exactly what that means. We'll describe wimpy and tyrannical behaviors so that you can decide for yourself whether you fall on one side or the other – and we'll also describe how assertive management looks when it's done right.

## WIMPS

Managers who are wimps often let their desire to be nice trump their fundamental obligations as managers, like holding the bar high and expecting people to adhere to it, warning them when they're falling short, and taking action when warnings don't work. Ironically, many wimpy managers are just trying to be liked, but over time the opposite happens: as problems go unresolved, staff members grow frustrated and complain, and the best among them leave.

Signs that you might be a wimp include:

- Avoidance. Wimps avoid conflict and tough conversations like the plague. Most frequently, this plays out in managers not addressing performance problems or firing under-performers. But it surfaces in other ways as well. For instance, a conflict-averse manager may hesitate to make necessary course corrections mid-way through a project because she thinks doing so will upset her team.

- Indirectness. Wimpy managers often present requirements as mere suggestions. Staffers end up confused about expectations, and managers get frustrated when "suggestions" aren't acted upon. For example, an unassertive manager who wants to look at a letter before it's sent out might say, "Feel free to show me that letter before you send it out," leaving the staff member with the mistaken impression that the manager has no preference.

- Masking indecision as consensus building. Because many nonprofits are working for a more egalitarian, inclusive society, they sometimes talk about the need to "be the change" – to model in practice the values they hope to see spread more broadly. In practice, we've seen "be the change" actually "impede the change" – such as when managers interpret "be the change" to mean that decisions should be made by consensus or majority rule, an approach that confuses everyone *having a say* in decisions with everyone *making* decisions. While there are certainly times when building consensus is important for an organization, too frequently we see organizations in which difficult decisions don't get made and no one takes responsibility for moving work forward. Frequent punting in favor of reaching consensus often indicates a lack of assertiveness on the part of the manager.

Your staff members themselves will recognize the distinction – most want a chance to give input and to have their opinions considered and then will want the right person (often the manager or the "owner" of a particular area) to make a final decision. Use your staff's input to inform your decisions, but remember that when it comes to making tough calls that will lead to good results, that's your job! (If you struggle with this area, you might read the article we list at the end of this chapter, "Fair Process: Managing in the Knowledge Economy.")

---

*"I used to think in order to get extremely talented people to work together, you needed their buy-in in terms of a decision-making structure, that you needed more of a consensual decision-making structure. What I've learned is that you can build an extremely dynamic team of these kinds of people while still having a hierarchical management structure in place. The mixture of a highly collaborative, transparent culture combined with a clear hierarchical structure has been the magic mix. Earlier in my career, I tried getting together the people I most respected and having everyone be co-directors and taking equal management and decision-making responsibilities, but we eventually realized that often it's best to have a single decision maker. Sometimes consensual processes place enormous demands on time and energy and sometimes result in compromises that are lower quality than following any single vision.*

*"A more structured hierarchy has been highly effective, and far from people feeling less bought in because they don't have equal decision-making power, people have felt more excited and more engaged because the team as a whole has performed better."*

*- Ricken Patel, Executive Director, Avaaz*

---

- Overfriendliness. Managers who are overly concerned with being liked by their employees can compromise their effectiveness if employees get mixed signals about the nature of their relationship. Ironically, this can lead from wimpy behavior into tyrannical behavior: if an employee pushes the envelope with you, taking advantage of the friendship, you may feel your authority is being challenged or undermined and end up reacting too aggressively.

## TYRANTS

Managers who are tyrants get things done through rigid control, negativity, and a climate of anxiety and fear. Employees often fear interaction with them.

Most tyrants don't set out to be mean, but they don't trust that they can get the results they want any other way. However, tyrants aren't as effective in either the short-term or the long-term. Staff members who are distracted by fear or anxiety won't bring up new ideas for fear of being shot down and won't be honest about problems. Additionally, very few great people with lots of choices are going to want to work for a tyrant. Not only will good employees leave, but once a manager gets a reputation as a tyrant, not many good people will want to come to work for her in the first place.

Signs that you might be a tyrant include:

- Passive-aggressive criticism. Rather than offering direct, constructive feedback, tyrants sometimes criticize in indirect asides, making it hard for the staff member to respond. For example, a manager given a memo only a minute before a meeting might walk in and say, "I don't know why I'm just getting this memo now, but I guess we should go ahead and talk about it." If you have feedback, make a note and talk to your staff member directly when the time is right.

- <u>Defensiveness</u>. Tyrannical managers often respond defensively when their decisions are questioned. They may also squash dissent, making employees less likely to suggest new and different ways of doing things, and are prone to shooting the bearers of bad news, which means that staffers will avoid sharing negative information. When you're secure in your authority, you aren't threatened by dissent, and you might even recognize that – gasp! – others' ideas are sometimes better than your own.

- <u>Yelling</u>. We hear with surprising regularity about bosses who yell and scream. Managers who yell demean and humiliate the person being yelled at and actually diminish their own authority because they look out of control. After all, a manager confident in her own authority doesn't need to yell because she has far more effective tools available to her. Don't yell.

- <u>Unreasonable demands</u>. Tyrants cross the line from holding their staffers to a high standard to pushing their staffers to the brink. For example, a tyrannical manager might insist that staff members work over the weekend to complete a project that isn't time-sensitive, or might demand that a staffer do the truly impossible (such as getting a replacement part for a computer when all the stores that sell it are closed).

  It's difficult to give a hard-and-fast rule for finding the line between holding people to high standards and being unreasonable, but a good

> **The Wimp/Tyrant Combo**
>
> Oddly enough, we see many managers who are both wimps and tyrants in one. Typically, the manager starts out as a wimp, not being direct enough about what she expects. When her staff doesn't properly interpret her too-subtle signals, the manager gets frustrated and yells. Later, she feels badly about yelling, and presents her next set of expectations as mere suggestions, and the cycle repeats itself when her expectations aren't met.

guideline is to weigh the business need against the hardship the demand may cause. If it's the night before a board meeting, it's reasonable to ask staffers to stay late to make sure everything goes smoothly, but it's presumably not reasonable to insist that staffers work through the weekend when a project isn't crucial and time-sensitive.

## ASSERTIVE MANAGERS

Effective managers are neither wimpy nor tyrannical. They act with the confidence of their position – directly laying out expectations and holding people to them, operating in a fair, positive, and straightforward manner, and backing up their words with action. We'll call them "assertive managers."[1]

Signs of assertive management include:

- Directness. Assertive managers simply say what needs to be said, directly and straightforwardly. They don't shy away from difficult or awkward conversations, and they know that addressing problems head-on is a key part of their job.

- Calm. When giving an employee feedback or talking about a problem, an assertive manager may sound concerned but rarely angry or hostile. For instance, in talking to a staff member who has been forgetting assignments, an assertive manager might say, "I've noticed recently that some of the projects we agreed you'd take on fell off your radar screen, and that's a serious problem. I need to be able to rely on you to remember the assignments we discuss, because I can't check back in

---

[1] In *Assertive Discipline*, a book about classroom teaching, Lee and Marlene Canter present a very similar framework for teachers, distinguishing between nonassertive, hostile, and assertive styles.

on every item. How can you make sure it doesn't happen again?"

- Openness. Because assertive managers know they aren't infallible, they're open to the possibility that they may be mistaken or that there may be a better way of doing something.

- Comfortable in charge. The best managers see their authority as simply one more tool for getting things done. It's neither something that makes them nervous nor something that they lord over others.

- Following the golden rule. What effective managers are often doing is just treating people as they would want to be treated themselves. For instance, you would want someone to tell you if you weren't doing a good job, so don't wimp out on giving feedback to your staff. At the same time, you'd want to be told in a respectful way, so don't yell or talk down to people.

> "One of the things I've found toughest about managing people is that I'm very close in age to my staff, and it's been a challenge for me to be both an authority figure and a peer. Sometimes I'll tell my staff, 'I've been you more than I've been me'– meaning that I've been in their shoes in whatever scenario we're in quite a bit and I understand where they're coming from, but sometimes you have to deal with it and do what the boss wants."
>
> *- Alexandra Acker,*
> *Executive Director, Young*
> *Democrats of America*

---

### **Wimps, Tyrants, and Assertive Managers in Action**

<u>Situation #1</u>. A new receptionist is chronically late, leaving others covering for her.

*What the wimp does*: Very little. She may complain about the behavior to others or be silently irate, but she doesn't address it with the employee directly.

*What the tyrant does*: Calls the employee into her office and says to her loudly enough for others to hear: "This is not hard! How do you function in life? If you don't get your act together, you're gone."

*What the assertive manager does*: Addresses the person privately as soon as it's clear there's a pattern: "Kate, you've been late four times in the last two weeks. When you're late, Alex and Jill have to cover for you. I need you to make sure you're here by 9:00 from here on out. Can you commit to that?"

<u>Situation #2</u>. A manager is growing concerned that a field organizer is falling short of her recruiting goals for the year.

*What the wimp does*: Hopes to herself that the field organizer gets back on track by the end of the year.

*What the tyrant does*: Comes down hard: "Do I have to do your job for you? Can't you do anything right?"

*What the assertive manager does*: Addresses it directly: "I'm concerned that our recruiting numbers are lower than they should be at this point in the year. Let's meet this afternoon to talk about what you could do differently to get back on track toward this goal."

<u>Situation #3</u>. A communications director scores an editorial endorsement for the group's legislation from a major newspaper.

*What the wimp does*: Responds more like a friend than a manager: "Sweet endorsement!"

*What the tyrant does*: Barely acknowledges it, if at all. Or possibly takes the credit.

*What the assertive manager does*: Quickly praises the communications director for the victory and the work that went into it: "Great coup! All that outreach to the editorial board and the pitching you did really paid off."

---

## JUST BE NORMAL

Ultimately, our advice to you is to *just be normal*. Don't over-think it. Be yourself. If you're someone who uses humor in your personal life, don't be afraid to use it in your work life, too. If you're on the quiet side, you don't need to lead office cheers. Just be normal.

Of course, one response to this is to say, "Well, I *am* kind of a tyrant (or a wimp), so if I'm supposed to be myself, I'm going to be tyrannical." But people are rarely tyrants across the board. What's more common is selective tyranny. Few people are tyrants toward their own bosses, for instance, or toward funders, or toward their loved ones. So perhaps the rule of thumb here is to be yourself *within the confines of bringing out the right pieces of yourself.*

### Gender Dynamics and Authority

Women managers may at times confront the reality that authoritative women will sometimes be seen as "bitchy," while men displaying the same behaviors are seen as resolute, strong leaders. In our experience, this is a very real, and unfortunate, dynamic. But until society changes, our advice to female managers is to do precisely what we recommend throughout this chapter: Be normal, be assertive, and be neither a tyrant nor a wimp.

---

*"The first time I had to talk to an employee about errors she was making, I was really nervous. At first, I wound up just doing the work myself because I didn't want to tell her that she wasn't doing it right. But I finally realized that I just needed to talk to her about it, even though it felt strange being the one reprimanding someone. I realized that when bosses have taken the time to help me learn to do my job better, it's been such a favor to me, and now I see it in that light when I need to tell someone that I want them to do something differently."*

*- Nydia Swaby, director of grants and VIP outreach, Marijuana Policy Project*

### Key Points

- The best managers we've seen aren't wimps or tyrants but are simply normal, assertive people.

- Managers who are wimps often get that way by allowing a desire to be nice trump their fundamental obligations. These managers – who avoid difficult decisions or topics, are uncomfortable asserting authority, frame requirements as suggestions, and/or overvalue consensus – create environments where problems go unresolved, no one takes responsibility for moving work forward, and good staff members get frustrated and often leave.

- Managers who are tyrants generally don't trust that they'll get the results they want any other way. These managers – who get things done through rigid control, negativity, or a climate of anxiety and fear – create an atmosphere where staffers won't raise new ideas or be honest about problems and where good employees won't stay long-term.

- Effective managers act with the confidence of their position – directly laying out expectations and holding people to them, operating in a fair, positive, and straightforward manner, and backing up their words with action. They are open to feedback, have a matter-of-fact attitude toward being in charge, and treat people as they themselves would want to be treated.

## 📖 Additional Reading

- Lee Canter and Marlene Canter, "Response Styles" in *Assertive Discipline: Positive Behavior Management for Today's Classroom* (Solution Tree 2001), pages 25-38.

- Jim Collins, "Level 5 Leadership" in *Good to Great: Why Some Companies Make the Leap... and Others Don't* (Harper Collins 2001), pages 17-40.

- Joseph Grenny, David Maxfield, and Andrew Shimberg, "How to Have Influence," MIT Sloan Management Review (Vol. 50, No. 1), Fall 2008.

- W. Chan Kim and Renée Mauborgne, "Fair Process: Managing in the Knowledge Economy," Harvard Business Review, January 2003.

## *Chapter 10*
# Time and Systems

It's the unspoken secret among managers: we all struggle with the seemingly simple job of staying organized and using our time well.

If you're like many managers we know (and us on bad days), this may describe a typical day for you: You arrive at the office and begin sorting through your e-mail. A staffer drops by with some questions about a project, and just as she leaves, you get a phone call from a volunteer with feedback on a recent event. When you're done talking to her, you begin reviewing a draft of a mailing, but when you're halfway through, you're interrupted by a stressed-out staffer who needs help prioritizing her workload. Before returning to the mailing, you check your e-mail and find a handful of urgent messages to respond to. The day continues like this, and by its end, you haven't managed to touch the two biggest things you had hoped to get to that day.

Sound familiar? When you become a manager, the flow of *stuff* coming at you increases exponentially – e-mails, reports, questions, meetings, materials to review. As a result, systems that used to be adequate for juggling it all may no longer suffice.

How you manage yourself and your time and how you stay organized will seriously impact what kind of results you're able to get. There are many good books that do organization systems more justice than we can do here, so in this chapter we'll simply synthesize what we've seen work best. First, we'll talk about how to think about where your time should go (and how to make sure your intentions don't get crushed by circumstance), and then we'll move into some specific tips for staying organized and managing your time.

## HOW TO THINK ABOUT WHERE TO SPEND YOUR TIME

At its core, time management is about clarity – clarity about your purpose in the organization and what you're trying to accomplish. Yet in the hustle of daily work life, with a steady flow of demands coming at you, it's easy to lose sight of the most important contributions you're there to make.

In this section, we look at some ways to think about where your time is best spent.

### Focus on the big rocks

The biggest time management mistake that most managers make is spending their time on what's immediately at hand or what's most comfortable to work on, rather than what's most important. If you don't make time for the important things first, you may never get to them, as this parable from Stephen Covey illustrates.

*One day, an expert in time management was speaking to a group of business students and, to drive home a point, used an illustration those students will never forget. As he stood in front of the group of high powered overachievers he said, "Okay, time for a quiz."*

*Then he pulled out a one gallon, wide-mouthed Mason jar and set it on the table in front of him. Then he produced about a dozen fist-sized rocks and carefully placed them, one at a time, into the jar. When the jar was filled to the top and no more rocks would fit inside, he asked, "Is this jar full?"*

*Everyone in the class said, "Yes." Then he said, "Really?" He reached under the table and pulled out a bucket of gravel. Then he dumped some gravel in and shook the jar, causing pieces of gravel to work themselves down into the space between the big rocks. Then he asked the group once more, "Is the jar full?"*

*By this time the class was on to him. "Probably not," one of them answered. "Good," he replied. He reached under the table and brought out a bucket of sand. He started dumping the sand in the jar, and it went into all of the spaces left between the rocks and the gravel. Once more he asked the question, "Is this jar full?" "No," the class shouted.*

*Once again he said, "Good." Then he grabbed a pitcher of water and began to pour it in until the jar was filled to the brim. Then he looked at the class and asked, "What is the point of this illustration?"*

*One eager beaver raised his hand and said, "The point is, no matter how full your schedule is, if you try really hard you can always fit some more things in it."*

*"No," the speaker replied, "that's not the point. The truth this illustration teaches us is: If you don't put the big rocks in first, you'll never get them in at all. What are the 'big rocks' in your life? Your children, your loved ones, your education, your dreams, a worthy cause, teaching or mentoring others, doing things that you love, time for yourself, your health, your significant other? Remember to put these big rocks in first or you'll never get them in at all. If you sweat the little stuff (the gravel, the sand) then you'll fill your life with little things you worry about that don't really matter, and you'll never have the real quality time you need to spend on the big, important stuff (the big rocks). So, tonight, or in the morning,*

*when you are reflecting on this short story, ask yourself this question: What are the 'big rocks' in my life? Then, put those in your jar first."[1]*

While this story is about getting priorities straight across your life, it applies at work as well. You could easily fill most of your days with small things and never get to the big-picture goals that will significantly move your work forward. How often have you agreed to spend an hour at a meeting that wasn't crucial for you, when your to-do list was filled with high-impact but less urgent needs, like checking in on a project you've delegated or talking to an employee about a performance problem?

> *"The question you need to ask yourself is not am I getting everything done, but am I getting the most important things done?"*
>
> *- Ricken Patel,*
> *Executive Director,*
> *Avaaz*

Figure out what one or two items are most important to accomplish on any given day and make those your priorities. Whenever possible, do them first before other things have the chance to intervene. The details will fill in where there's room.

One of the best ways to free up time to focus on the "big rocks" is by delegating anything else you can. Let's talk about what that means.

**If you *can* delegate it, you *should* delegate it**

We talked in depth in Chapter 1 about *how* to delegate, but how do you know *what* you should delegate?

There's a very simple principle for knowing when you should delegate something:

> If you *can* delegate it, you *should* delegate it.

In other words, work should flow downward to the lowest level person who can do it well enough. That's right – we said "well enough," not

---

[1] As related in Stephen R. Covey, A. Roger Merrill, and Rebecca R. Merrill, *First Things First* (Fireside 1994).

"perfectly." Your assistant may not proofread as flawlessly as you do, but your time could likely be far better spent on say, talking with a major funder, than on proofreading documents yourself. (That said, occasionally you may have a document so important that you do choose to proofread it yourself – but this should be the exception rather than the norm.)

If you're like a lot of managers we know, this may make you nervous. It can be painful to delegate things that you know won't be done as well as you yourself would do them. However, think back to your Econ 101 class and keep the idea of *comparative advantage* in mind. You might be a bit better than your assistant at proofreading, but given your experience and role you're probably far more effective than she would be at talking to the media, cultivating donors, and hiring a new head of the communications department. You should be spending your time in the areas where you're *much* better than your staff, because the pay-off will be greater.

Of course, this doesn't mean that you should accept mediocre work. Continuing with our example, you should use the delegation principles we discussed in Chapter 1 and make it clear to your assistant that when she's done proofreading there should be no typos, and you should spot check her work and hold her accountable. And if she wasn't a better proofreader than you to start, hopefully over time she will become that.

> *One executive director we know described his feelings this way: "I've been told that I should let my staff take the calls from most of our volunteers and activists. But I feel like by doing it myself, I'm panning for gold. All sorts of nuggets come out of those conversations, and I don't want to miss those." While we like that the executive director was getting his hands dirty enough to know what was going on in the field, by spending his time taking all of these routine calls, he was letting entire gold mountains go unexplored, as he greatly cut into the time he had available for overseeing strategy and raising funds.*
>
> *He has since shifted out of this mode and generated several sizable contributions that might not have otherwise happened.*

### You're a manager, so spend time managing

The corollary of delegating as much as you can is that, as we noted in Chapter 1, while you *do* less, you should *guide* more. And guiding takes time. Whether it's reviewing drafts and giving feedback, having check-in meetings to help your staff members sort out their priorities, visiting the field so you can see how your team's work is playing out in real life, or preparing for a coaching out conversation, a sizeable portion of your work now is to shape the work of others.

Many new managers fail to make the shift from doing to guiding. They spend just as much time as they used to on their own work, and they try to squeeze in managing others between the cracks, almost treating that part of their job as an inconvenience. They end up in a vicious cycle, where work they delegate gets done poorly because they don't invest the time to manage it well, so they take on the work themselves and then have less time to supervise other work they have delegated, which in turn goes poorly so they take that work on, too.

Avoid the trap of the manager who doesn't manage: change how you allocate your time so you can get the benefits of having others working for you. It's simple leverage: if you have a team of five people and you can make each of them successful, you'll get much more done through them than you will if you try to do all the work yourself.

### Manage your calendar; don't let it manage you

If you let it, your calendar can fill up with meetings and other obligations to the point that you don't have any time left to work on your biggest priorities. If this is happening to you, start making appointments with yourself. Rather than just hoping time will become available, ensure that it's deliberately built into your schedule – set aside a few three- or four-hour work blocks per week to do your most important work, or half an hour at the start of every day to touch base with your staff about a key project, or a two hour "meeting with yourself" to write that update for the board, or whatever best meets your needs.

**Manage interruptions**

As a manager, you're going to get a lot of requests for "just one minute to ask you something." If you can save a staff member hours of struggling by providing a few minutes of advice, it makes sense to allow the interruption.

However, if you're constantly being interrupted and it's disrupting your ability to focus on your real priorities, you might look at whether or not you've delegated broadly enough and given your staff sufficient ability to move forward without constantly checking in with you. And while you should err on the side of being accessible, you also might consider setting "non-office hours" (i.e., the reverse of office hours), or times when your staff knows not to interrupt except for true emergencies.

**Teach your staff to use your time well**

Be explicit with your staff about how they should and should not use your time. For instance, you might ask them to do the following:

- Save up non-urgent items rather than bringing them to you piecemeal. This way, you can talk about everything at once, rather than in five separate interruptions throughout the day or week.

- If you're unavailable, they should leave you the question in an e-mail or a voice mail, so that you can respond when convenient.

- As we noted in Chapter 1, your staff should make it easy for you to give quick input so that they are still "owning the monkey." For instance, a staffer might e-mail you, "Here's the situation with X. Here are three options for responding, here are the pros and cons, and I propose we do A. Does this sound good to you?" This allows you to respond much more quickly than if you had to generate and analyze options yourself.

## (Almost) never stuff an envelope

Don't feel silly or awkward about focusing intensely on the areas where you bring the most value and not spending time on the areas where you don't.

For instance, some nonprofits have an ethos that everyone should pitch in on projects like stuffing envelopes. This may be egalitarian, but it's not a good use of resources. Your budget will go farther if you hire temps at $10 an hour to stuff envelopes while you stay focused on the higher-level work that only you can do. If you feel uncomfortable about this, it's worth explicitly explaining that it's not about "pulling rank" but rather about responsible use of limited funds. (In rare cases, pitching in like this can send a nice symbolic message that you're all in the work together, but this should not become something you do on more than the very infrequent occasion.)

## Know when you should get more involved

Despite everything you'll do to protect your time, there *are* times when you should get more involved than you would in the normal course of business. You may recall the story we told in the introduction of the manager who stepped in to do the job of his regional manager when that person was not moving as quickly as he needed to. Like that manager, you don't want to be hands-off if there's a crisis or something important going awry. One manager we know describes this approach as the "helicopter theory": you circle the land in a helicopter, watching to make sure everything is moving along smoothly. When you spot what looks like smoke, you swoop in to engage.

**Make the Most of an Assistant**

Having an assistant is an incredibly powerful tool for making yourself more efficient – *if* you utilize the role effectively. Here are five tips to maximize the relationship:

1. In our experience, the best assistants tend *not* to be career assistants but less experienced workers who are smart, hyper-efficient, energetic, and ambitious. This type usually won't stay in the position for more than a year or two, precisely because of the talents that make them excel in the role. But because a really good assistant will learn the job in just a few days, it's worth it to accept some turnover in the position every year or two.

2. Be explicit from the start that it will be crucial for the assistant to have air-tight systems that ensure 100% follow-through so that absolutely nothing can fall through the cracks. In order to rely on her to the extent you're going to, you need to have perfect faith that once you transfer an item from your plate to hers, it won't disappear.

3. Also be explicit from the start that you're going to delegate to her plenty of things that you could do yourself. This is important, because managers often feel embarrassed to ask an assistant to do small tasks that they could easily do themselves, such as printing documents, formatting a letter, or scheduling a meeting. So set the stage from the beginning. You can even say that you feel awkward about it but are going to force yourself to do it anyway, since you're a bottleneck in the organization and therefore need to get anything off your plate that isn't something only you can do.

4. Speaking of scheduling meetings, setting them up often takes a lot of back and forth. Utilize your assistant for scheduling anything but the most uncomplicated appointments.

5. Maximize the organization's use of the assistant. We've rarely seen an efficient assistant who wasn't able to support multiple executives.

Of course, when you need to swoop in like this, you should be examining *why* you need to be so involved. Is it because you're short-staffed? Is there a problem with a particular staffer? For instance, if you see that an event coordinator is letting important planning elements fall through the cracks, you should involve yourself to whatever extent necessary to ensure that the event is a success… but you should also make sure the coordinator knows you shouldn't have needed to be involved at that level and that she isn't meeting the bar you need from her.

## Establishing Strong Systems

Now that you know how to use your time, you need to find a system for organizing the many pieces of information, to-do items, and commitments that will be coming at you throughout the day.

> *"Learning simple tools like making a weekly to-do list and starring the most important items, and checking in with yourself at the end of the week, tracking whether you're being overly ambitious or hitting your targets, has made an enormous difference. I get to feel much more satisfied, because at the end of week I'm able to look at a work plan and feel comfortable that I've accomplished it. If you lay things out that way, and can say you've accomplished the things that were prioritized, you can enjoy your weekend without having to worry about the things you didn't get done."*
>
> *- Ricken Patel, Executive Director, Avaaz*

If you're like many managers when we first encounter them, you have a full calendar, multiple to-do lists, sticky notes on your computer and phone, thousands of e-mails in your inbox, and a code-red stress level from the need to remember numerous items stored in your head.

As you are likely painfully aware, it's pretty tough to see beyond the day-to-day and be a resource to your staff members when you're struggling to stay afloat among the daily demands of your work. Fortunately, there are systems that will organize the overwhelming morass and allow you to comfortably track and store all the important information in a way that will free up your time rather than demanding more of it.

**Criteria for a good system**

There are lots of different systems that work well (and plenty of books[2] and office supply stores that stand ready to sell them to you), but any good system should meet these five criteria:

1. Every piece of information should have one designated home. And floating around your head does not – we repeat, does not! – count as a home. A good test of whether your system meets this standard is whether you can answer things like:

   - A colleague calls you in the middle of a meeting and you say you'll call her back. How will you ensure you do?
   - You have an idea over lunch that you want to follow up on when you get to the office. Where do you capture it?
   - A friend recommends a good book that you want to read next summer. How will you remember?
   - You receive an agenda for next week's staff meeting via e-mail. What do you do with it?

2. Your system should funnel all the things coming at you into as few places as possible. If you have eight different lists to consult, you'll inevitably stop consulting all of them and things will get missed.

3. Your system should be easy to maintain and should make your life easier, not harder. You don't want a system that is a project unto itself.

4. Your system should focus you on the most important work at any given moment.

5. If you travel for your job, the system should be portable and accessible on the go.

---

[2] We like *Getting Things Done: The Art of Stress Free Productivity* by David Allen (Penguin Books 2001).

## The Three Homes System

You'll want to come up with a system that works well for you. But if you're stumped or if you want to see an example of one system that works well for many people, grab your computer, three different-colored folders, and a legal pad. We'll give you a detailed look at a system that meets the five criteria above – and has saved the sanity of many a harried manager!

The three homes system is built on three basic types of homes that take care of all the papers, e-mails, and pieces of information that come across your desk. The first type of home is the **list** (or plan), which keeps track of all your action items and helps you identify what you should be spending your time on at any given moment. **Folders** are the second type of home and store the key materials you need to do your work. Finally, the **calendar** captures every item with a date. Your lists and three thin folders go where you go, along with a legal pad for your notes.

In the sections below, we'll take a look at each component in more detail.

### *Lists*

If you're picturing the many lists scattered around your desk, bag, and home and thinking that the last thing you need is another list, please keep reading – lists are the essential element of this system, but there are only three of them (and frankly, you can get by with just the first two). The **daily** is simply a list of things you'll do *today*, and it's the only list you look at more than once a day. The **weekly** is a separate list that captures active projects you'll work on tomorrow or later. The separation keeps you from constantly reading over things you have to do in three days, which may not be relevant for today's work and can easily become a distraction or source of stress. The **mid-range** plan is a bigger picture document for your broad strategic priorities that informs your weekly, and in turn your daily. It keeps you on track so all the specific tasks you do get you where you need to be.

282

Keep things easy by having a Word document for each list. When it comes time to revise and update, pull items from other lists by cutting and pasting. Don't bother saving old versions. This is about getting things done, not documenting what you did.

*How to use the daily.* The action items you're committed to doing today go on this list. Highlight, bold, or underline the two or three big rocks of the list and do them first. You can add a section on your daily for "quickies," or items that will take just a couple minutes to take care of, such as forwarding a document your colleague asks you to send or making reservations for a lunch meeting.

Tuck your daily under the last page of your legal pad so you have it with you and ready to jot down new items that come up during the day (but only if you'll really do them today – if not, the items go on your weekly). Before you shut down for the night or first thing when you arrive in the morning, spend five minutes revising and updating this list for the day ahead by pulling from your weekly and looking at your calendar.

One helpful tool for your daily is the "waiting for," or "w/f" section.[3] W/fs are items that are due to you, in contrast to items that require action from

---

**Your Daily List in Action**

- Your colleague calls you in the middle of a meeting and you say you'll call her back. To ensure that you do, add it to your daily as soon as you hang up the phone.

- Later that day, you ask a scatterbrained colleague in another department to send you some data you'll need by the end of the day, and you're not confident he'll remember. Write "w/f data from Josh" on your daily list so that if you don't receive the data, you'll remember to pester him.

- You have 30 free minutes between meetings. Pull out your daily and find your most important remaining item that you can make progress on in 30 minutes. Spend your time on that, rather than flipping through e-mail.

---

[3] David Allen, "Organizing: Setting Up the Right Buckets" in *Getting Things Done: The Art of Stress Free Productivity* (Penguin Books 2001), pages 149-50.

you. Reports you request, work you delegate, and phone calls you're expecting all fall in this category. By getting your w/fs on a list and out of your head, you can better track items you're waiting for and have a lot less anxiety about things falling through the cracks.

*See page 293 for a sample daily list.*

*How to use the weekly.* The weekly is a list of items you plan to accomplish this week. You should update it at the end of the week, drawing from your mid-range plan. You might divide the weekly list into "buckets" of work, with sections for different projects or areas of responsibility. When compiling the list, think critically about what you can do the following week to move work forward. For big or unwieldy items, take the time to figure out specific, actionable next steps. For example, putting "plan gala dinner" on your weekly is less helpful than breaking the project into tasks such as "gala dinner: call printer for cost estimates on invitations; call hotel to confirm data; set up meeting with John to discuss program."

---

### Your Weekly List in Action

- In a meeting, you agree to write a memo about the fundraising plan for 2009. You know you won't get to it today, so you flip quickly to your weekly plan and add it to this week's list.
- You edit a letter for your development director and cross the task off your daily. Add "revised draft of letter from Julie" as a w/f on your weekly, and you'll remember to follow up if you don't receive a new version before Friday.

---

Keep a printed copy of your weekly right behind your daily so you can add to it as necessary. Remember, though, you should look closely at this list only when updating your daily each morning (or evening), so that it keeps you on track day-to-day but doesn't distract or worry you. As with your daily, your weekly can have a w/f section for things you're waiting for, in this case items that are due beyond the current day.

*See page 294 for a sample weekly list.*

*How to use the mid-range.* The mid-range plan captures what you will do in the next quarter to make progress on your annual objectives (of course, some other timeframe may make more sense for your particular circumstances). Keep a copy in your key documents folder (see more below) to reference when redoing your weekly.

One piece that we've found particularly helpful for either the weekly or mid-range list is the "someday/maybe" section.[4] This is where you capture items you aren't committed to acting on yet but that you want to remember and consider at a later time. Recommended reading, interesting projects, and random ideas that strike you in the middle of the night go here.

---

**Your Mid-range Plan in Action**

- A friend recommends a great book on management that you don't have time to read right now, but that you don't want to forget about. Make a note on your "someday/maybe" so that when you do have time, you remember the title.

---

*See page 296 for a sample mid-range plan (note that this is the same plan we discussed in Chapter 4).*

### Folders

As a manager, you're probably in and out of meetings, sometimes in the office and sometimes not. You don't want to carry around a ton, but it's essential that you always have what you need at your fingertips. The

---

[4] David Allen, "Organizing: Setting Up the Right Buckets" in *Getting Things Done: The Art of Stress Free Productivity* (Penguin Books 2001), pages 167-70.

solution is to create a few key folders to funnel things into and to then take them with you everywhere.

*Key documents.* The key documents folder is a thin file that stores the few documents and materials that you reference often or want to keep on hand. In addition to your mid-range plan, this folder might contain a list of important phone numbers, your annual goals, and the one-page overview about your organization that you find yourself using over-and-over in external meetings.

*Action.* The action folder is where you file all the materials you need for current and upcoming work as those materials come in. If most of these materials – like agendas and relevant notes from previous meetings – come to you by e-mail, print hard copies to keep in your folder and file or delete the e-mail (more on managing e-mails below). Don't hesitate to put something for the holidays in this folder when it's only July. You'll want it at your fingertips come December – you won't want to go digging through your computer or desk to find it. If your action folder gets too thick, which it probably will, split it into two – one ("action – this week") that goes with you and holds projects and meetings for that week, and one that stays on your desk with stuff for future weeks ("upcoming – longer-term").

---

**Your Folders in Action**

- You receive an agenda for this Tuesday's staff meeting via e-mail. Print it out and put it in your "action – this week" folder.
- A vendor gives you a document that you'll need when filling out an expense report next month. Put it in the "upcoming – longer-term" folder on your desk.

---

*Read.* Finally, create a read folder for, well, things to read. Carry it around so you can take advantage of your commute or down-time between meetings. Note that having a current, portable read folder means printing materials so you have them on hand. This requires two things. First, you have to be honest with yourself about what you will actually read. Be ruthless about simply deleting e-mails that you might read in an ideal world, but that you really don't have time to do (like your aunt's four-page e-mail about her trip to Savannah). Second, you're going to have to kill some trees. We'd all like to move to a paperless world, but if you try to keep everything in electronic form only, you're just going to be less efficient (think of all that time spent brushing your teeth when you could be reading, too!). Donate to a worthy environmental organization to even the score, and be aggressive about printing out things you need to read.

### Storage

Your folders will contain the materials you need for current and upcoming action items. Everything else should be kept in files that are easy to access. Adopt a categorization that works for you (alphabetical, grouped, etc.) and resist the temptation to overstuff your file cabinets: if you can't find something easily or drop something in a file, you are less likely to use your system (David Allen suggests keeping your file cabinets at the most three-quarters full). Set yourself up for success by getting a new file cabinet or re-organizing what you have so you know where to find and file everything you need.

## *Calendar*

In addition to lists and folders, the only other piece you need is a calendar to record everything with a date attached. Start with the basics, recording all your meetings, trips, and deadlines in the calendar. Beyond that, though, use your calendar to trigger actions with any sort of timeframe, even ones not associated with hard dates. For these items, enter them as "all day events" (if you use Outlook) and they will show up in the gray space above your scheduled appointments.

# My Calendar

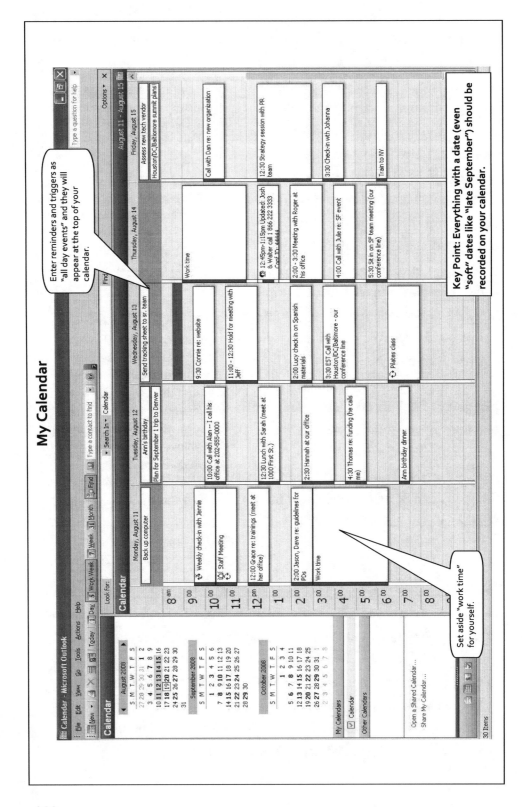

Enter reminders and triggers as "all day events" and they will appear at the top of your calendar.

Key Point: Everything with a date (even "soft" dates like "late September") should be recorded on your calendar.

Set aside "work time" for yourself.

---

### Your Calendar in Action

- You contract with a new vendor and intend to assess your satisfaction with her services in a few weeks. Flip ahead a month or so and enter "Assess new tech vendor" on your calendar.
- You have an important trip in September. Mark a day in mid-August to plan for it.
- Every month you're supposed to turn in your expense form. Record a monthly reminder and set it to recur on the fourth Thursday of every month.

---

Given the volume of information and requests you receive every day, it will require a bit of discipline to funnel each item into its proper place and keep your lists up to date. But we can't overstate the value of organizing your work to make the most effective use of your time. Try this system for at least three weeks, tweaking it to meet your needs. Whether you stick with this system or find another, we guarantee a good system will help you get better results and make you less stressed, because you won't have to worry about what you may have forgotten.

## Taming the E-mail Beast

Answering e-mail could sometimes be a full-time job in itself, if you let it. We've seen managers drowning in e-mail with no system for processing it – an in-box with thousands of unanswered (or even unread!) e-mails, a constant worry about what might be in those messages, and a feeling that as soon as one e-mail is dealt with, five more arrive to take its place.

Here are some tips to get control of your e-mail.

- Check e-mail only at defined periods. Consider turning off your "new messages" indicator so you aren't tempted to cheat on this.

- Apply the two-minute rule – if you can do a task in two minutes or less, don't wait. Do it now! Reply right away, forward it to someone else to deal with, print it and put it in your "read" folder, or otherwise figure out what next action must be taken to move it forward.

- Don't create work for yourself. If you ever look at the number of e-mails you get while you're on vacation, you'll notice that the total (apart from spam) decreases significantly with each passing day. You might get 120 on day one, then 100, then 80, then 40. This is a sign that when you're around, you're creating work for yourself! Reply to e-mails in a way that makes clear who should drive what steps and how you want people to move forward so that they don't need to keep coming to you for every tiny step.

- Don't use your in-box as storage. Use it only for messages that still need to be dealt with. All others should be deleted or filed. Otherwise, you won't be able to quickly differentiate between what you've already processed and what you still have to deal with.

- Utilize e-mail folders. For instance, if you're managing a project and are expecting feedback from six people, create a folder for the project, put all related e-mails in that folder, and then set a reminder on your calendar to deal with that input. (That reminder is crucial, since you shouldn't kid yourself that you'll spontaneously read through folders other than your in-box without a trigger.)

Follow these rules and you'll typically have fewer than 10 e-mails remaining in your in-box at the end of the day.

You'll find some great resources online for managing your e-mail so that it doesn't back up. In particular, we like 43folders.com's "Inbox Zero" series, at www.43folders.com/izero.

## Key Points

- How you manage yourself and your time and how you stay organized will seriously impact what kind of results you're able to get.

- At its core, time management is about clarity regarding your purpose in the organization and what you're trying to accomplish.

- The biggest time management mistake that most managers make is spending their time on what's immediately at hand or what's most comfortable to work on, rather than what's most important. Figure out what one or two things are most important to accomplish on any given day and make those your priorities. Whenever possible, do them first before other things have the chance to intervene.

- If you *can* delegate it, you *should* delegate it. Work should flow downward to the lowest level person who can do it well enough.

- Remember that as a manager, you should be spending your time managing.

- There are lots of different organizational systems that work well, but any good system should (1) ensure that every piece of information has one designated home; (2) funnel all the things coming at you into as few places as possible; (3) be easy to maintain and make your life easier, not harder; (4) focus you on the most important work at any given moment; and (5) be portable if you travel for work.

## 📖 Additional Reading

- David Allen, *Getting Things Done: The Art of Stress Free Productivity* (Penguin Books 2001).

# ✎ <u>Tools</u>

- Sample daily list

- Sample weekly list

- Sample mid-range plan

## Sample Daily List

### My Daily List
### August 11

> Take five minutes at the start or end of each day to update your daily list. Keep any necessary items from yesterday and cut/paste new items from your weekly and from your calendar.

<u>Today will be a success if</u>: The majority of prep for Ohio site visit is completed.

> At the top of your daily, write down the key thing(s) you need to accomplish in order for the day to have been successful.

**Action:**

- **Prep agenda for message training for RDs/CDs in Ohio**
- **Review preparations for Ohio site visit with Jennie, including materials, tickets, hotel**
- Delegate to Jennie: compile a shortlist of good PR firms that might work for our needs
- Review draft agendas for summits in Houston/DC/Baltimore
- Meet with Jason, Dave re: guidelines for PDs for principal meetings
- Birthday card for Ann
- Call Sue back – stress importance of deadline

> Put personal to-do items on your daily, as well, so everything is in one place.

**W/f:**

- Data from Josh by COB

**Quickies:**

- Forward newsletter to Walter

> Your daily should be short and contain only the work you want/need to get done that day. Keep other projects on your weekly or mid-range lists so they don't clutter your daily.

## Sample Weekly List

### My Weekly List
### August 11 - 15

**This week will be a success if:** Plans for Ohio and SF event are finalized; summit materials are sent out.

> To clarify for yourself what's most important, write at the top of your weekly what your "big rocks" for the week are.

### Development:

- **Final revisions of plan for San Francisco Bay Area event (need final plan by Monday; event is 8/26)**
- Write memo about fundraising plan for 2009

> Items in bold are "must do" this week.

### Recruitment & Selection:

- **Prep agenda for message training session with RDs/CDs**
- **Get tickets, hotel for site visit to Ohio**
- Latino marketing: meet with Lucy to measure progress against goals (basic materials available in Spanish by 8/30, look into focus groups and decide on plan by 9/20). Mention meeting James last week—possible partner/resource?

> Regular font items should be done this week.

### Alumni:

- **Materials for summits in Houston/DC/Baltimore – due 8/15**
- **Review draft agenda and talking points, edits to be incorporated by COB Wednesday**
- **Final read-through of binder**

### General marketing:

- **Web site**
  - *Public site: identify contacts for recruitment, HR, development by 8/22*
  - *Train all contacts by 9/30*
  - *Maintain quality control of public and CMA Web site per system established – ongoing*

> Italics items don't have to happen this week but need to happen relatively soon.

- Print PSA distribution (ongoing as we get requests)
- Consider creating guidelines for PDs for principal meetings – talk to PDs, have recommendation for Thomas by 8/25
  - Meet with Jason, Dave on this

**PR:**
- Explore hiring firm to help on the PR front for short-term. Convene meeting with Connie and Thomas by 8/29.
    - Delegate to Jennie: compile a shortlist of good PR firms that might work for our needs
- Full transition to Johanna of basic procedures/processes/responsibilities and basic media inquiries by 8/29
    - **Schedule 2 meetings w/ Johanna – this Friday to check in on transition so far and in one month to follow up**

> These categories are your main areas of work and can be taken from a longer-term plan (in your case, these might include each department, fundraising, board, etc.).

**Team:**
- Jennie: delegate finding a PR firm, review preparations for Ohio site visit
- David, Jason: guidelines for PDs for principal meetings – describe need, ask for input, get sample?
- Johanna: review last week's media inquiries
- Lucy: Spanish-language materials –step-back, timeline (James)
- Staff meeting: my Ohio trip, vacation schedules

> Keep a section for your recurring meetings, including check-ins with your staff.

**Personal:**
- Submit dental reimbursement
- Mom birthday
- Call AF, JW, LT
- Buy the Book of Hard Choices

> In a good system there are as few homes as possible. Keep one list for both your professional and personal to-do items.

**W/f:**
- Web site materials from Johanna
- Revised draft of letter from Julie
- Goals from Alan

> Use a w/f (waiting for) section to keep track of the tasks you've asked others to do, and a someday/maybe section to capture items for future consideration.

**Someday/Maybe:**
- Summer reading – Bel Canto; End of Poverty
- Holiday cards and/or party?
- Refresher course for Spanish
- Team hike
- Casa Oaxaca (restaurant recommendation from SK)

## Sample Mid-range Plan

**Julie, VP Marketing, 3-Month Plan**
**July – September 2008**

> You should draw from a mid-range plan like this one when you prepare your weekly list.

**Goal 1: 85% of senior staff from teams we support (Regions, Recruitment, Alumni, Development) feel the Marketing team consistently delivers high-quality products on time (as measured by end-of-year survey)**

- Create guidelines/best practices for regional galas (event and diaries) (*nice-to-have – if so, by 9/30; at minimum, start informal running list of ideas*)

> Organizing mid-range plans by goal helps keep the ultimate end in mind so you can be sure your activities listed below align with it.

- Create materials for summits in Houston/DC/Baltimore – due 7/15
- Revise Continuum (contingent upon hiring new Dir of Alum Comm)
- Hire new Director of Alumni Communications – create job description and place ad on Idealist and craigslist by 9/1
- Ensure Lynette develops letterhead (without address/vision statement) for press kits/development packets/recruitment packets, etc. by 8/15

> Clear due dates will make it easier to determine at a glance which items need to go on your weekly.

**Goal 2: All written materials reflect our desired messages and 80% of staff (as determined through random sampling) can deliver concise, accurate messages on basic questions about our organization**

- Conduct message training for RDs/CDs (I go on at least 2 site visits and work one-on-one w/RDs)
- Revise guidelines and templates for regional matriculation packets, ensure Lynette completes new version by 8/31
- Web site
  - Public site: identify contacts for recruitment, HR, development by 7/15
  - Maintain quality control of public and CMA Web site per system established – ongoing
- Ensure new ED training on media/PR is ready for ED conference 9/2

**Goal 3: Increase in significant national and regional press hits – i.e., stories about us, not just mentions in passing – by 50% (from 8 to 12 national and 52 to 78 regional)**

- Explore hiring firm to help on the PR front for short-term. Convene meeting with Connie and Thomas by 7/15
- Web site
  o Have press center up and running by 9/30
- PR strategy finalized (*may change per PR consultant/agency*)
  o Prepare calendar of announcements
  o Capitalize on annual round-up stories (i.e. *NY Times* Giving section—November deadline; *Worth Magazine* 100 Best Charities; *Chronicle of Philanthropy* Year-end Round-up)
  o Establish PR advisory board (top targets: Ms. Jackson at ABC Bank; Mr. Goldstein at MSNBC; etc.)
  o Finalize more detailed plan for all of this by 8/15

**Goal 4: New glitch-free Web site that reflects our identity and desired positioning and enthusiastically signed-off on by top 3 execs in the organization launched by December 31.**

- Ensure Juan gets phase 2 of Web site up by 9/1
  o Online giving capabilities
  o Replace regional "supporters" list with regional one-pagers
- Redesign regional pages (content and layout) to be more effective/engaging by 8/1

*Longer-term (on hold for now):*

- Explore possibility of desk side briefings with Abby/Wendy (around issues, studies)
- Redo 2008 national brochure (winter/spring as part of annual report)
- Corporate sponsorship guidelines (with development)
- Early planning for national alumni summit
- Welcome packet for new alumni

> Specifying what you will NOT do helps you get aligned with your manager and your staff about what your priorities really are.

## Chapter 11
# Managing Up

Up until this point we've talked about how to manage people who report to you. But unless you're a rare exception, you have a boss, too. Even executive directors typically report to a board. And just as you can get better results through effective management practices with those who report to you, so can you maximize your results by using the right practices with the person who manages *you*.

We want to be clear: managing up isn't about manipulating your boss or managing her perceptions; rather, it's about working with your boss in the way that will produce the best possible results for the organization, while at the same time decreasing your stress level.

In this chapter, we'll talk about how to structure the relationship, how to make it easy for your boss to manage you, and how to be emotionally intelligent when it comes to your relationship with your manager. We'll also talk about some concerns unique to managers who are in a second-in-command role.

### SET IT UP RIGHT

Just as in delegation, the first step of managing up is to agree on expectations. This means you and your boss need to get on the same page about what you'll do, how you'll do it, and how the two of you will work together. Ideally you'd do this at the start of your relationship, but you can also do it right now if you're struggling in an existing relationship.

- Get clear about expectations. Talk explicitly with your manager about the following:

  1. What are your goals for the year? What would success look like for you this year? What's top priority, and what's a "nice-to-have?"

  2. What responsibilities fall to you, and what falls to your boss? Establish a clear division of labor. *See page 308 for a sample division of labor plan.*

  3. What decisions of yours should she be kept informed about? What can or should she be consulted on? Given final approval on? *The MOCHA (manager-owner-consulted-helper-approver) model on page 19 is a helpful tool for talking this over.*

  Once you've figured out the answers to these questions, raise some hypothetical situations and talk through how they would be handled. For instance, you might discuss how to handle a low-performing staff member, or how to involve your manager in the development of a new press strategy.

- Decide on a communication system. Establish a system for checking in and getting questions answered. For instance, you might have a regular weekly meeting, plus ad hoc conversations throughout the rest of the week as the need arises. Alison is a devoted fan of keeping an ongoing list in her e-mail program of issues, questions, and information for her executive director, which she tweaks throughout the day – so when they can grab a few minutes to talk, her list is organized and waiting. Whatever system you decide on, err on the side of investing a good amount of time talking in the beginning; you can reduce it over time.

**MAKE IT EASY**

As a manager of others, you know the time and effort that it takes to manage someone well. Once you and your boss have agreed on general expectations and how you'll work together, make things as easy as possible for *your* boss by doing the following:

- <u>Apply the principles of delegation upward</u>. When you delegate a responsibility to a staffer, you articulate the desired outcome, constraints, and prioritization. Do the same thing when your manager gives *you* a responsibility, in order to make sure you're on the same page. For instance, if your manager asks you to oversee the development of a new logo, you might say, "So we're looking for a logo that's professional and modern, with a global feel. It sounds like the budget needs to be kept under $2,000, and I'm thinking I shouldn't tackle this until after we're done with the spring conference. Does that sound right?" Once you're both aligned, take the two minutes to do a "repeat-back" e-mail afterward, so that weeks later you both remember what was decided upon. And just as with when you're delegating to others, help your boss stay engaged by checking in on an ongoing basis, offering updates and giving your manager chances for input as the project unfolds. For instance, you might agree with your manager that once you have developed five good options for the logo, you will run them by her to get her views.

- <u>Whenever possible, suggest solutions</u>. Just as you want to keep your staffers from handing you the monkey (see Chapter 1), keep your own monkeys off your boss' back. Saying, "What should I do about X?" puts the problem on her. You make it easier for both of you if you say, "Here's the deal with X. I've thought about A, B, and C, and I think we should do C because... Does that sound okay to you?"

- <u>Have your act together</u>. We hear from a lot of people who think their managers are overly controlling or "micromanagey." Most managers don't like being control freaks, but that they become that way when they don't have confidence that things will get done otherwise. It follows then that if your boss is a control freak, the easiest way to solve the problem is to give her confidence that things are under control. In other words, stay on top of things, do what you say you're going to do, take good notes on the subtleties of what your boss asks you to do so you do it right, ensure that your boss only has to tell you something once, don't let things fall through the cracks, and generally be someone she can rely on. You might be surprised how much easier your boss becomes to work with when you have your act together.

## BE EMOTIONALLY INTELLIGENT

Beyond being a good "delegee" on specific pieces of work, don't forget about the personal side of things. You can keep the relationship healthy by keeping these principles in mind:

- <u>Focus on your sphere of control</u>. There will be some things you can't change or control. Try to move past these, and rather than focusing on things that you may not be able to do much about (like a busy manager who cancels your regular weekly meeting), think about what you *can* do (such as saying, "I know you're really busy – but can I talk to your assistant and get 10 minutes on your calendar?").

- <u>Don't stew in silence</u>. The most effective managees tend to see the responsibility for making the relationship work smoothly as theirs. If you're frustrated about something, such as your manager undermining a decision you made, raise it, talk about the impact, and discuss how it could go differently in the future. Mistakes will happen – use them as opportunities to strengthen your systems. (Of course, be smart about this: you'll get better results if you raise these issues at a moment when your boss has time to consider them, and it's worth thinking about your delivery ahead of time, just as you would if you were speaking to a subordinate about a sensitive issue.)

- <u>Don't take it personally</u>. There will be times when you have a different point of view than your manager on something where she is the ultimate decision-maker. When this happens, you should advocate for what you believe, and if you think your boss is making a mistake, part of your job is to explain why. But if your boss ultimately picks a different route, it's helpful to have reasonably thick skin: don't take it personally, and keep your ego out of it. (It's a bonus if you can find the humility to recognize that she might even be right!)

- <u>Don't forget your boss is human</u>. Sometimes managers are extremely emotionally intelligent about the needs of the people under them but forget to apply the same sensitivity to the person above them. Don't lose sight of the fact that your boss is human. There may be times when she is grouchy, frustrated, or frazzled, or times when she would appreciate hearing that she handled something well. Additionally, realize that in the same way you might have sensitivities about the relationship, she may, too. For instance, if you're taking on responsibilities that used to be hers, she likely won't appreciate hearing that they used to be a disaster until you came along. All of which is to say, be thoughtful.

## SPECIAL CONSIDERATIONS FOR SECOND-IN-COMMANDS

More and more organizations are moving to a structure with an executive director and a "second-in-command." These number two's might have the title of managing director, chief operating officer, deputy director, or chief of staff. While the specifics of the labor division vary, typically a number two's role is to ensure that the organization hits its goals, with all that that entails, including managing people, checking in on progress, and overseeing organization-wide systems. The number one's job, in turn, is to make sure the goals are right in the first place by overseeing strategy, to engage internally on high-priority tactical issues, and often to do significant amounts of external relations.

Regardless of the exact set-up, being the second-in-command can be tricky. Because you're often speaking for your boss or exercising authority that stems from her, the situation can produce a unique set of frustrations, such as a boss who reverses your decisions when staffers go around you to her, or needing to hold people accountable when they're working more closely with your boss than with you.

Because of this, it's especially crucial that a number one and number two are aligned and on the same team – and that other staff members know it. If staffers start to worry that you're pursuing your own agenda rather than your boss' agenda or that you don't speak for her, you may get a frustrated, disgruntled staff or a staff trying to go around you to get things done. And you don't want to make decisions that your number one will later feel compelled to reverse, since this will undermine your authority.

Here are four keys to making a second-in-command position work smoothly:

1. <u>Get explicitly aligned</u>. If you're managing the execution of the agenda your boss drives, it can be fatal if you're on different pages about priorities or desired results. In order to make sure you're truly aligned, you and your manager should routinely talk about priorities – what's most important, what's good to keep moving forward but is not in the top priority bucket, and what can be put on the back-burner.

Beyond priorities, you and your boss should get aligned on how to handle tricky, new, or potentially controversial situations. Over time, you'll likely find that you've jointly established core principles that will apply from one situation to the next, so you'll be able to act in more and more situations without needing to check in as often. You should still continue to get aligned on particularly sensitive situations, however.

2. <u>Do your aligning behind the scenes</u>. Just as effective parents show a united front to their kids, you and your boss should try to do your aligning in private – and in advance when possible. Of course, if you didn't talk something through beforehand and you discover while meeting with others that you disagree on an issue, it's fine to have divergent opinions – but you should be sure you ultimately send a clear signal to the staff about which way to head, and you should ensure that the two of you are clear about which of you has the final decision-making authority.

3. <u>Expect a learning curve and debrief regularly</u>. We can almost promise you that things won't go perfectly smoothly right at the start. You might make a judgment call that your boss thinks was a mistake, or she might inadvertently step into your sphere of authority, particularly if your position as number two is a new thing for the organization. This is normal. Don't get discouraged or too freaked out by it – and in fact, see these bumps as useful opportunities to help you clarify expectations and get more aligned. To make sure that you actually do this, agree on a time in advance (say, from 2-3 p.m. on the first Friday of every month) when you'll review some specific examples and talk about how things are working and what you both could do differently. Not only will this strengthen your operations overall, but doing this will help you get more inside your boss' head so that you become more and more instinctively aligned with her over time.

4. <u>When you're in the middle, bring the ends together.</u> While you'll be able to resolve many situations on your own, it's important to differentiate between when your job is to solve something yourself and when your job is to get the right people to talk to each other so that the problem gets solved. This often simply means ensuring that the right people get together and that the right questions get asked. For instance, if you notice that your boss frequently makes extensive edits to the op-eds written in her name by the communications director, don't get caught up in being a go-between, ferrying messages back and forth or trying to guess what's driving your boss' edits. Instead, facilitate a meeting between the two – and rather than focusing just on the most recent set of edits, ask questions to help your boss articulate the underlying principles driving her edits.

## Key Points

- Managing up is about working with your boss in the way that will produce the best possible results for the organization.

- Talk explicitly with your manager about goals for the year, communication preferences, and how she wants to be involved in decisions.

- Apply the principles of delegation upward, by articulating the desired outcome, constraints, and prioritization to make sure you're on the same page, as well as checking in to provide chances for input.

- Have your own act together.

- Be emotionally intelligent, by focusing on what you can control (rather than what you can't), speaking up when you're frustrated, not taking things personally, and remembering that your boss is human.

## 📖 Additional Reading

- Nathan Bennett and Stephen A. Miles, "Second in Command: the Misunderstood Role of the Chief Operating Officer," Harvard Business Review, May 2006.

- BoardSource (www.boardsource.org) – articles, books, tools, and training for nonprofit boards. Some content is available to members only.

## ✏️ Tools

- Sample division of labor plan

## Sample Division of Labor Plan

**Division of labor between:**
**Ruth Johnson,** Founder and Executive Director
**Alan Alperowicz,** Chief Operating Officer

| FUNCTION | RUTH'S ROLE | ALAN'S ROLE |
|---|---|---|
| | *Functions should be all the areas where there is any role confusion or potential role confusion.* | |
| **Board** | Manage board relations and serve as point person | Support Ruth as requested |
| **Fundraising** | Owns 2008 fundraising goal; lead strategist and pitch-maker | Ensure Ruth has support she needs (help develop plan & manage execut'n effectively); be a resource to Ruth |
| **External relations** | Lead spokesperson for and face of organization | Serve as spokesperson on occasion and own key external meetings |
| **Issue and campaign management** | Consult on "major" decisions and (rarely) use veto power to stop a particular action; give input/suggest ideas on day-to-day issues | Responsible for making decisions on all day-to-day issues, figuring out process for decision-making (including what meetings need to happen and how they should be run) and consulting Ruth as needed; get Ruth's input on all major decisions |
| **Staff management** | Manage Alan and back him up once decision has been made; use veto power sparingly over management decisions | Manage all day-to-day operations, including Office of the CEO, Comm., Dev., Research, Finance, and HR; determine appropriate staff roles and reporting lines; evaluate staff; make hiring and firing decisions, consulting Ruth as appropriate |
| **Annual plan** | Give up-front input on and have final sign-off on plan | Manage to annual plan and ensure goals are met; drive next year's goal-setting process |
| **Strategic vision** | Set strategic vision | Be resource to Ruth in setting vision |
| **Legal compliance** | Consult on key matters | Manage legal team around relevant issues in order to ensure legal compliance |
| **Budget** | Provide up-front input and sign-off on final budget | In consultation with Ruth (especially on relevant development issues), develop budget and manage to it |
| **Special projects** | Develop new ideas and consult on implementation | Ensure projects are executed well, with emphasis on building needed capacity (e.g., hiring top talent to carry out special projects) |

308

**Summary of Ruth/Alan division of labor:**

> This summary page serves as a kind of job description and would typically be put together after the chart on the first page is prepared.

**Ruth**

On all major decisions that Alan owns, give input and ask hard questions. Use veto-power on rare occasions. Once decisions are made, back-up Alan 100% – with staff as well as external audiences.

- Board: Manage board relations and serve as point person for board members
- Fundraising: Lead strategist and pitch-maker on development; owns 2008 goal
- External relations: Lead spokesperson for and face of organization
- Issue and campaign management: Consult on major issues, give input
- Staff management: Manage Alan (check in regularly, provide feedback, evaluate performance)
- Annual plan: Give up-front input, final sign-off
- Strategic vision: Set strategic vision
- Special initiatives: Develop new ideas

**Alan**

Overall, make sure we hit our goals. Manage all day-to-day operations, including managing all staff, while consulting Ruth on all major decisions.

- Issue and campaign management: Manage organization to annual plan and ensure goals are met; make decisions and consult Ruth on major topics
- Staff management:
  - o  Manage all day-to-day operations, including Office of CEO, Communications, Development, Research, Finance, and HR
  - o  Determine appropriate staff roles and reporting lines
  - o  Evaluate staff
  - o  Make hiring and firing decisions
- Legal compliance: Ensure organization stays in legal compliance
- Budget: Ensure organization stays within budget
- Special initiatives: Ensure that initiatives are executed effectively
- Other: Serve as a resource to Ruth

**General principles:**

Ruth and Alan should get aligned on the relative prioritization of what's on Alan's plate on a regular basis (e.g., at least weekly) and make explicit choices about what's urgent and what can wait.

**Outstanding issues:**

- Division of labor around annual conference

> Flag areas where there remains potential for role confusion for future discussions.

## *Conclusion*
# Personal Qualities of a Great Manager

In the preceding chapters, we've talked a great deal about the *practices* of great managers, but we haven't talked much about their *personal qualities*. That's because great managers come in many different packages, and we don't believe that you need to become someone you're not in order to excel as a manager.

That said, before closing, we'd like to take a look at what kind of person it takes to do well the sorts of things we've talked about here. As you read on, keep in mind that in our experience, even managers who don't start out with all of these qualities end up bringing them out in themselves as they internalize the practices covered in this book.

So what personal qualities do great managers have or grow to have? If you've read this far, it won't surprise you to learn that we don't think that being a great manager is about having the most charisma or giving motivational speeches. Those things can be nice, but ultimately they're not necessary. What being a great manager is about is *being someone who cares passionately about getting results*.

And that can't be faked. If you are truly determined to get results, it becomes the fire that fuels everything you do – overriding ego, and overriding the discomfort of having hard conversations, and even overriding the desire to be liked. It leads you to do the sorts of things we've talked about previously: rather than delegating and disappearing, staying involved to make sure there's no implementation gap… making sure that people are clear about their goals and that those goals represent significant progress… holding people accountable for meeting high performance standards… and being aggressive about moving out staff members who don't… because that is how you get significant, sustained results.

No matter what the rest of the package looks like, in our experience, this intense determination to get results leads great managers to display the following personal qualities:

- Great managers *constantly worry about the real impact of their work, rather than appearances*. They have deep integrity about their missions, which leads them to pick goals and projects that will represent truly meaningful progress, not just an easy success with which to impress funders.

- When they run into roadblocks that might deter the average person, great managers *persist – and persist, and persist –* until they find a way past the obstacle.

- Because great managers are determined to be successful, *they make hard decisions that may be unpopular* (such as abandoning a strategy that isn't producing results) *or personally painful* (such as letting go a loyal but lower-performing staff member).

- While they may never be entirely comfortable having difficult conversations, great managers *put aside their personal discomfort* and have them anyway. They make themselves use words like, "I'd like you to do this differently," or "I'm concerned about something I've noticed recently," or even, "If this doesn't change, we will have to let you go."

- Great managers are *almost ruthless when it comes to identifying ways the organization could perform better* (beginning with themselves), and they tend to display a *deep commitment to learning from experience and adapting their approach* to make it as effective as possible.

- Because of this, they are *willing and even eager to take feedback and genuinely want to hear dissent.* They don't get defensive or shut out differing opinions; in fact, you may hear them thanking a staff member for sharing complaints or concerns – and they really mean it.

At their heart, all of these qualities come down to one thing, which is the same place where we started: that relentless, even obsessive, determination to get results. It's a prerequisite for great management, and everything follows from there.

We hope this book has shown you how to best harness that determination to achieve significant, dramatic results – results that will help you change the world.

# Acknowledgements

We would like to thank the many people whose feedback and patience assisted in the creation of this book.

Many of Jerry's former colleagues at Teach For America were enormously helpful. Among others, Elissa Clapp, Kriste Dragon, Steven Farr, Rebecca Helmer, and Maia H.M. Levner not only read and commented on portions of the text, but more importantly, put up with Jerry while he was learning to be a decent manager. And Teach For America's founder Wendy Kopp taught Jerry, if not most of what she knows about management, at least most of what he knows about it.

At The Management Center, clients far too numerous to name served as guinea pigs for early versions of this text. Our original guinea pigs, Julie Stewart and Mary Price at Families Against Mandatory Minimums (FAMM), though, deserve special thanks for their patience and support, as does Jon Cowan at Third Way for his insightful comments on the text. At the staff level, our colleagues made critical contributions to developing the concepts and the content. Ethan Fletcher gets much of the credit for the tools inserted throughout the book, several of which former intern Lydia Poon originally helped create. Abigail Kim drafted significant portions of the chapter on time and systems, proofread the text, and took care of the layout and printing. And neither this book nor The Management Center would exist without our unofficial co-author, Rebecca Epstein.

The Management Center also would not exist without its founder, benefactor, and spiritual guide, Peter B. Lewis.

Finally, Jerry's wife Liza not only edited parts of the text but also put up with his ruining several weekend excursions by dragging the manuscript along with him.

On Alison's end, she would not have been able to work on this book were it not for MPP executive director Rob Kampia's graciousness in permitting her both to take time off from MPP and to engage into bizarre schedule contortions in order to set aside time for the project.